Letters

J.R.D. TATA

Edited by

Arvind Mambro

Rupa & Co

The Publisher would like to thank Mr. Rajendra Prasad Narla (Senior Archives Officer), Ms. Freny J. Shroff (Senior Archives Officer) and Mr. H. Raghunath (Archivist) of the Tata Central Archives, Pune for their generous help.

We would also like to thank Mr. Fram Petit for his invaluable assistance in providing rare material for this book.

Published 2004 by

Rupa . Co

7/16, Ansari Road, Daryaganj,
New Delhi 110 002

Sales Centres:
Allahabad Bangalore Chandigarh Chennai
Hyderabad Jaipur Kathmandu
Kolkata Mumbai Pune

Typeset in 12 pts. Weiss by
Nikita Overseas Pvt Ltd
1410 Chiranjiv Tower
43 Nehru Place
New Delhi 110 019

Printed in India by
Gopsons Papers Ltd.
A-14 Sector 60
Noida 201 301

Contents

Editor's Note

Among Indian industrialists, J.R.D. Tata was, probably, the most prolific letter-writer. He often said he had an "intense dislike" for making speeches. But he loved writing letters.

There are over 40,000 letters by JRD in the Tata Central Archives (TCA), Pune, which are broadly arranged under the following heads:

- Family Correspondence
- Master Files
- Alphabetical Files
- Project Files, and
- Miscellaneous Correspondence.

JRD's family correspondence covers the period 1913-1926. He started handling business correspondence when he joined Tatas in 1925. While his correspondence increased substantially after he became Chairman of the Tata Group in 1938, the peak period, when he wrote the largest number of letters, was from the 1950s to the mid-1970s.

The range, breadth and depth of his interests and concerns are reflected in the huge cross-section of people these letters are addressed to: family members, his colleagues in Tatas, business associates, ministers and bureaucrats, friends in India and abroad, as well as others who were not known to him. He was punctilious in answering the letters of such "unknown" people if he felt they seriously wished to learn his views on matters of importance.

JRD's correspondence reveals various facets of his personality, his relationships with different people, the projects he was involved in, his views on various issues, his kindness, forthrightness and sense of humour, his attitude to life, his concerns as a citizen, the values he lived by, and his personal interests.

Mr. Tata's lasting friendships emerged from his business contacts, some of them dating back to the pre-Independence days. It is fascinating to see the development of these friendships. His letters followed a typical pattern in interpersonal communication. Initially, he addressed his correspondents by their surnames, later he used their first names and ended by addressing some of them by their pet names. Here are some of them: Dinos (Dr. Doxiades), Munne (Dr. Zahir Hussain), Doug (Dr. Douglas Ensminger), Goku (Dr. M.G.K. Menon), Nanja (B.K.N. Rao), Nikka (M.I. Qadir), Bachu (D.M. Ghia), Kini (Ms. Ella Millart), Bhoothy (Dr. S. Bhothalingam). "Chinn" was Chinnappa and "Cinni" was C. Sundaram. It is interesting to see that initial letters to Dr. Robert McNamara start with "Dear Mr. McNamara", continue with "Dear Robert" and end up with "Dear Bob". Mr. Tata also insisted on his friends calling him "Jeh" ("I'm Jeh for you, not Mr. Tata," he would write) and often corrected them if they called him "Jay" (a noisy bird) or "J".

In JRD's letters, what appeals to the reader most is what may be called the "directness" in his communication. He was very particular about his choice of words to convey his message and often referred to both British and American dictionaries for the right word. By 1975 his letter-writing had decreased. By then, most of his close friends and associates had quit the scene. The age factor may also have contributed to this.

Usually, in his serious letters JRD followed a particular pattern: as and when he decided to write to someone, he weighed the pros and cons of the matter under consideration thoroughly and arrived at a conclusion which he communicated to his correspondent. If he agreed or disagreed on any issue he said so in clear terms and gave reasons for his views. Through these letters, therefore, you can see Mr. Tata's thoughts, feelings and judgements, and, what is more, the way he arrived at them. You can almost hear his voice.

Each section of this anthology provides its own special insights, but the aviation correspondence of Mr. Tata has a special significance. While due importance has been given so far to his pioneering efforts in starting India's first airline, some of his best letters in this section belong to the period from the 1950s to the 1970s, when he was largely involved in taking major policy decisions regarding Air-India and getting them implemented. This correspondence includes his letters to the manufacturers of aircraft, Presidents of foreign airlines, Union Ministers of Aviation (with whom he often disagreed on important matters) and Air-India executives.

All these aspects have been taken into consideration while making this selection, which includes about 300 letters. A few replies have been included to give the reader the background of the matter under discussion. Needless to say, important letters, which figure in Mr. R.M. Lala's biography of JRD, *Beyond the Last Blue Mountain*, are included here.

JRD became a legend in his lifetime. It is my hope that both the man and the legend come alive for the reader through these letters.

While every effort has been made to ensure the accuracy of the footnotes describing the correspondents, since the letters date back many decades, any errors and omissions are regretted. Also, editorial changes have been kept to a minimum to retain the original flavour of the letters—especially those written in JRD's early years.

I am grateful to Mr. R.M. Lala for his help and advice since the inception of the project, as well as for his Introduction and the Profile of JRD. I also thank Mr. T.R. Doongaji and Mr. S.N. Batliwalla for keeping in touch with the work in progress and the officers of the Tata Central Archives—Mr. H. Raghunath, Mr. R.P. Narla and Ms. Freny Shroff—for their invaluable help. And Mr. Hemal Vaid and Ms. Hufriz Karkaria for translating some of JRD's letters from French into English, Ms. Pervin Mahoney for making useful suggestions while preparing the book for publication, and Ms. Anahita Khambatta and Ms. Minaz Jokhi and Ms. Anahita Lentin for secretarial assistance.

A word of gratitude to the team at Rupa & Co. for its efforts in bringing out this anthology. There are several others who helped me in this project. I am grateful to them and regret not being able to thank them individually.

Arvind Mambro

About the Editor

Associated with the Tata Central Archives, Pune since its inception, Arvind Mambro had done research for *Beyond the Last Blue Mountain*, a biography of J.R.D. Tata written by R.M. Lala. He has also updated *Keynote*, compilation of J.R.D. Tata's speeches edited by S.A. Sabavala and R.M. Lala.

Introduction

By R.M. Lala

The refined art of letter-writing is fast receding into the background, yielding to the distraction of speedy e-mails, cell phones and instant worldwide communication. The grace, the charm, the depth, even the affection that was once expressed through letters, has been overtaken by the unholy hurry creeping into our communications. Moreover for a future historian the absence of letters is going to prove a major impediment to a more complete picture of the times we live in and of the personalities who function.

Letters are a permanent source of information and the primary source for any biographer. Through one's letters, thoughtfully written or dictated, a man has time to think and bare his soul and his mind—and in the case of lovers their heart—to the other person. Letters display or rather reveal not only a man's thoughts but his likes and dislikes and reflect the times he lived in. They express his views on men and matters. Lord Chesterfield's letters to his son are famous. Nehru's letters to his daughter Indira from jail intended to educate her proved to be the source of his book *Glimpses of World History*.

In JRD's case, his letters to his father are revealing. JRD lived in an era where letters mattered and the credit partly goes to his father (then in India) who insisted that JRD from France sent him detailed letters about himself and his siblings' activities. This not only improved his command of the language but also inculcated in him the habit of writing longish letters. Sometimes he also gives at length his reasons for his decisions.

When writing the biography of J.R.D. Tata, I requested access to his sixty-odd years of letter writing. I was sent to the basement of Bombay House where in one steel cupboard were packed the letters. Mostly they were the master files of those written by him. I guessed that there were about 20,000-25,000 of these letters (they turned out to be 40,000). With my task as full-time director of a leading Tata Foundation, I thought it would be impossible for me to go through each one with the care and thought it needed. And so I requested Mr. Arvind Mambro to help me. I suggested that he first select all correspondence with important personalities or connected with important events in JRD's life or that of the companies he handled. Secondly, he should keep his eye open for any letters that showed the humour and humanity of the man.

As Mr. Mambro waded through the letters, every few days we would sit together and he would show me some flagged letters in each of the files. On that basis, about 900 letters were selected. Between them, they gave me a fairly clear picture of the man, his views and his activities. Though I may have finally quoted from only five to ten per cent of these letters, the insight they gave me as a biographer was invaluable in writing *Beyond the Last Blue Mountain*. Alas, the letters of his childhood, which constitute the beginning of this book, were not available to me then. They were discovered, some time after JRD's death, in a small suitcase in his home, forgotten by their writer and by the march of time. By then, *Beyond the Last Blue Mountain* was published.

During JRD's lifetime, along with his close colleague Mr. S.A. Sabavala, I edited his speeches, given over a period of approximately half a century. We chose to divide the speeches thematically rather than chronologically so that one could follow his thinking on a particular subject. I requested Mr. Mambro to keep the same style in the presentation of his letters, so that they would harmonise well with the book of his speeches called *Keynote*. In *Keynote*, before every section, was also a summary giving the highlights of what each section held.

There was one outstanding quality about JRD. He took every letter seriously as well as every office memo. Sudha Narayana Murty was a student at the Indian Institute of Science in 1974 when she saw an advertisement for an engineer in TELCO with a line at the bottom: "Lady Candidates need not apply."

She wrote off a postcard to JRD that Tatas have always been pioneers and "I am surprised that in such a company you can make a distinction between men and women." She posted it in anger and forgot all about it. "Within ten days, I received a telegram stating that I had to appear for an interview at TELCO Pune, at their expense." She got the job. TELCO explained its difficulties about accommodating the first lady to be on the shop floor but hired her. She writes:

"I consider JRD a great man because, in spite of being an extremely busy person, he valued one postcard written by a young girl, who was asking for justice and questioning him. He must have received thousands of letters every day. He could have thrown mine away in a dustbin. But he didn't do that. He respected the intentions of that unknown girl, who had neither influence nor money, and gave her an opportunity to work in his company. He did not merely give her a job, but also changed her life and mindset forever."*

With his own people JRD was big enough to admit his errors. In a letter to Sumant Moolgaokar, the man who made TELCO reach its heights, he wrote by hand:

"I apologise for my outburst. I have been under great pressure at home and on my trip to Jamshedpur and am a bit of an insomniac to boot! So I am unduly sensitive and was hurt by your criticism which I know was well meant. My affection and admiration for you will never change."**

Over the spell of a decade or more through which I worked closely with him as a director of the Foundation, a letter or a memo went to him on Friday afternoon, and came back by Monday morning on my desk with his very clear comments. There was no ambivalence in his replies. It was a clear-cut decision. If he had seen a letter of some worth, there was always a "Thank you" with his initials. If it needed a reply, which was typed, that would take a day or two longer. This courtesy and promptness, which he extended to those who wrote to him, were in keeping with his concern for the dignity of people, who, he felt, deserved to be promptly attended to. During most of his life he was Chairman of the largest industrial group in India. He was virtually the head, from 1932, of Tata Airlines, and later of Air-India International

---

* From Sudha Murty's book, *How I taught my Grandmother to read and other stories* (Puffin, Delhi, 2004).
** This is from one of the 15 letters only Mr. Moolgaokar had kept with him. On his demise his son Anil Moolgaokar gave them to Mr. D.R. Pendse for his book, *Giants by any Measure – Sumant Moolgaokar and J.R.D. Tata* (Parchure Prakashan Mandir, Mumbai, 2004).

till 1978. He also was a very active Chairman of the then largest company in India, Tata Steel, and he kept track of some of the largest companies of India. This only highlights his competence and his thoughtfulness where his letter-writing is concerned. This is also demonstrated by the fact that even after his colleagues retired he occasionally wrote and kept them informed of significant developments that would interest them. After all they were not just his colleagues. They were friends he could never forget. In his official letters he had the great ability to switch his mind from one company to another or from one subject to another and give it his intense concentration. He was totally focused on the letter or work he had at hand. He was a perfectionist at choosing the correct words in his letters and speeches.

An instance worth noting is that when an obscure school-teacher from Calcutta enquired from him what the guidelines of his life were, he spelt them out with great clarity and conviction (under the section *Personal: Guiding Principles*). It is not as if he had the time to attend to each one but he made the time because, to him, individuals mattered. This was the man. He went beyond the pressures of the bottomline to the hearts of people and that is why he is so fondly remembered even today, more than a decade after he is no more. The tributes and even the hoardings that appeared on his death indicated that. The one that would have pleased him most was that of his former company Air-India, whose hoarding read:

> *He touched the sky and it smiled.*
> *He stretched out his arms and they encircled the globe.*
> *His vision made giants out of men and organisations.*

Another hoarding said: "The spirit of JRD lives on". In some ways, the spirit of JRD also lives on through his letters and hence the value of this prized collection that Mr. Mambro has taken the trouble to select. The letters, as the reader will make out, cover a wide spectrum of subjects. JRD followed his own guideline: "to think things out for oneself". He had an endearing trait. He once told me, "I never take myself too seriously." He was full of fun and even mischief, which comes through in some letters like the one to his Delhi representative Kish Naoroji (under the section *Managing Men: Managing Business*). At the same time, he could be profound.

Nothing escaped his eagle eye and unlike most of us he never reconciled himself to the conditions of incompetence that prevail around us. On one motor ride with him he commented on the state of the roads and the condition of buildings; on another when he saw a man with a bundle on his head poorly dressed he said with feeling, "This is probably all he has". Though he drove in a Company's Mercedes he never lived in the comfort zone. His letter to the General Manager of Bombay Telephones Mr. P. M. Agerwala is a model (under the section *City, Nation and Beyond: A Citizen's Concerns*). He notes, "As soon as the road is finally repaired your people pounce on the same spot again and dig it up." "Obviously," says JRD, "they keep close watch on it." Then he gives a solution to this way of functioning. He took national and local concerns all in his stride.

He was in some ways also a seer. In the 1950s Communism was at its very height. With confidence in its material power, and above all the power of its ideology, it had reached its peak of arrogance. It was the decade during which Nikita Krushchev told the West: "We will bury you." In January 1955, JRD addressed a letter to Jayaprakash Narayan, who was then a convinced Marxist.

"I must confess that I do not share your understanding of the capitalist system or its place in history. With great respect, I wonder whether you are not making the mistake of viewing the capitalist system as it was many years ago and not as it is today or in the form into which it is clearly developing all over the world....I believe that in most parts of the world the system of free enterprise, far from dying, will be given a renewed lease of life in recognition of its ability and willingness to serve the community well and also from a revulsion against the unpleasant reality—as distinct from the myth—of state socialism."

This was thirty-five years before the collapse of the Berlin Wall and the disintegration of the Communist system in the Soviet empire. A decade later, even conservative and adamant China was opening its doors to the market economy.

In March 1991, when I showed JRD his own letter to JP he studied it carefully and read aloud twice the last lines. Majestically, he handed the letter back to me. "Not too bad," he said. He claimed no credit that history had vindicated his words. Once when discussing with me his favourite theme—of reincarnation—he was thinking aloud: "Now where would I like to be reincarnated? In the West?" He dismissed it. "There are few challenges left there. Russia will be interesting but it won't be the same as it is today. It is too large, for the Soviet Union to exist as it is today."

Again he was right.

He had a bitter-sweet relationship with Nehru. He was bitter because Nehru never consulted him on economic matters. But it is to his credit that it never interfered with his personal affection for the man. He could keep the two separate. He knew Nehru since 1924 and before Independence they were good friends. This book contains the handwritten letter of Jawaharlal to JRD specially inviting him to the wedding of his daughter. I still recall him telling me, years after Nehru had passed away, "I was very fond of him". He never felt the same affinity to Mahatma Gandhi. The Mahatma on the eve of JRD's leading an industrial delegation at the end of the War told the press:

> Ask them to wait till leaders are free. Freedom will come only after big business forgo crumbs from Indo-British loot.

This was in May 1945. Strangely, in that delegation was also Gandhiji's blue-eyed boy—G.D. Birla. JRD issued a statement regretting that the Mahatma had not taken the trouble to seek any clarification from them and wrote a pained letter to him to which the Mahatma gave an ambivalent reply (under the section *Towards Freedom and After: Industrial Mission, 1945*). The episode blew over. The person who hurt him perhaps the most was Morarji Desai. On 25 January 1978 when Morarji Desai received JRD he gave him no indication that when the Air-India Board was to be reconstituted on 1 February JRD would be dropped. The government had not the courtesy to inform him and Morarji called an employee of JRD, Air Marshal P.C. Lal, then the head of a company in Jamshedpur, and asked him to take over as Air-India's Chairman. Officially, the 9 o'clock news confirmed what Lal had privately told JRD earlier the same day that JRD was removed and P.C. Lal was appointed Chairman. When there was a public uproar, Morarji Desai tried to cover up with a letter, on the original of which JRD put pencilled question marks. It added insult to the injury (under the section *Aviation: Major Events*).

Courteous as JRD was, he was always unafraid to speak his mind. As one flips through the pages of this book, one rejoices in the childlike enthusiasm of JRD on getting his first racing car, the Bugatti. Enthusiastic as he was, the father was aghast, after having sanctioned the money for it, to see a car without even mudguards on it—the racing Bugatti. One observes the joys, the sadness, the perception, the humour, the care and humanity of the man through the pages of this book. Through it, the reader will conjure up his own impression of the personality of JRD and in a sense it will be for him or her a voyage of discovery.

J.R.D. Tata: A Profile

JRD was an interesting product of two continents. JRD's father was a Parsi and his mother French.

Born in Paris in 1904, JRD schooled in Paris, Bombay and Yokohama. Most of his education was in France. In order to improve his English before going to Cambridge, he was sent to an English "Crammer" School.

His mother was a very resourceful, intelligent and adaptable lady who—with five children—single-handedly packed up her household items in France and came to India to be with her husband, who was in the House of Tatas. As she went back to her home country every year or two, JRD's education was regularly disrupted. His grandmother was a very formidable lady. "Her husband was a humorist and after some time with her," says JRD, "the gentleman ran away as anyone would have, had he been married to my grandmother." Perhaps JRD inherited his sense of humour from his French grandfather.

After school, he was drafted for a year into the French army and assigned to a regiment in France called Le Saphis. At the end of his time there, he expected to go on to Cambridge where a place was reserved for him. But his father summoned him back to India to join the Tatas. It was to rankle with him for decades that he never went to a university. His father must have had a premonition, for he died nine months later and JRD took his place as director of Tata Sons, which controls India's largest industrial group. JRD was twenty-one.

Though he missed his college education, he undertook his own education after office hours, studying books on various aspects of business. When he was in his early twenties, while recovering from typhoid, he would come to his room at the Taj, throw himself in bed and study. When his sister Rodabeh pleaded, "Why don't you rest Jeh, you are tired and unwell," JRD replied, "I want to be worthy of Tatas."

Flying was a passion with JRD. Louis Bleriot, the first man to fly across the English Channel, had a house on the coast of France near the Tatas' country home. Bleriot's pilot, who used to land a small plane on the beach, once gave JRD a joyride. It was then that the fifteen-year-old boy decided that one day he too would fly. He had to wait ten years for it to happen, but when it did, he was the first one to qualify within India to fly. He got his licence, which bore on it Number 1, on 10 February 1929. When I asked him what was the greatest adventure of his life, he replied, "The flying experience. None can equal that." He added, "When you are on your own in that little plane at the control without an instructor, and the plane speeds on the runway and finally takes off—you know you are in the air on your own."

In 1930, the Aga Khan Trophy was offered for the first Indian to fly solo from India to England or vice versa. JRD competed, taking off from Karachi to London. When he landed at Aboukir Bay in Egypt, he found that Aspy Engineer, the other contender, flying from London to Karachi, was stranded in the desert airfield for want of a spark plug! JRD sportingly parted with his spare one and they continued their journey in opposite directions. Aspy beat him by a couple of hours. "I am glad he won," said JRD, "because it helped him get into the Royal Indian Air Force." Later, Aspy was to be the second Indian to be the chief of the Indian Air Force.

JRD recalled that in 1932, "One October morning as the sun rose on the eastern horizon, a single-engined Puss Moth plane took off from Karachi with a load of mail for Bombay. As the plane hummed and rose the pilot said a word of prayer." And so India's first airline—the Tata Airlines—was inaugurated.

In 1948, JRD went on to start Air-India International. Within ten years he was president of International Air Transport Association (IATA). Though the airline was nationalised in 1953, he remained at the helm of Air-India till 1978, making it one of the most efficient airlines in the world.

In 1938, at the age of thirty-four, he became the Chairman of the largest industrial group in India, which he led with distinction for fifty-two years. When I asked him why he was appointed at such a young age as Chairman of Tata Sons, when senior, more distinguished men like Sir Homi Mody and Sir Ardeshir Dalal were on the board, he shrugged it off and said, "It was an aberration." When pressed for a reply, he said, "Perhaps, because I was hard-working."

With his limitation of formal education, how did he discharge his responsibilities? "Because of a lack of technical knowledge, my main contribution in management was to encourage others." He elaborated on how he dealt with each man in his own way and brought out the best in people, "At times, it involved suppressing yourself. It is painful but necessary.... To lead men, you have to lead them with affection."

With more than sixty years of experience in top management, he developed his own philosophy and method where leadership was concerned. "One of the qualities of leadership is to assess what is needed to get the best results for an enterprise. If that demands being a very active executive chairman, as I was in Air-India, I did that. On the other hand, in one of our other companies where I know that the managing director likes to be alone and will get the results that way, I argued with myself and decided that it will be stupid for me to come in the way when the other person has a capacity for focusing his genius and producing the results. Often a Chairman's main responsibility is to inspire respect." And then he added, "Don't forget, I like people."

JRD's sympathies were wide. Unlike some of us, he never accepted the poverty around him. He wanted the best for India and her people. Though he headed a group of almost 100 companies, he could also care intensely for individuals.

One of the most memorable evenings for those attending it was on the spacious grounds of the National Centre for the Performing Arts, when JRD was being felicitated by Tata employees on the Bharat Ratna awarded to him in 1992. Towards the latter part of his speech, this patriarch, then eighty-seven, addressed his people, "My friends, I should say my children...". Every eye was moist because they knew he meant it. Then the man who had done so much to give India economic strength went on to say, "An American economist predicts that India will be an economic superpower in the next century. I don't want India to be an economic superpower. I want India to be a happy country."

In the 1960s and 1970s Tatas were not growing as fast as some other industrial groups were. All the major schemes JRD put forward to the Government of India from 1960 onwards, including the manufacture of cars and the setting up of a suitable fertiliser complex in Mithapur, were stymied while other industrial groups were given licences to grow. I observed to him in 1979, "Could it not be said that the other industrial groups have grown faster than Tatas over the last years?"

JRD replied with feeling as well as firmness, "I have often thought of that. Had we resorted to some of the means that some other companies did, we would have been twice as big as we are today. But I would not have it any other way."

JRD's strength was that he applied his beliefs in practice. Vasant Seth, founder of Great Eastern Shipping, while in college was once standing at a bus stop with three women colleagues. A limousine rolled up at the bus stop. The driver asked if anybody wanted a lift. The girls hesitated but Seth hustled them on to the rear seat of the car while he perched himself next to the driver. To impress his lady friends he turned to them and said, "Do you know whose car we are travelling in? We are travelling in the car of Mr. J.R.D. Tata." The distinguished man at the steering turned to him and said, "Young man, this car does not belong to J.R.D. Tata. This car belongs to the Tata Iron & Steel Company."

JRD was one of the most highly decorated Indians with many awards bestowed on him. Yet till the end of his long life, he regretted not being sent to college. Eight months before JRD died, while driving to the airport, I asked him, "Sir, you are genuinely modest and humble, but suppose you had been to Cambridge, would you have been as humble and modest as you are today?" He thought for a moment and replied, "I think I would have been even more humble because although I may have been a Doctor of Engineering from Cambridge, I would have known how little I knew of other subjects."

JRD preferred to spend a good deal of his time in what appeared to be his study. There was a whole shelf of books on aviation, another on military ventures and warfare, and one on sports cars and motor racing. He liked to read crime fiction, lighter books like David Niven's *Bring on the Horses*, and books by Louis L'Amour. JRD was not just a collector of books but was an avid and enthusiastic reader. After one of my first interviews at his home, I returned with three of his favourite books including one by Alexander Woolcott, which JRD was keen I should read. (One area in which he had not read and thought about enough was religion, he admitted. At almost our last interview we dwelt at length on the subject of God.)

For my interviews connected with his biography we used to meet in what I thought was his study. About three years later, I discovered that this room was not only his study, but also his bedroom! I ventured to say, "Sir, nobody in your position would live in a room as small as this." He replied, "Why? It suffices me."

Though very fond of children, he and his wife had none of their own. Even in his eighties, he worked till late in the office. When his secretaries would say, "Sir, it is late. Would you not like to go home now?" JRD would answer, "What have I to go home to?" Neither children nor grandchildren were there to greet him on his return. There was his wife in the wheelchair with a nurse and his pet dog to receive him. In some ways he had everything, in other ways, nothing. He lacked some of the simple joys of life but it never dampened his spirits.

At the end of his life, he was searching for a deeper faith in God.

I had my most moving interview with him two weeks before he left India forever for Geneva. He was discussing with me a hymn he liked, "Abide with Me". "God has to look after 800 million people in this country and six billion in the world, how can I expect him to look after me or abide with me?" I replied, "It depends on your understanding of God. If God is your friend, you would." Then I quoted the lines:

> *He walks with me*
> *He talks with me*
> *He tells me I am his own.*

"It is beautiful," he said, paused and then added, "Walk with me! I think it is damn cheeky to say that. He has so much to do. Why should he bother about me?"

He said that he had prayed more in the last year, though he had prayed earlier when someone near him died, but never for himself.

This was in mid-September 1993.

On 4 November, JRD was removed to the Geneva State Hospital with very high fever and a urinary infection which was brought under control. He knew he was nearing the end and he wanted to go. He told a friend in French, *"Comme c'est doux de mourir."* (How sweet/gentle it is to die.)

On 26th November, two of his doctors, Dr Dalal and Dr Farokh Udwadia, both from Bombay, met him. Dr Udwadia asked, "What is your major complaint, Jeh?"

"Don't you know, my dear Farokh, it is age. After all, I am eighty-nine." JRD had given up eating a couple of days earlier. "Don't behave like a child," remonstrated the doctor. "You must eat." "Why do you want me to eat at my age? Why should I eat? Why should I not just shut my eyes and go?"

Later the same day, Simone Tata met JRD in hospital. JRD seemed somewhat brighter. Between spells of drowsiness and alertness, he suddenly opened his eyes and said in French to Simone Tata, "I am about to discover a new world. It is going to be very interesting, very interesting."

"As he said it," Simone Tata recalls, "his eyes were sparkling as if he had seen a glimpse of that new world." After that, he went back to sleep.

Three days later, in the early hours of the morning, he passed away.

Based on *A Touch of Greatness: Encounters with the Eminent*
by R.M. Lala
Penguin, Delhi, 2002

PERSONAL

Family Letters

★

Personal Views and Preferences

★

Home Workshop and Other Interests

★

Guiding Principles

This section is divided into four parts.

Part I comprises a section of the family letters. This correspondence, which is between JRD and his parents, is handwritten and has been published without making any corrections.

JRD was born in 1904 in Paris. His father—RD—was a Parsi and his mother Suzanne (Sooni after marriage), French.

RD was a Director of Tatas and a close colleague of Jamsetji Tata, founder of the house of Tata. Jamsetji selected RD and Dorab as his two partners in Tata and Sons in 1887. His second son Ratan was too young then, but joined later.

RD's work demanded his presence in Bombay. Most of JRD's school days till the age of twelve were spent in Paris. Following this there was a three-year (1916-1919) spell in Bombay and Yokohama. Later he spent a year in England and one-and-a-half years in France. At twenty-two, he arrived in India and lived here for the rest of his life. Some of JRD's early letters in French were written in pencil. The earliest written by him was to his mother when he was nine. The family letters were discovered after his death in 1993, and some of them have been translated into English for publication in this volume.

JRD was ten when World War I broke out. His mother began voluntary service as a nurse. The strain of the War and bringing up five children resulted in her getting afflicted by tuberculosis. She passed away in 1923 and her husband in 1926.

Part II: "Personal Views and Preferences"—includes JRD's letters to various people in India and abroad on diverse topics: God, literature, sculpture, sports, painting, cosmetics, etc. His strong likes and dislikes are reflected here.

Part III: "Home Workshop and Other Interests"gives us an insight into one of JRD's major pastimes: working in his workshop at home. He was also a fitness freak and a lover of the English language.

The last part, "Guiding Principles" on which he built up his life, includes letters which specify these principles.

Family Letters

TO MOTHER[*]

19, Boulevard Delessert
Sunday, 23 February 1913

My Dearest Little Mama,

I think of you often. We are all very happy that you are returning soon. I hope that you will have a good journey.

I embrace you with all my heart.

Your Little Jehangir

---

[*]   Original letter in French at the age of nine.

TO FATHER[*]

Saturday, 11 April 1914

My poor papa,

I am so disappointed as you had written in the letter which we received this morning about not to have written a word of tenderness but I hope that you are fine to forgive me. My poor papa I see how you must be sad and disappointed.

I ask you to forgive me not to have written to you either on Wednesday or on Thursday but truly it was not my fault because in the morning it was calculation composition period and afterwards history composition and in the afternoon another composition and we left at 4 o'clock. But on entering we were told that Mumma and Navajbai[**] were coming so I dressed up and once dressed I heard the door bell ring and I was told it is Mumma and Navajbai but nay it is Jamie who came to tell us that Mumma and Navajbai have not come and as Taleron and Louisette...(two little school girls) had told us that if we could come to the spot outside....We played our piece of piano with four hands and afterwards Mumma sang and I put the music in order until Navajbai's departure...I hoped that I would not start again and I followed just the same. I think and hope that you are fine. I embrace you with all my heart.

Your dear Jehangir

---

[*]   Original in French.
[**] Navajbai (in Gujarati).

TO FATHER

My Papa,

I have gone to the Champs de mars to play with my friends but it was very cold then came back at 15 minutes to 6 and I was coughing much then Gannie told me that I would not go to the school tomorrow if I would cough like that, I hope I won't cough like that tomorrow because I should not like not to go to school. I hope you are well, the others are going well. I do my exercises everyday and pray everyday well. My dear papa when you will come back will you teach us some other prayers and you will also when you will come back take us to see something new, it is so nice to go for a walk with you and you give so great attention to us. Oh Papa! I was so glad when the last day before your departure for India you went for a walk with us and when we went to the Pantheon with you. Oh Papa, my heart palpitates! I kiss you very nicely.

Your Jehangir

TO MOTHER[*]

Val-Mont
Territet
June 1919

Mami Dearest,

It is with joy that we yesterday learnt that you were leaving today for Hardelot with the young ones, because it is a sign that all the many big troubles have been overcome, the servants and home arrangements, and above all because now that the young ones are settled down we will not have a long time to wait before seeing you again here near us, because you know it seems to me that Val-Mont is more sad since you are no more here.

I have a lot of things to say to you, so much so that I do not know which end to begin from! Ah! At first, health, I am fine, although I have only increased by 50 grams today in these last three days...

Now moving to things more important in life. Sylla and I have each bought a racket, Driva 13 ozs...and we build our stamina without tiring ourselves, because we play only one set per day and do not go there every day! It is inconvenient to play with a collar and tie.

Day before yesterday and yesterday we had horrid weather, dreadfully dull, abominable, disgusting fog, could not see a thing for five metres, and ceaselessly drizzling. On the contrary today we had bright weather and marvellous clearness, it was at the same time very hot.

---

[*] Original in French written at the age of fourteen. The letter refers to R.D. Tata's first visit to France after World War I, hence the reference to recouping his health.

Papa is better. He sleeps better and scratches himself much less. That makes us very happy and I hope that he will be cured quickly. Besides, everyone finds him changed so much, he has a better appearance and refreshed features. It is to you Mamerette dearest to follow this good example. I would so much like to see you in all good health and well rested. You have another example here, it is Aunt Bianca. She has put on weight so very rapidly that I am astounded by it!

How are the young ones? Kiss them well from me and Gannie also I hope that they have received my three cards.

I believe Mamie that this is a little close to all that I had to say to you, also I stop myself here, and I am sending this letter immediately wanting you to reply to it before your departure.

I kiss you a million times very tenderly and I am waiting impatiently for your return.

Your son who loves you,
Jehangir

TO FATHER

Sal mubaruck,* my dear Papa,

Though you must have already got the letter containing my wishes for a merry Christmas and a happy new year, I renew my wishes in this letter. You were the only one today, of us, that did not get our wishes, and so when I wish you happiness and health, though it is through a letter it gives me a little the impression that you are among us, or at least not so far.

There is the birth of a new year, and I hope it will bring us many things. First I hope it will keep us all in good health and specially you who need it so much to keep up the work you are doing now. Then I hope it will bring your return to France and for long. Thirdly success in your business and plenty of happiness for you and all of us. These are the principal. Then I hope also to succeed well in my studies for the better I work the sooner I shall replace you in the business. My trimestrial notes were not very brilliant as you may see in the note we got from school and which I am sending to you with the letter. You will see the remarks of my teacher Mr. Cury and of the Censor. Latin and Mathematics are especially the feeble points but I promise you that my next trimestrial notes will be better than these. Mami will go and see Mr. Cury for my Latin and see if I shall have to take private lessons....

Goodbye, dear Papa, till next Thursday, I enclose in this letter lots of love and kisses.

Lovingly yours,
Jehangir

---

* Happy New Year (in Gujarati).

P.S. The apartment is getting on fine and the carpets are already put down in the dining room, the bibliotheque, the two drawing rooms and Mami's room. One of Touton Louis' paintings is nailed on the wall and looks and is really beautiful. Another one will be ready on Thursday next and the last one two weeks after.

TO FATHER

140 *Avenue V. Hugo*
19 May 1920

My dear Papa,

You must be by now very near to Bombay and if everything goes well, you will be there day after tomorrow. I hope it will be after a very good voyage and after having had a pleasant time on board. I hope that you have met nice people and even some friends of yours.

How fine wouldn't it be if the boat was going the other way and that you were instead of going to India, already coming back to France!

First of all I have news to tell which I am sure will please you immensely. Darab and I are accepted at the "College of Normandie". Isn't it fine? The director, Mr. Dedet, has already come to see Mami and everything is arranged! You can't imagine how happy I am though still doubting. Well you see I have been refused thrice already and had lost all hope of being accepted, by now, so you may judge of my surprise and joy. I am sure you will be glad too, especially for Darab, who like that won't be too shy and to whom the first days won't seem so hard....

We are all well, Mami is getting on very well and I find her fatter and very much better. Sylla too is improving, and miracle, she is writing letters like she has never written in her life. I hope it will last!

I won't write more today my dear Papa, and will stop here, hoping you are in perfect health. I hope we will soon get news from you and know that you have safely arrived to Bombay. Goodbye, Papa dear, I join to this letter all the best and most loving kisses from your

Affectionate,
Jehangir

TO FATHER

Hardelot
3 August 1921

My dear Papa,

We got a letter from you yesterday and I thank you ever so much, to write sometimes like that directly to us. I know how terribly busy you are, and what little time you have to spare, so it seems to me I am happier still when I get them, and I read them with more gratefulness.

You say in your letter that I shall have to go to India in 1922. You can't imagine how glad I am, for I would even want to go this year with Sylla. But I understand that I positively can't go before I possess more thoroughly the English language and really now I am incapable of holding a serious conversation in English. And that is why I want to ask you something which I think really very important. It is to leave definitively my French studies which are absolutely useless for my future, and to go for a year in England,* after which I will be better prepared to go to India.

Please don't think, Papa, that it is only a passing fancy. I have thought all the time of that since I am in Hardelot and I really feel I must go to England....

As I promised you when you left I am doing regularly exercises every day two or three times, and I have bought a sandow exerciser with which I develop my chest and its muscles. I have already made good progress. But the hardest part of my body to improve in shape and colour is my face; for though I feel I am getting much stronger, though I eat like ten hungry soldiers at every meal, though I sleep so much and often, that I have acquired a strong reputation of laziness, my face is still pretty

---

* His father took due notice and got him admitted to a "Crammer" so that he could learn the English language fast.

thin though not half so pale. And unluckily it's the face that people generally see first...

Maman's health is improving in Swithzerland and we all here are also in very good health...

I hope my dear Papa, that you too are keeping in health and that all your affairs are behaving to your satisfaction. How much I would like to begin at once to work in Bombay so as to be able to unburden in a few years of a part of your work.

Hoping you will consider my demand I shall stop here, dear Papa, and end this long epistle by sending you my best love and kisses.

Jehangir

TO FATHER

Southwold, Suffolk
11 October 1921

My dearest Papa,

Here I am in England since a week tomorrow, and settled in this seaside place in Mr. Hope's school. I won't talk to you much of the school because I suppose you know everything about it. Let me just tell you that Mr. Hope is very nice to me and that everything is getting on very well.

As for all these English boys here, all of them from 16 to 20, I was rather disappointed in them as well as regards to their manners as for their mentality. They are all insincere and thoroughly false. And if I had not an Indian friend, Chakravarti here, I wouldn't know what to do. Anyway everything is all right and I will get along very well.

As the weather has been simply marvellous since I am here and until today I bathed every day and had lovely swims. But the weather is changing now and I don't think I'll bathe any more this year.

Now to progress by order I will first tell you about my work and then about games and sports.

Work starts in the morning at 9¼ and goes until one o'clock. Then we have the whole afternoon for games and work starts again at 5¼ until 7¼. Dinner is at half past seven and three times a week I work sciences that is chemistry from half past eight to half past nine. Now about the work itself: I do some French, English, History, Chemistry and Mathematics. I do 3 hours of French a week, 9 of English, 6 of History, 3 of Chemistry and 9 of Maths. That is how my time table is now and I think it is definitive. I had three more hours of French put into three of Maths.

I hope you will like my doing a lot of Maths. As a matter of fact it is what I like best here.

Now in games and sports I have taken up boxing (twice a week) and football. And perhaps I will take up golf too. Of course when the season will come, football will be replaced by tennis. The thing I am most keen on is boxing, and the teacher, Sergeant Button, said I would be very fast. That is a main point in boxing. And I will owe it to my year and half of fencing. As for fencing, I think I will have to give it up here, because there isn't any good professor. And I would rather console myself with the thought of boxing...

I heard from Mama that you had been ill with malaria. I really hope that it was nothing very serious and that you have got over it by now and that you are quite well again. I would be dreadfully sorry to know you to be ill and so far from us all....

I hug you thousands and thousands of times with all my heart.

Your son that loves you,
Jehangir

FROM FATHER

Bombay
21 October *1921*

My dear Jehangir,

I received your letter of 29th September from Bonneville S/Tonques at Suzors. I am glad you enjoyed there so well & also at Hardelot. I now hope that you will put in the same zeal, energy & time in your work in England as you did in dancing & other amusement all throughout the summer. Do you know for your age your handwritings are abominable? You must improve them. Now I was extremely pained to learn that you have become very negligent since I left. It seems that through your negligence your bicycle costing 700 francs was stolen, that you lost a *gold* watch & gold chain & a gold pencil. I cannot think without feeling distressed that my son who is going to come to help me in business can be so negligent. You know your father works like a nigger in such a climate to keep & maintain his family in comfort. The presents that my children get don't think that they cost me nothing. I have to return—in presents—to everybody that has given you whenever an occasion arises. Most painful to me is your conduct towards me, your father, in keeping everything secret from me. Is this the recompense you are giving me in return for all that I do for you—riding, tennis, golfing, fencing, etc.? You know very well that I excuse & pardon everything if you tell me at once. The only recompense I want from you is to take your father into all your secrets & never keep anything from him. I shall then become your friend plus father & will always give you good advice. You must now promise me to do all this. Poor Maman must also be very much distressed now that you will be in England. I hope you will devote the short time you will be there in your studies. I have written to Mr. Treble that if my boy wants to have his long nose broken let him learn boxing.

I am delighted to learn that you have gained 3 kilos in weight & 12 centimetres around the chest. The weather in England is very treacherous, always cover yourself immediately after any exercise in the open. Are you doing the exercises I had shown you? Do them everyday at least once. Do you pray?...

In the school & outside be very polite with everybody & never tell untruth whatever happens. Take care of your health & also of your clothes.

Au revoir mon enfant, je t'embrasse de tout coeur.

Papa

TO FATHER

My dear Papa,

I am writing to you just before lunch, and lunch is just before the fancy dress hockey match we are going to play today in benefit of Southwold's hospital. I don't remember if I told you in my last letter, anyway I say it now. I did not mean to join because I did not know how to dress and I had nothing. But as players were wanted I accepted yesterday and I will appear dressed as a girl. A lady in town who helped us all a great deal for this match, lent me a dress, a sun hat (I look charming in it), a blouse and a pair of stockings. We had notices put in town, and the town crier announced the news yesterday and today, so I hope there will be lots of people. I had asked Mama for an advise a week ago but I had no answer, so I will stick to that dress. I am sure we will make a most comic and interesting group and I wish you would see us. As soon as the match is over and we have come back home I will continue this letter and let you know how everything happened.

Well, my dear Papa, I just come from tea, after having played in the match. It was a great success; in fact it turned out far better than we thought it would, and we collected over three pounds for the hospital. I never had such fun in my life and I enjoyed the game thoroughly. Photos have been taken of us, and I will buy some and send some to you and some to Mama. I hope they will be good ones....

I am going on very well here, as well as my work. I have started boxing and I like it immensely. Physically I am feeling very well and I am sure that this outdoor life and out of town, is doing me a lot of good....

Goodbye dear Papa....

Many many kisses and lots of love from your loving

Jehangir

FROM FATHER

Bombay
4 November 1921

My dear Jehangir,

I was very pleased to receive your first letter from England. I hope you know that these are the last 12 months of your student life & that you will take full advantage of the opportunity. In sports you will know the character of the English boys from every side, but then you must go with an open mind and not with "prejudge" opinion. I was very sorry & pained to see that before you were hardly a week at school you judged all the boys as "thoroughly false" and "insincere". If you are going to judge people so hastily & so haphazardly when you will go into the world as a man I am sure you will be a failure in the world. There are 2 sides to a shield. It seems you don't want to see the better side. So I as a father, strongly advise you to try & become friends with some of them, instead of standing aloof with prejudiced opinion & I assure you you will find these boys quite different. I shall be glad to learn that you are following my advice....Frankly join the sports & be a *camarade* of everybody. I am glad you had swims & also have taken up boxing. Don't have your beautiful big nose broken. Football I am afraid won't be nice for you. You must consult a doctor for it. You must also do a lot of chemistry along with plenty of mathematics. You were right to give up fencing as the English fencing is quite different to the French....

Write me every week & everything. Don't hide anything from me. I am not only your loving father but also your best friend. You must tell me even if you had done anything wrong.

Goodbye my dear child, I hug you with all my heart. Be good, nice & polite to all.

Your Papa

TO FATHER

Southwold, Suffolk
10 November 1921

My dear Papa,

When I came back from London on Sunday in Mami's letter I found yours and I thank you very much for it.

But I must say that though I was awfully happy for the bright two days I passed in London and for having telephoned to Mami, I was very much cooled down on reading your letter and in fact I felt very unhappy. For you were a bit hard on me, and I hate giving you any cause to be angry or dissatisfied with me.

I don't understand why I did not write to you about all the misfortunes that happened to me in form of the losses of many things during the summer, because I told it to Mama and I would certainly be more afraid of her for such cases than of you. But don't think that I wanted to hide anything from you. I don't think I hid anything ever from you and I don't want to begin now. I was almost sure that I had told you about the loss of my bicycle and how the whole thing happened.

But if I didn't and for the other things too I am very very sorry and I want you to pardon me and not be any more angry with me.

Another thing is that you must not think that I have been negligent in all my losses. For it is only the loss of my watch which is due to some negligence of mine. I ought not to have taken such a watch in a tour to the battle fields, and I ought never to have left it in the car with my waistcoat while visiting a cimitery. I don't know if it has been stolen during that time, or if it slipped through a hole in the coat afterwards.

But for the bicycle you may ask Sylla who will tell you the circumstances under which it was stolen, and you will see that it was not all through my fault.

As for the coat, I never knew how it happened, for I had left it in its place hooked on a hanger…where all the coats were, and I never found it again.

Why also do you also ask me every time if I pray, or do the exercises you showed me? I promised I would and it seems that you have very poor faith in my words. Anyway you may believe me I do the exercises every morning and some others too.

As for praying I don't think I could possibly go to sleep without doing so. So on that too, dear Papa, you may be quite at rest…

Hoping again that you have forgiven me for all my grievances to you, I kiss you over and over again with all the tenderness and affection of your ever loving son,

Jehangir

P.S. I am playing a lot of games here: football, hockey and boxing (by the way my nose is not yet broken) and I have plaid this afternoon in football with our team against the Southwold reserves.

J.

TO FATHER

My dear Papa,

I have received your long letter, and I thank you very much for it. I was very happy, especially that as there is a short time I got a letter from you, I did not expect another one so soon.

I admit my dear Papa, that I was a bit hasty in forming an opinion of the boys here, but I was vexed and angry then, and one never ought to issue an opinion when angry. N'est-ce-pas?

All the fellows seemed very nice to me in the beginning and they asked me to lend them my bike, and this and that, while behind my back they said all sorts of things about me and made fun of me.

I was foolish enough to take offence and to be vexed, and I must owe that I judged them all rather haphazardly. But there was some sense in what I said.

Don't be afraid Papa that we talk all the time about politics or such things. In fact we never do, knowing too well how dangerous a subject it is...

You say, Dearest Pa, that I ought not to play football. But what must I play then? All the boys play only football and hockey, each once a week, and so do I. I haven't notice any harm it may have done to me and I hope you won't mind if I go on playing. I don't think I will take up golf just now, but perhaps next term.

I am very glad you said that you would travel with me in England next year, though I think I prefer France, but I don't mind, and as long as I am with you I don't care where I go.

But what I don't understand is your saying that it would be better for me to stay in England for the holidays. Who with? I don't know a soul here out of the Trebles, and I how could I possibly stay away, when Mami, home and everything I like is so near at hand?...

Goodbye, dear Papa, be sure that I am doing all I can to please you in every sort of way. And that I always will...

Jehangir

TO FATHER

My dear Papa,

This letter will reach you very near Christmas so I load it with all the wishes for a Happy Christmas and new year my heart has prepared for you.

I hope that it will be a happier year than this one, and that we won't be each in a corner of the world, as now, but all together and all very happy.

I hope that all your affairs will work better and that they will leave you more time to rest and take care of your health. I hope all sorts of things for your happiness and health. I hope that when I will enter the business, you won't be dissatisfied with me, that I will prove to have the stuff of a businessman and that later you will be quite proud of me.

Yes I hope for all that and more, and I pray every night for them all. This Christmas again like last year you are away from us, but may god let us be together for next, and pass a happy time together. I am going Saturday to France by aeroplane. Maman permitted me if I paid the difference of price between the usual way and air way...

I am awfully keen on driving it and very glad. I will tell you next week how I liked it and how I felt.

If only it was not so dear, wouldn't it be splendid?!

A term has passed now in Southwold, and still two to come. At the beginning I felt rather lonely and *dépaysé* (disoriented). But now I have become used to it. The air is so pure and healthy. The town is calm and the daily life and work is good and regular. I have been working well I think and if not as much as I did in Paris at least better and more regularly. But I will work still more next term now that I am well in the "routine" of the thing. The only thing I really like here is Mathematics...

As I told you in a previous letter I am doing the games very regularly and am enjoying football and hockey very much.

I don't know if I am fatter (I am certainly not thinner) but I feel much better than in Paris, and haven't been once really tired since I am here, not even after a game.

By the way how many of your cars did Sylla smash? Why don't you buy a pedal one for her?

Goodbye, dear Papa, I will go to bed now and repeating all my wishes, I send you also my best love and kisses.

Your loving son
Jehangir

TO FATHER

My dear Papa,

I am writing this letter today to ask you something. And this something is the biggest thing I ever asked for and a thing which there are nine chances on ten you will refuse. But as miracles do happen sometimes and that you don't consider me now as a child I take my courage in both my hands as we say in French, and ask you for a motorcycle!

I know that you will at first get angry or shrug your shoulders, but please Papa think about it long before you take a decision and for heaven's sake don't mention it to Boman Bheram or I am done for.

I know what I ask you is terrible, considering your ideas and Mama's on a motorcycle which to you both is simply an instrument of accidents and death.

But then you sent me to England to live with English people and take their habits. Well England is the country of motorcycles, and of ten English boys, there are easily nine who have, had, or will have one, and there, it is only considered as a mode of locomotion better than an ordinary bicycle and less expensive than a car. Then there is a reason, other than that I am very keen on having a bike. It is that Saturday afternoons and Sundays are simply deadly in Southwold, as we are not allowed to do anything or play any games on Sundays. So that if I had a motorcycle there would be at least something to do. Of course if you don't want me to I won't buy a powerful and speedy machine but a very moderate one such as 3½ HP.

I won't speak any more about it now, dear Papa, but please don't make a hasty decision and remember that I am, perhaps stupidly but really tremendously eager and hopeful. And don't say "Ask Mama", for she said, "Ask Papa"!

If it is yes, by chance, I could use it for nine months until we go to India. Another thing very important: The prices are of course like cars, very high, and the best bikes cost 150 or 160 £. But I wouldn't buy so dear, so please let me know what prices you will allow.

I will be dreaming and hoping until I get your answer, and I pray god I may not be deceived....

I read Sylla's letter about all the festivals in Bombay, and I was delighted that you both enjoyed it very much.

I am so glad now that you have one of us with you now, and that you are less lonely.

Do you remember when we were Sylla and I both with you when Mama was still in Japan? How we used to sit down with you at your dinner every night and talked over all what we did during the day! Happy time!

Mama told me you were in very good health now. I am very glad, and I hope you will always be thus, as well as Sylla.

Yours very affectionately,

Jehangir

FROM FATHER

Bombay
23 December 1921

My dear Jehangir,

I was very pleased as usual to hear from you. I am very happy to see that you write me very regularly & everything. You said in this letter that the boys in your school said all sorts of things about you behind your back & made fun of you. O.K. But my dear boy how did you know that the boys were so mean to say bad things of you behind your back? Somebody must have carried you such stories. Why do you mind, my dear boy, about such petty things? In life, when you will be little older you will have to go through such serious things & matters that you will yourself laugh at what you now take seriously. In life we must mind our own business & continue to act & think as your conscience dictates when you are old enough. At present mind your studies, enjoy your student life & act according to the advice of your parents.

If it pleases you & if you are told that you are physically strong you can play football....

You will have plenty of opportunities to travel in France while it will be rare to do so in England. So if I come over to England we will travel & see the country a bit.

You must now be in Paris for the Xmas holidays & must be happy to be with Maman & children. Sylla is content & happy here & enjoys herself. Next year she will come back with you & then you 2 can enjoy here more. Our new house will then also be finished.

I wish you a merry Xmas & a very happy new year.

I hug you my dear child with all my heart.

Papa

FROM FATHER

Bombay
29 December 1921

My dear Jehangir,

I was delighted to have a long letter of 8th Dec. from you. This year's Xmas has come & gone & we shall enter into a new year of 1922. I sincerely hope & trust this new year will bring to all of us health, happiness & prosperity which we sorely needed in 1921. The present year had been a very unlucky year for us, however I am thankful to God that the whole family remained intact & safe. You know, the year 1922 will be an eventful year for you. When (1) you will leave your student's life & (2) you will enter into a business career where your intelligence, your nerves, your courage & your morals will be severely tested by the eventful life that you will be leading. You will there understand the seriousness of responsibility. I doubt not that my Jehangir will eventually come out successful through his high moral qualities. You will find in your path many pitfalls & temptations which you will have to shun & jump over though with great difficulties. If you always keep before your eyes Truth & Honesty whatever happens you will come out safe; at least you will never be discredited or dishonoured. May God always protect you from all temptations. You should never forget that you have a mother & a father to whom you should courageously go for advice even if you had made mistakes or when you find yourself in difficulties. You must for your own sake take them as your confessors, guides, friends & *camarades*. Keep this letter with you always and read often even if I did not exist in this world & follow my advice. Never forget that you have the best of mothers who adores you all & who has made immense sacrifices in her health & peace of mind & who will do everything to make you happy. Worship her & always go to her for advice.

I was extremely pleased to read in your letter "I hope that when I will enter the business you won't be dissatisfied with me, that I will prove to have the stuff of a businessman & that later you will quite be proud of me."

Papa

FROM MOTHER[*]

23 January 1922

My Dear Big One,

A word in haste that forwards all my affection...
Work hard my dear child, think of the happiness you give us and always be under God's protection.
My most loving kisses,

Your Mami

---

*   Original in French.

TO MOTHER[*]

Mama Dear,

I received your long and sweet letter and I thank you for it with all my heart. I was absolutely grieved to learn that Papa will not be able to come again to France this year. But is it absolutely definite? The changes in business are so frequent, that it is necessary that he comes. It would be sad if he didn't come and I understand how hard the shock of this sad news must be. The only compensation that I find in my sadness is the thought that I will be travelling only with you and I will have you all to myself for 15 days! It is so rare that I have the luck to be alone with you for long. But at the same time I had so much hoped to pass summer altogether with Papa again at the centre of the family for once entire!

I am very happy that you have overcome your sadness and that you have accepted this cruel news with your habitual energy. When I think of all that you suffered and tolerated during your life and the things that you have known how to overcome, you cannot imagine how proud I am to be your son, and to be able to call you Mama! There are times in which I would have desired to talk about you to the whole world and to show them how superior you are to other ladies and especially to the English women, but they would not understand…

As a matter of fact, I will be able to use only the train ticket to Paques, since in July I will be 18 years old and the classes end here a few days before this date. Now in order to go there and return to London, that would cost me eighty francs

---

[*]   Original in French.

more than what I will spend during the stay in the city. That it would not be a big advantage and may be even a loss. But if you believe that it will be better if I go there tell me in your next letter and before the reply is received from London, if it is necessary I will go.

I am very happy that the young ones are well because at the same time you can also take rest. I was also very happy to know that the doctor finds you better because if you are going to the Indes in winter it would be necessary that you are entirely well and strong to stand the few months that you will stay there to resist the climate that is not good.

You have a good reason to keep Sylla close to Papa during summer...She is also a support for Papa because she deprives him of some solitude and I am sure that he would be unhappy if he had gone himself in April.

Do not torment yourself on small things here, mama dearest. I am very well... I have started once again hockey and football and I play tomorrow in a match of...

I am going to stop myself here because I have a lot of work. My best wishes to all our friends and to you, Mamerette, all my tenderness and affection, big kisses.

Jehangir

FROM MOTHER*

5 July 1922

My Dearest,

What joy I felt to know that you arrived without discomfort because I like to believe that you are a good sailor. I wanted to write to you at length, thanking you for your very loving affectionate letters but we are leaving on the 10th for "Charville". We had to make the plan to go this week!...

Naruseh has sent his photograph for you that I will send you tomorrow or later. Thank Sylla for her letter dated 16th June which followed the one of 11th May! And she tells me that she excuses herself for having missed 2 couriers. The naughtiness! Anyway, hug her tight and tell her to send me one letter immediately regarding the linen from Bombay and the table size for the sheets.

I hug you very tight, my dear big one and Lylette also.

Write to me at length about the details of your life.

Tari Mami Sooni**

Cultivate music and your stomach.

---

*   Original in French.
** Your mother Sooni (in Gujarati).

TO MOTHER[*]

Poona
21 July 1922

Mama Dear,

Like you see I am still in Poona and I am coming to Bombay only on Monday with Papa who comes this evening...

On Monday, I will go for the first time to office to work there. Let's hope that very soon Papa will have every reason to be happy with me and that he will have all that he expects from me. As for me I am very willing and hopeful. You will know in my next letter what were my defects (how my beginnings have been).

Yesterday Dorabji and Meherbai returned from Bangalore and came home for lunch....They brought back a young gentle fox terrier with a willing heart to play all the time but feeling violently attracted by the fringes of our carpet. It was necessary to tie her up!

You must know that Dorabji has a beard now. He does not look worse, but in fact better. Meherbai is always the same, shining in bright and conspicuous colours to bring out the fineness of her silhouette. Besides they were both in fairly good humour.

I have nothing interesting or important to say as absolutely nothing special has happened and every day has been the same as the previous one. Once in Bombay I will have lots of things to tell you about.

You must at present be all well settled in the countryside, and I see the younger ones running and romping happily in the middle of flowers and greenery.

---

[*]   Original in French.

And you Mama, I hope that you take rest and rapidly regain all health and the kilos that you desire since such a long time.

We are all well here and the temperature and weather is truly very pleasant at present.

I am going to stop here, mama dear, and hoping to receive good news from you soon. I hug you very hard and a million times with all my heart and also the young ones.

Your son,
Jehangir

FROM FATHER

Winter Palace
28 December 1922

My dear Jehangir,

I am very much delighted to receive your letters regularly & full of news. I hope you will continue to do so. I am preserving these letters to be useful to you for future reference. The great success you have achieved is that Peterson is very much satisfied with you. By this time you must have met the Viceroy & I am anxious to know all about his visit to Jamshedpur. It is a real pity that neither Dorabji nor I was present to receive him.

About the knotty question of Jamshedpur labour, I will wait to discuss it till my return. During your stay in Jamshedpur I hope you have got some inkling of how the things are managed there so that next autumn when you will go to stay there some length of time (at least 3 months), you can go there deeply & study every department. Up to that time you will have got some general knowledge of the business. As I have already written to you you must always put health first & then business. Without health the business is bound to be neglected or done in a slipshod way. Never miss some outdoor exercise or sports in a moderate way. Don't pray neglect the advice of mine.

You can never write me *too many* details. I want them to keep myself thoroughly *au courant* with all that is going on. I am surprised that only 5% of the import of Iron into Japan is from India. We must try to work & get hold of some portion however small of the rest 95%. I am glad to learn that the D furnace is in blast now...

I am glad you have fixed up with our architect the changes proposed by Maman in the new house.

Wishing you my dear Jehangir, a very happy new year full of health. I hug you with all my heart.

Papa

TO FATHER

Papa cheri,

I have received and thank you immensely for your letter dated 18th July which Sylla forwarded to me together with hers…

I thank you for your kind wishes for my birthday. I know that half of this new year of my life will be spent in my paternal fatherland. You need not fear, dear Papa, my not liking it. I have lived in it and been happy there long enough to *love* it. If we consider the climate and amusement or distraction I admit frankly that I prefer France, but for work and the life we lead there I could not by any means wish for something better and grander. And I have more friends there too….

I have read in the minutes of one of last month's Tisco's board meetings that you were expecting Mahatma Gandhi* at Jamshedpur. Did it come off? I hope the effect of that visit was good and that you were satisfied. It must have pleased and impressed labour. I wonder what his opinion of Jamshedpur in general and labour questions in particular, was.

A year ago today, I embarked on my typhoid. Gosh, but I did feel rotten that day! I am glad I am better than that today! I am keeping very well but I am sure I would be much better if I were at home. For I have a good appetite, but I am getting fed up with this food and I am not eating as much as I could and would if it were good. I will take my revenge in three months! 85 days left today! How many of them will go by before you join us Papa?…

---

* Mahatma Gandhi visited Jamshedpur at the invitation of the management and labour leaders of Tata Steel.

I don't know why, but I haven't much to tell you this week. Nothing interesting seems to have happened....So I will say goodbye here. I hope you are always in very good health and are keeping in spite of all your troubles...the invincibly high spirits for which you are so envied.

Good bye, Papa cheri...

Jehangir

TO FATHER

Vienne

13 August 1925

Dearest Papa,

Thanks very much for your letter of the 23rd July.

I was filled with admiration at reading of your dancing feats! I honestly think you are perfectly amazing to be able to stand the strain of business all day, and then finding it not sufficient, spending your nights banqueting and dancing. Men even one-third of your age would not bear up long! I certainly wouldn't! I think you are the consecration of what a healthy life and physical culture can do for a man. It makes me laugh when I compare you to all our Indian friends, who although younger than you, are all decrepit & finished physically....

I thank you dear Papa for having given a dinner for my 21st birthday. I would have loved to be present at it instead of being here. However next year will see me in Bombay and I hope we will be together for all our birthdays. Unfortunately Darab and Jimmy will be absent.

You say that if by ill-luck you can't come to France this autumn I will bring back the girls to India. Why Papa, do you mean to say that you are afraid not to be able to absent yourself from Bombay. That would be awful, and I do hope you will soon contradict this. I was counting already that in a month you would be on your way to Marseilles. You must come! I know it is useless my saying that, as you must be doing all you can for that, for if you could not come, you would suffer from it more than ourselves, being all alone in Bombay.

I am sending your letter on to Sylla and I am expecting yours to her today or tomorrow.

…I am afraid this disaster will deal a bad blow to the fate of Hardelot which will now be classed as a dangerous seaside resort….

The night before last was the worst I spent at the Regiment*. I had to go and sleep at the Chambre and fought all night with *bugs*. Again! I only slept an hour in the whole night and next morning I had at least 200 bites on me! If it had not been cold and raining, I would have gone and slept outside but could not do so for that reason. I caught a cold on the stomach not having my shawl and being half of the time out of my bed shaking my sheets and near an open window. I took calomel this morning, wore my shawl around me whole day and night and am quite well now….

The General, Inspector-General of Cavalry is coming to inspect our Depot next Wednesday. Our commandant is to meet him at the station with his car. And as he has no chauffeur I believe he is going to ask me to drive! Great guns! It is a Renault and I will have to drive slowly, but still I will enjoy it as there is a long time I haven't done so. I will go round bends on two wheels and skid into the entrance. I think not!…

I have never been so much interrupted in a letter as I have been over this one. Owing to the coming of the General and also owing to the escape of a prisoner from here there was a lot of work to do today. Being the only man who types in this beastly place every letter or document to be typewritten is given to me. It is the only useful thing I will have learnt in the army, typewriting fairly well. However I must say that isn't my vocation for I am getting fed up with it. I would much prefer being whole day doing some work outside rather than spending my time sitting in an office.

We have had perfectly magnificent weather today, sunny and warm. A weather that makes you feel that…this world…is full of good things. My liberation seems to me nearer on such days….

I hope the weather is improving in India. The thick of the monsoon must be over and it is less damp now. Still it would be so much better for your health if you could spend a few weeks in France or Italy. In India you can never get away from business and its worries and if you don't come this year when will you be able to come next? And if you do come alone, it won't be the same as being with your five kids around you. That is why I pray to God that you may come in September.

---

* As per the law, JRD spent a year in the French army.

Meanwhile I hope you are keeping very well. Don't be anxious about me. I am getting on very well. The children are well too.

Goodbye Papa Dear, I hug you with all my heart and very affectionately.

Your son,
Jehangir

TO FATHER

7 September 1925

Dear Papa,

I have not yet received the news from you which must have come by last mail....
I have received however mail from the office, mainly the speeches made by Mahatma Gandhi and concerning his visit to our works. I see it was a very great success and was quite an event in India. I must say I was very glad to see your name mentioned so often and to see how responsible and important was your position. If a son can compliment his father I can say I was devilish proud of you! And I feel rather awed when I think that one day I will have to take your place. It will be a terribly heavy and great "heritage" and I pray to god that I may have the brains, the willpower and the shoulders to bear the weight of it.

I hope your concessions to labour will not have been in vain and that now the relations between the latter and the Management and Board will have relaxed into easy & friendly cooperation. I know that, on principle, labour, all over the world like to consider themselves and pose as victims of capital, and as you often said in certain cases they are to a degree justified. But I hope that your generosity towards them and your fatherly appreciation of them will destroy this belief in the mind of our labour. Anyway it will surely have brought back in our favour the opinion of many people whose opinion was that Tatas and all industrialists simply exploited their workmen.

I wonder why the Board have refused to sanction the Rs.250 for a Baby Clinic in Jamshedpur. It was not much but would have perhaps reinforced the effect of what you have done at J'pur...

I read in the *Matin* yesterday that 20,000 Mill workmen have gone on strike in Bombay owing to a reduction in salaries. The paper says also that some mills were attacked by strikers throwing stones. It is very unfortunate and you must be very worried again....With such varied interests and affairs one is constantly worried with one of them. When one goes well something goes wrong with the other....

I especially hope that I am wrong in fearing that this strike might again retard your departure. That would be desperately hard luck. I am impatient of getting the *Weekly* that will give me details of what is happening in Bombay....

The cold wave has passed and since yesterday the weather is much warmer but cold has given its place to rain. I hope to goodness it won't rain Saturday, as long runs on wet roads and in the middle of rain are no fun. It is time that the Bugatti is practically incapable of skidding & it is a great asset....

I went to a perambulating circus last evening with some other fellows. It was not up to much naturally, but I enjoyed it like a kid and laughed loudest of all at the clowns' old, old and ever-repeated jokes. Poor Papa, you sent to France almost a man last year and you will find back a child asking to be taken to the circus or *guignol*. This is what army life has done of me!...

I hope Papa cheri you are in very good health and not having too tiring a time in Bombay.

I am very well myself.

Jehangir

TO FATHER

Dear, dear Papa,

I have received this week through Sylla two of your letters to each of us and one to Dabeh. They made me all very sad as they expressed your worries and your sorrow at being unable to come to Europe this year & having to remain alone for months yet. Fate is terribly and obstinately hard and I assure you, dearest Governor that my heart bleeds when I think of all that you are suffering.

We can't do anything to relieve you of your business worries but we can relieve you of your desperate loneliness and longing for your children. I wrote yesterday a letter to Sylla entreating her to take the first boat for India after Darab and Jimmy's entrance at the "Normandie" without waiting for me. I will myself spend in Paris just the necessary number of days to prepare for my departure, seeing the doctor, dentist, buying a few things and will follow if possible on the 14th of November. I am liberated as you know on the 7th.

After receiving your two last letters I am sure Sylla must have had the same idea and if she possibly can there is no doubt that she will leave as very soon as possible. If she can, she, Dabeh & Signorina ought to be with you, at last, in a little over a month, whilst I will join the three of you in 2 months & a few days.

I try and be glad when I think that you will soon have your daughters with you but I wish desperately that they could be with you *allready*!

I was very worried to hear of your fears about Rudhra but was really aghast when I read in the papers the very important proportions taken by the textile strike in Bombay. Heaven, won't your worries never stop. How I regret being as young and still useless to you! My only & dominant thought now is to join you as fast as I can and be of some help to you however small it may be.

I must say I am also very anxious at the danger you may run in Bombay with those thousands of strikers probably out for a riot and trouble. Unfortunately the papers here are very brief & short on the subject & I don't want to send you a wire for fear of worrying you. You must be sufficiently worried as it is! I am afraid even to think of it....

As for your so kind and sad "reproaches" on my "inconscience" at spending money for my pleasure at such moments, they make me terribly sad as they are so very just and justified. They make me realise how stupid unexperienced and thoughtless I am still in spite of my 21 years and the example I have in you. And I am filled with remorse. You will think I am stark mad, but if I find a chance of selling that beastly Bugatti before sailing I am determined to do so....

If I can't, I have indeed hopes of doing so in India as there are no such cars there and there must surely be some other mad fellow like myself to go in for such a car. As a matter of fact I have told Bugattis that I would try and sell some cars for them in India.

If I did not want to wait till my departure to buy a car it was principally to avoid paying the enormous import duty on *new* cars when entering it in Bombay....

You say Papa that our stay in France will have been useless, morally it certainly has been so for me. But physically I don't think it will have been totally useless. I think I am better than before and once I can eat good and nutritious food according to my appetite I am sure to progress distinctly. I have no more trouble with my throat, and since my typhoid last year I have never had any trouble on the stomach side. However future will show wheter I have really made any progress and I hope I have....

I suppose you know that our cousin Jeanne Tribout is getting married (at last!). Sylla & the boys will be in the cortege. And they wrote to me asking me to come too. But you may understand that I hardly feel like travelling 1,000 kilometres to attend a wedding, unless it was mine of course! So I have replied that I tried all I could but found it impossible to get leave. What a lie!

No more shooting for me thank you! I try to joke, but really I have the blues since a few days. I long so much to be with you again that every hour seems to me an invaluable loss!

It is getting dark though it is only 6 o'clock on account of the...weather and the lights are on only at 7. So I will stop now, Papa cheri. I hope that in spite of your worries you are keeping in good health and I pray to god and Mamma with renewed strength to protect & keep you from worries & unhappiness. Goodbye, dear father, your loving Jehangir kisses you with all his heart.

Jehangir

TO FATHER*

Jamshedpur
Sunday, 14 March 1926

Dear Papa,

We arrived yesterday morning at 2 o'clock after an uneventful journey. We found Jamshedpur fairly cool & cloudy and I must say the dryness of the place is very pleasant.

At 10 o'clock Peterson & I went to the office & Peterson had a general talk with Alexander, especially on the rounding up of the plant & the question of the figures to be wired to Tilden Smith on Monday.

He had a talk with Sawday on all the subjects on the agenda regarding sales. Nothing important to report.

We saw also Temple & Percival. In the afternoon after sleep Peterson played golf & I played tennis with Kisan & two other chaps from the works. Kisan seems alright and is as usual frightfully popular with everybody.

He & Sawday came to dinner & Captain Foster of Kilburns came from Calcutta.

Kisan & I went to a Bengali drama played mostly by the Institute Students. It was quite funny as I did not understand a single word.

This morning Peterson & the "big bugs" had a meeting with Foster on the coal question. I wanted to attend but Peterson sent me around the Plant with Kisan.

I had a long talk with Keenan, the Blast Furnace Superintendant, or rather he had a talk with us! Talked my head off with technical points. He is an extremely fine fellow I think & is quite mad on his beloved Blast Furnaces. He is out to break all records.

---

* This is JRD's last letter to his father available in the Archives.

He is doing some of that already. No. "C" averaging nearly 700 tons a day with record low coke consumption. The estimates were 450 tons a day!

Then we went round the Duplex & Sheet Mill both of which were not working owing to it being Sunday. There is great excitement on the Sheet Mill as it was suddenly decided yesterday to fire 25 Englishmen!

This evening I played tennis with Kisan, Mr. Bryant & Mrs. Townsend. The latter is the niece of Sawday and married recently Townsend of the Tinplate Co. I knew her 3 years ago when she was Miss Edwards....

Monday

I suddenly remembered while writing last night that I must be up at 7.30 this morning as Kisan was taking me around the new plant which I had never seen working. So as it was 1 o'clock I precipitated myself into bed & closed my eye with a bang.

This morning therefore I saw all the new mills & the Duplex Plant. I do not think that there is anything more wonderful to watch than the Bessemer Converters blowing. It must be absolutely marvellous at night and I intend going there after dinner. I believe one can read a mile off with the glow. On the whole I was greatly impressed and *proud* and very enthusiastic.

One thing I was glad to notice is that labour seems to be very content & the women who earn something like 5 annas a day are especially jolly & cheerful. I think Kisan has a very fine grasp of all the labour and everyone of them likes him & respects him. He certainly has a lot to do with their presence, peacefulness & content.

I am playing tennis again this afternoon. There is a weekly dance at the club tonight but I think I will rather go to bed or go & see the Duplex.

I have booked today one seat for Bombay for Sunday next. Peterson is probably not going to Calcutta....

I am keeping very well & do not feel tired a bit after walking miles in the plant & then playing tennis in the evening.

I hope you are all very well in Bombay & having a good time. Are you still leading a shamefully dissipated life?

Good bye, papa cheri, I send you all my most affectionate kisses.

Jehangir

Personal Views and Preferences

TO MISS PIROJA NANAVUTTY[*]

Bombay
22 December 1943

Dear Miss Nanavutty,

Thank you very much for sending me a copy of your little book of translation of Parsi prayers. I much appreciate your kind thought but I wonder if you would have carried it out if you had known that I am anything but a good Zoroastrian, at least in the sense of being a practising one. While I am certainly not an atheist and not even an agnostic I do not believe in the outward, priest-created manifestations of religion and in fact hold the view that they have been for centuries and are still today one of the principal causes of disunity and backwardness amongst people, particularly in our unhappy country....

I believe in God but not in a man-made one nor in all the paraphernalia and rites invented by priests....

But I do think it was very kind of you to have sent me your book and, as I have said, I much appreciate the thought, although I am incapable of appreciating the gift as I am sure it deserves to be!

---

[*]   Copy of handwritten letter.

With best wishes for a happy new year (one of the five new years I celebrate in every twelve months!).

Yours very sincerely,
J.R.D. Tata

TO LT. COL. A. INNES COX

Bombay
15 September 1945

My dear Col. Cox,

I found your letter of the 20th June on my return from England and the States. Many thanks for Shaw's *Everybody's Political What's What.*

I generally agree with your views on the book. The trouble with Shaw is that in everything he writes he has to live up to the reputation of being the greatest wit of two centuries, and of being endowed with the most phenomenal cheek. That is of some advantage in the case of his plays, but is somewhat irksome when he deals with serious subjects....

Yours sincerely,
J.R.D. Tata

TO L.P. VACHEK[*]

Bombay
11 January 1949

My attention has been drawn to the fact that during the Christmas and New Year Eve nights at the Taj, the band played a number of Christian religious hymns, such as "Silent Night, Holy Night".

As such hymns are played in churches as part of religious services, I feel that their being played as dance music in a hotel may wound the susceptibilities of some people. Also it is not in good taste.

I shall therefore be obliged if you will kindly instruct our band to avoid playing in future any tune which forms part of religious services.

J.R.D. Tata

---

* General Manager, Taj Mahal Hotel.

FROM JAMSHED BHABHA[*]

Bombay

10 February 1951

My dear Jeh,

I am enclosing, in duplicate, a character sketch of you which Minoo Masani pressed me to prepare for the article promised for the French Magazine *Réalités* (which now also appears in translation in the U.K.). The write-up will also be sent to the American publishers of a volume entitled *The World's 100 Most Important People — And Why*, whose request for biographical material and other data has been referred by Tata Incorporated to the Public Relations Department. Minoo holds the view that since the publishers intend to include you in their list of 100, the question of getting your approval for sending them the necessary material does not arise. He feels that if we refuse to cooperate with the publishers, they will get their material in any case, but from less accurate sources.

Minoo did not think it was even necessary for me to send my sketch for your approval. I am doing so, however, as you may think it advisable to leave out certain passages....

As Minoo wants the material very urgently, could you please return it within a day or two of receiving it?...

Yours,

Jamshed

---

[*] For some years there was resistance on the part of JRD to allow editors of "Who's Who" to include his name and life sketch in their books. This is one instance.

TO JAMSHED BHABHA

Geneva
20 February 1951

Just received excellent obituary sketch which should be safely preserved until appropriate occasion stop meantime publication my lifetime will provoke immediate legal action for inverted defamation of character stop positively prohibit my inclusion in worlds hundred most whatnot people although would have no objection if number reduced to ten

Jeh

TO P.L. BHANDARI*

Bombay
20 *December* 1952

Dear Mr. Bhandari,

Many thanks for your letter of the 2nd December asking for information in connection with a threatened article on myself in the *Readers' Digest*.

I have throughout my life avoided publicity except when I could not escape it, in the interests of the Tata organisation, at official meetings and functions. I therefore feel very uncomfortable at the thought of what the editors of *Readers' Digest* may be preparing when they ask you for "a mass of biographical data" for an article on my "life, endeavours and achievements"!

I cannot of course stop the editors of *Readers' Digest* from going ahead with their scheme with the same persistence as the author of a recent book published in the States entitled *The Hundred Most Important People*, but I would like to make a suggestion which I would appreciate your forwarding to the *Readers' Digest* for their consideration. The story of the House of Tata as a whole and in particular of its founder, J.N. Tata, who was a real pioneer and whose life provides ample human interest would, in my view, provide a much more interesting subject for an article. In such an article, the editors of the journal would of course be free to devote such space and attention as they feel is called for in regard to my own position as Chairman of the firm. I wonder whether this idea will interest them....

Yours sincerely,
J.R.D. Tata

---

* Public Relations Officer, Embassy of India, Washington D.C.

TO Dr. K.T. GAJJAR[*]

Bombay
10 May 1954

Dear Dr. Gajjar,

I am sorry to worry you again about happenings at Juhu.

The trouble now lies with the excessive barking of the dogs in your house or compound. I myself am a lover of dogs and quite understand that a healthy dog must give vent to its feelings from time to time, but continuous barking at nothing in particular for long periods at a time can be disturbing, particularly when it happens late at night or early morning or after lunch when one tries to get a little sleep. I think the nuisance in this case is principally the black female dog who loves to bark endlessly at the sea or at people on the beach which she no doubt considers her personal domain!

My wife and I would be most grateful if you would kindly give instructions to your servants to keep this particular dog tied up at least during the hours I have mentioned....

Hoping you are well,

Yours sincerely,
J.R.D. Tata

---

[*] A noted pathologist whose house was next to JRD's shack at Juhu, Bombay.

TO MRS. M.E. TATA CHESTER[*]

Bombay
16 October 1956

Dear Mrs. Chester,

    It is kind of you to have written and told me about the strange and amusing coincidence by which we happen to bear the same name, Tata. I am also interested to know that you pronounce it in the same manner. While strange, I doubt if there is anything very mysterious about the phenomenon. It is perhaps a happy reminder that we are all in the same world and that these national barriers that unfortunately divide the various peoples are not so fundamental after all.

    Thank you once again for writing.

With kind regards,

Yours sincerely,
J.R.D. Tata

---

[*]   A lady from Sydney, Australia.

TO FRANK MORAES*

Bombay
24 November 1958

My dear Frank,

How nice of you to have sent me a copy of *A Beginning*,** on receipt of which I promptly put my "engaged" sign on and spent the next half hour reading every one of those lovely poems!

I have always been, in a humble way, a lover of French and English poetry but having been weaned on classic verse, I usually find modern poetry somewhat less congenial to my old-fashioned taste and more difficult to understand. When, however, it is not too "avant-garde" and, as in the case of Dom's, "sings" and responds to the subconscious sense of sorrow and loneliness which I suppose exists in every man, I find deep pleasure in it. If Dom fulfills, in the coming years, the promise of his first collection, it is obvious that he will make a great name for himself. Thanks again....

Yours sincerely,
Jeh

---

* Frank Moraes (1907-1974); Editor, *The Indian Express*, Bombay; earlier Editor, *The Times of India*, Bombay.
** A collection of poems by Dom Moraes, son of Frank Moraes.

TO F.H. NALLASETH*

Bombay
3 December 1958

My dear Feroze,

When I stayed at the Ashoka last, I promised I would let you have my comments on the hotel, the accommodation provided, the food and the service. I am doing so in the attached note in which I have jotted down my views, based mainly on my observations during my wife's and my stay there on the occasion of the IATA A.G.M...

Suggestions for improvements in the Ashoka Hotel.

Dressing Tables: Every dressing table should be provided with a stool and a light above or on each side of the mirror. The lights which were added at my request in the bedroom in Suite 442 are both decorative and useful.

Electric Bulbs: No 25-watt bulbs should be used in any room or suite. The minimum should be 40 watts, and preferably 60 watts.

Curtains: Venetian blinds should be fitted to windows or, in their absence, curtains should be of thick material or have an opaque lining so as to shut out the daylight which is disturbing early in the morning.

Cupboards: The cupboard accommodation in large suites is totally inadequate. An additional cupboard should be put into the central lobby of the suite. The best and cheapest arrangement would be to have a built-in cupboard in the corner of the lobby

---

* In-Charge, Ashoka Hotel, New Delhi.

as a permanent fixture painted the same colour as the wall and with mirrors on the doors.

Twin Beds: The twin beds in large suites should be modified so as to be independent of each other. At present they form in effect one single double bed. The occupants of such expensive suites are usually middle-aged or elderly people who are light sleepers and disturb each other in a double bed.

Shower Curtains: All bath tubs should be provided with shower curtains.

Telephones: At present the two telephones in suites—one in the bedroom and one in the sitting room—are on one extension so that both ring at the same time and the conversation on one is also heard on the other. Under this arrangement, occupants who may want to rest or sleep in the bedroom are constantly disturbed. It is a simple matter to have a switch put on to the bedroom telephone wire which would enable the bedroom occupant to disconnect his phone when desired while leaving the phone in the sitting room in use....

Incidentally, the telephone service at the Ashoka is the least satisfactory of all the services provided. The fault does not I think lie with the staff, but with the insufficiency in their number....

Uniforms: The uniforms of some of the supervisory staff at the Ashoka are not in keeping with a hotel of this importance and status. In particular, the reception clerks and cashiers should be allowed to wear more attractive clothes....

Reception and Hall Porter Desk: In all hotels in the world, the reception or registration desk and the hall porter's desk are wholly separate and the functions of reception clerks and hall porters are clearly separate and well defined. That is not done at the Ashoka and I suggest it should be....

Meal Service: In every first-class residential hotel in the world there are two menus. The Table d'hôte menu, which is usually included in the daily residential charge, and an À la carte menu from which residents or outsiders can order anything they like. The À la carte has always a far greater choice and is also more expensive. While the Ashoka does provide alternative courses on request, there is no separate À la carte menu. This I feel should be provided....

Band: Except for dancing, the band in the dining room of the Ashoka is far too big and noisy. Except at dinner dances, meal time music should be background music and should not unduly interfere with conversation for those who want to talk. The orchestra should consist of not more than four to six musicians....Incidentally, the

Ashoka is the only hotel I know which plays Indian music during meals for the entertainment of its guests. I had my doubts about it at first, but I find it is popular and I compliment them on this innovation.

Jeh

TO S.M.*

Bombay
19 January 1962

You have asked me to state in what respects I did not consider the air-conditioned bus we exhibited at Delhi up to the high standards expected from Tatas.

I was of course not referring to the technical and performance qualities of the bus, about which there can be no doubt, nor its exterior appearance which is quite good. I referred to its interior appearance, décor and finish. Unfortunately, as I did not keep any notes at the time, I cannot make any detailed comments. Speaking from memory, however, five points struck me forcibly.

The chairs, both in design and upholstery, were much below what I would consider minimum standards. The chairs in Birla's Alwyn luxury coach, although still not up to the mark, were superior to ours. I see no reason why we could not fabricate at Jamshedpur wholly satisfactory seats....

I stated earlier last year, when I saw this bus body still under construction at Jamshedpur, that we should not use any wood finish at all either in the form of panels or of strips. I still strongly adhere to this view. Apart from being old-fashioned, except of course when using luxury and exotic woods, wood is an unsatisfactory material because it needs constant repolishing or varnishing, and tends to crack as a result of expansion and contraction under temperature variations. It was widely used at a time when other materials were not available. Substitutes are now freely available. Wood strips can be replaced by aluminium or steel, while wood panels can be replaced by various modern materials including Formica or by hardboard painted or covered with rexine and other fabrics.

---

* Sumant Moolgaokar, Director-in-Charge of TELCO, 1949; later Vice-Chairman and Managing Director; retired as Chairman of the Company in 1988.

I thought the lavatory quite below minimum standards....

I do not think it is an advantage to keep the driver completely separate. In fact, a tourist coach of this kind would normally carry a guide or manager of some sort accompanying a group of tourists, who would sit next to the driver and be accessible to passengers during the journey....

J.R.D. Tata

TO HANS A. STOEHR[*]

Bombay
22 April 1963

My dear Stoehr,

When I wrote to you on the 2nd of February to thank you for the loan of the F12 you had so kindly sent me for my use while I was in Geneva, I said that I would write again after I had returned the car if I had any suggestions or comments to make.

The car is such a delightful and sound vehicle as it is, that it is difficult to suggest improvements. The only material one I can think of is that of giving it a little more power. Although it does perform quite adequately with its present engine, I feel that in view of its weight an extra 100 or 200 c.c. would bring out the full potentialities of its size, carrying capacity, suspension, road holding, etc., which are today substantially in excess of the car's actual performance. Perhaps because of its 2-stroke configuration, the engine particularly lacks torque at low R.P.M.s which a little more cubic capacity would, I think, remedy. I personally remain unenamoured of the 2-stroke cycle for anything but very small cars. I think that owners of a car of this class would prefer the increased power at low R.P.M. as well as the slightly better fuel consumption of a 4-stroke engine than the extra smoothness and freedom from vibration of a 2-stroke one which, after all, is purely a luxury.

Although it is true that the automatic mixing of oil and petrol provided on the new cars is a great improvement, which relieves the owner from the additional repeated trouble of putting in oil every time he puts petrol in its tank as in the past,

---

[*] A staff member of Daimler-Benz who organised the automobile division of TELCO in Jamshedpur. He lent a vehicle to JRD for use during his stay in Geneva.

it is still one additional thing to watch and bother about and also a potential source of trouble which does not exist in a 4-stroke-engined car.

While on this subject of oil addition, one minor defect I found in the F12 was that the dashboard light, which is supposed to come on when the special oil tank content is low, flashes on and off quite often even when the tank is full, thus causing a certain amount of doubt and worry to the driver!

There were two other minor defects I found in the particular car I had. One was a great difficulty in engaging reverse gear. This, however, was largely remedied by the Auto-Union Agent in Geneva. The other, which persisted, was a difficulty in closing the doors. If you did not slam them hard enough the latch did not engage fully, and if you slammed them too hard they bounced out of the inner latch on to the outer one! Maybe it was because the car is too well made and air pressure intervened! I found, in fact, that I had to keep the windows open to get the doors closed at all, which is a bit of a nuisance when it is cold and raining or snowing!

Otherwise, I can only praise the car as a beautiful and mechanically delightful job, and congratulate you and Auto-Union on such a good product....

With best wishes and renewed thanks,

Yours sincerely,
J.R.D. Tata

TO MRS. SIMONE TATA[*]

Bombay
30 January 1964

Dear Simone,

Many thanks for sending me eight samples of Lakmé products for men and asking for my comments.

The Cologne, After Shave Lotion and Talc are excellent. I would, however, give the Cologne a slightly less anaemic colour by making it a little darker in tint.

The Hair Dressing Cream is not right as it is too thick and sticky. Its consistency should be nearer that of Brylcream, although the colour could be a little on the creamy side, if preferred.

As I do not shave with a blade, I have not been able to test the three Shaving Creams....

That leaves only the Pre-Electric Shave Lotion, which unfortunately I do not normally use! Its perfume, however, seems quite pleasant.

On the whole, I feel you have evolved an excellent range of products.

What about a good range of Deodorants? There is nothing we need more in our country! I have tried a number of deodorants made in Europe and America. As you know, they are mostly of three types: spray, roll-on and stick. As the roll-on bottles presumably cannot be made here, we could only produce the stick type, or the simple spray type (not aerosol variety) in a plastic bottle. I hope Lakmé are working on this product. They can count on me as a regular user!

Yours sincerely,
Jeh

---

[*] Wife of Naval Tata; Managing Director, Lakmé Ltd., 1964; Chairman, 1982; later Chairman, Trent Ltd.

TO MRS. PILLOO POCHKHANAWALA*

Bombay
24 August 1973

Dear Pilloo,

Many thanks for sending me a copy of the lovely brochure on your sculptures. How nice of you to want to educate a philistine like myself! I hope I am not too old to learn, and I do appreciate at least the ingenuity and imagination displayed in your sculptures and those of other talented artists. Would it be wrong, however, to impose on all creative art, including sculpture, painting, music or poetry, the test of how it is likely to be considered a hundred years, or even a thousand years, from now? I cannot help feeling that, if any of the type of figurative or semi-abstract sculpture, which you and others have been creating, were to survive by then, it will be considered by the people of those days as being little more than a light-hearted interlude indulged in by their ancestors of the second half of the 20th century in the continuous process of serious creativity from the beginning of time.

The sketches from your sketch book at the end of your brochure show so much craft and talent that I wish you would one day use them to create something perhaps less avant-garde but of deeper and more lasting significance....

Yours very sincerely,
Jeh

---

* Noted sculptor.

TO BERAM SAKLATVALA*

Bombay
2 April 1974

Dear Beram,

    I am sorry for the long delay in acknowledging receipt of your letter of the 12th February, forwarding a copy of the February issue of *History Today*, in which your friend Henry Marsh's article on "The End of Serfdom" appears. I have read it with much pleasure, although parts of it, and the pictures, are a pretty grim reminder that human beings were as cruel 500 years ago as they are today....

    All the best,

Yours ever,
Jeh

---

* Vice-Chairman and Managing Director, Tata Ltd., London.

TO MURAD FYZEE[*]

Bombay
5 January 1976

Dear Murad,

Many thanks for the two books, which I return herewith. I had already read *The Bermuda Triangle*. I am by nature totally skeptical of any miraculous happenings and I frankly cannot believe that some strange and so far unknown force has lured all those ships and planes to their destruction. In times gone by, countless sailors have navigated the globe by observing the sun and the stars and I cannot see how, even if their compasses went mad, the crew of any ship or plane operating within such a small area of the earth could not safely find their way to one or another coast. Anyway, I agree it makes exciting reading.

As regards the other book, I have always been addicted to short stories. Anatole France's *Procurator of Judaea* is hardly a short story in the usual sense, except for its punch line. Frankly, I much prefer Maupassant's *The Necklace* in the same book which is recognised, to use your own phrase, as one of the all-time classics of them all. Amongst the others I would rate O. Henry's *The Gift of the Magi* almost equal to it....

All the best, and thanks again for the books.

Yours ever,
Jeh

---

[*] Author of the book on JRD, *Aircraft and Engine Perfect* (Tata McGraw-Hill, Delhi, 1991).

TO JOACHIM ALVA*

Bombay
31 October 1977

My dear Alva,

I am sorry for the delay in replying to your letter of October 1st....

I note that you are completing your book on *Men and Supermen of Hindustan*. Had it not been for the fact that the *first* word of the title of the book defines a category in which I could be included, I would have excused myself from responding to your request!

Our Public Relations Department has put together a little material that may be of use to you, but I hope you will not describe me as a "representative of Indian Capitalism", in view of the fact that I have in the past 25 years spent nearly half my working time in running a Public Sector enterprise, and also that since the death of the original Tata founders there has not been a single capitalist in the Firm, in which all the Directors' functions are those of trustees and the senior Directors are, as you know, Trustees of the Tata philanthropic Trusts which today own a large majority of Tata Sons.

Hoping you are well and with all good wishes.

Yours sincerely,
J.R.D. Tata

---

* Journalist, author and Member of Parliament.

TO JEHANGIR SABAVALA[*]

Bombay
14 January 1988

Dear Jehangir,

Thank you so much for your letter of December 25, your good wishes for the New Year, and even more so for the lovely album of your paintings.

I must confess that I have upto now been somewhat of an ignoramus in my appreciation of modern art and particularly abstract art, in which I recognise your leadership. That is why I like best "The Rose" and, of course, that lovely "Portrait of Shirin" featured in the album! Thank you very much indeed for sending it to me....

With love to you both,

Yours ever,
Jeh

---

[*]   Noted modern painter.

TO DR. KARAN SINGH[*]

Bombay
1 October 1993

Dear Karan,

As you will remember, I spent a couple of days in Auroville in February this year when I had occasion to meet, or renew my acquaintance with, many members of the Aurovillian community who, naturally, talked to me about the situation in Auroville as they assessed it.

I was perturbed to find a rather widespread sense of discontent amongst them caused by the unsatisfactory relations between them and the Foundation's Secretary.... His treatment of every problem as a legal matter (in his own words: "as per law") is to them incompatible with the spirit in which Auroville was created....

I personally believe that the problem can be solved by replacing the present incumbent (whose term of office, I was told, in any case expires shortly), by someone spiritually and ideologically more attuned to the spirit and concept of Auroville's creation recognised by most Aurovillians. If you agree with this conclusion, as I think you will, you are obviously the best placed to recommend or decide upon another choice for the post of Secretary of the Foundation....

The mind of whoever is ultimately chosen should obviously be a sufficiently flexible one, familiar with the history of Auroville's creation and the views of

---

[*] Former Maharaja of Jammu and Kashmir; Chairman, Auroville Foundation, Pondicherry; had been Union Minister holding various portfolios since 1967.
JRD was a member of the Auroville International Advisory Council.

Sri Aurobindo and of the Mother for dealing with the kind of problems which may inevitably arise, in view of the substantial number of foreign and legally untrained elements of the Aurovillian community.

With warm regards,

Yours sincerely,
Jeh

Home Workshop and Other Interests

TO GIANNI BERTOLI*

Bombay
27 July 1953

My dear Gianni

Many thanks for your two letters about the photo flash and the bracket for the saw. The latter has been duly received. I am appointing a committee of eminent engineers to draft a detailed manual of instructions in view of your failure to send me the manufacturers' instructions.

In the meantime, I would like you to know that I have now a full-fledged workshop in which I combine the roles of chairman of the board, chief engineer, chief mechanic, chief sweeper and chief stooge. If you have any orders to place for any mechanical appliances from a wrist watch to an atom bomb, I shall be pleased to receive them in quintuplicate, as I am running rather short of paper, you know where!...

Yours in a rush,
Jeh

---

* Brother-in-law of JRD; husband of his wife's (Thelly's) sister Kitty. He was Air-India International's District Manager for Continental Europe.

TO RUFUS BURTON (B-BOY)*

JRDT HOME WORKSHOP INCORPORATED

"The Cairn"
Altamont Road,
Bombay 26.
14 December 1957

Dear Sir,

We have today despatched to you by airmail the nose wheel ordered by you from the undersigned for your Air-India Super-Constellation Model Airplane.

We much regret the delay in delivery due partly to a change in design involving the incorporation of a shock absorber and partly to the time involved in entertaining distinguished visitors and potential customers, such as Mr. Burton Senior who honoured us with a visit recently.

We trust that the nose wheel will prove wholly satisfactory in use and that you will meet with no difficulty in fitting it to the airplane. In the event that the upper rod is found to be a little too long thus preventing the main part of the leg and the two supporting cross pieces from fitting snugly against the bottom of the fuselage, the rod should be filed down slightly.

If the nose wheel does not fit properly, we suggest one of two alternative solutions: either you throw away both the airplane and the nose wheel or you send the nose

---

* One of JRD's American friends had a fourteen-year-old son, Rufus Burton, called 'B-Boy' He wanted a nose wheel to fit to his toy Super-Constellation and the order was sent to JRD.

wheel back to us with the airplane for adjusting and fitting here. We are glad to inform you that we can guarantee delivery in approximately twenty-four months.

As the undersigned had the good fortune of taking Mr. Burton Senior for a ride in a game of golf, as a result of which he disbursed more than the value of the nose wheel, we have decided to make no charge in this instance.

With good wishes for X'mas and the New Year and awaiting further orders which we undertake to treat with the same despatch, we remain,

Faithfully yours,
J.R.D.T. HOME WORKSHOP INC.
(J.R.D. Tata)
PRESIDENT

FROM RUFUS BURTON

Dear Uncle Jeh,

   Hope you are fine. The wheel looks nice on the aeroplane. Thank you for putting springs in the wheel. I think you are very clever to make it. I was skating over the weekend. I hope Auntie Thelley is very well.

Love from,
B-Boy

TO P.C. SEN[*]

Bombay
5 May 1965

My dear Punchie,

I am sorry for the delay in replying to your letter of the 12th February which reached here when I was abroad....

Coming to weight training and skiing, it is difficult for me to advise you on poundages in handling weights as that depends on the state of your own muscles and heart. The two exercises you must be careful about are the deep knee bend and the straight back dead lift. In the case of the former, the muscles of the thighs are so powerful that you need poundages of at least 100 lbs. to give them any real work-out. Lifting such a weight to your shoulders, although naturally you would start at less, doing five to ten repetitions, involves a good deal of physical effort and a problem of balance. That is why, when I do this exercise, I have a couple of servants standing on each side of me to make sure I do not drop it. It is not a suitable exercise to be undertaken in an upper floor flat, that is why I would recommend that you do instead the straddle lift which involves no risk and much less effort.

As regards the straight arm dead lift, it is an excellent exercise only if you have no trouble at all with your back which many men do after 50. It is not the straightening up that causes back trouble to some people but the stretching of the spine when bending down with straight knees. This is similar, only more so, to the effect of touching your toes with straight legs. If I were you, I would start with light weights not exceeding 50 lbs. and, if there is no adverse effect, gradually go up to 100 lbs.

---

[*]   A friend from Calcutta who, like JRD, was interested in skiing.

The Prone Press involves no risk at all and the pectoral muscles can take very heavy poundages without any strain on the heart or back. I do them with 100 lbs. but here again I need help to put the bar across my chest!...

With affectionate wishes to you and Pam,

Yours sincerely,
Jeh

TO L.N. TANDON[*]

Bombay
7 May 1970

Dear Mr. Tandon,

On my return from Australia, I was delighted to find what seemed to be a brand new drilling machine installed in my home workshop. Its overhaul and renovation has exceeded all my expectations. It runs extraordinarily smoothly and seems very accurate. I would like to test the accuracy with my dial indicator, and for the purpose I would appreciate your sending me, at your leisure, a test piece accurately ground as I find that none of the drills or end mills I have are sufficiently true for the job.

The finish given to the machine and its adjustable tables is superb and I am most thankful to you for the trouble taken in the matter.

I would very much appreciate it if you could communicate my personal thanks to those responsible for the overhaul job and its inspection...

With all good wishes,

Yours sincerely,
J.R.D. Tata

---

[*]   An employee of TELCO Machine Tool Division, Poona.

TO BERAM SAKLATVALA

Bombay
20 July 1970

Dear Beram,

I have for over thirty years used a dictionary of English synonyms by Richard Soule, printed in America and published in London by Frederick Warne & Company Ltd. Unlike *Roget's Thesaurus*, this is a straightforward dictionary which I find much quicker and easier to use. With my mania for always wanting the right word, I use it extensively for all my dictation.

The only drawback to Soule's dictionary is that it first came out in 1871 and was last revised in 1891! It therefore lacks many words in common use today.

My purpose in writing is to request that your office may please enquire whether there is a more recent edition of this dictionary. If there is a revised edition during the last twenty years, I would appreciate having two copies sent to me, as I keep one at home and one in the office. If, however, it has not been revised and is now totally out of print, there may be some other more modern dictionary of synonyms available and when I next come to London I would like to see one and buy it if I find it suitable....

Yours sincerely,
Jeh

TO HANS HERZOG*

Bombay
25 November 1971

My dear Hans,

You may perhaps be aware that on the happy day when Tatas and Daimler-Benz signed their Agreement in Stuttgart on the 2nd March, 1954, Dr. Koenecke, the then Chairman of the Vorstand, very kindly presented me with the gold pen with which the Agreement was signed by him and myself. The pen bears the Mercedes star, and was suitably inscribed before it was presented to me. I have used it ever since and have got very attached to it as a lasting reminder of a memorable and pleasant event.

The pen lately gave me a little trouble, in that the flow of ink through it was not right and also the decorative tip of the cap had become loose. I therefore sent it to Air-India in Frankfurt, to have it repaired, and was most disappointed to learn from them that it could not be put right as it was a model which was no longer manufactured.

Before I give up the use of this favourite pen for ever, and in view of the continuing sentimental link it provided between me and Daimler-Benz in general, and Dr. Koenecke and Arnold Wychodil in particular, I am taking the liberty of asking our Frankfurt office to send you the pen, in case Daimler-Benz's great prestige and influence might induce the makers to repair it for me....

Yours sincerely,
Jeh

---

* Of Daimler-Benz, Stuttgart, West Germany.

TO PROF. C.N.R. RAO*

Bombay
27 November 1987

Dear Professor Rao,

Re: Projected National Institute for Advanced Studies

The Dorabji Tata Trust has, as you know, established a number of pioneering institutions in areas of national need, following the far-sighted example of Jamsetji Tata, who conceived and planned India's first institution of science and technology, the Indian Institute of Science, of which you are now the distinguished Director. After the Tata Institute of Social Sciences and the Tata Memorial Centre for Cancer Research and Treatment which celebrated their Golden Jubilee last year, came the Tata Institute of Fundamental Research, and then, after an interval of about 20 years, the National Centre for the Performing Arts. Another 20 years have passed since this last institution was established, and the Trust is now planning the sponsorship of an Institute for Advanced Studies about which you are already well-informed.

A committee of eminent men of learning in the areas of science and administration have set out admirably the basic aims and objectives of this new institution in a Project Report,...It has been a heartening source of encouragement for my colleagues and me that our Prime Minister, Shri Rajiv Gandhi, welcomed warmly the idea of this new institution when I first spoke to him about it at a meeting in his office....The Prime Minister went so far as to issue instructions to ascertain if a building and a plot of land of sufficient size could be found in New Delhi or its vicinity to accommodate

---

* Director, Indian Institute of Science, Bangalore.

the new Institute. Unfortunately, however, it was not found possible to locate a suitable home for it in Delhi.

We have been fortunate, meanwhile, in having secured the services of your distinguished colleague, Dr. Raja Ramanna, as Director of the new Institute.

After considering various alternative locations for the new institution, my colleagues and I feel more than ever convinced that we would not be able to find a better base for it than in the vicinity of the Indian Institute of Science. It is possible that, since a large part of its programmes will be devoted to the humanities, arts, economics and other subjects outside the sciences, it may also serve the need of the Indian Institute of Science by way of complementing its science-oriented teaching and research programmes. As the projected Institute would require the construction not only of suitable lecture halls and faculty rooms but also of residential accommodation for some 50 participants, apartments for about five permanent members of the faculty and suites for other professors and eminent men from India and abroad visiting it, we have been advised that an area of about six acres will be needed for the requisite buildings.

Through this letter to you, I am addressing a request to the Council of the Indian Institute of Science to lease from its area a plot of about 6 acres abutting on a public road to the projected Institute....

I do hope that my proposal will be favourably received by the Council of the Institute, and make it possible to take early action to register the proposed National Institute for Advanced Studies as a public trust in the State of Karnataka.

With kind regards,

Yours sincerely,
J.R.D. Tata

TO PROF. M.P. GANDHI*

Bombay
22 December 1988

Dear Professor Gandhi,

Many thanks for your letters of November 25 and December 19...

I was touched by your flattering remarks, largely undeserved, about myself and my speeches. My deep and abiding love for the English language does indeed make me take perhaps excessive pains, in expressing what I have to say in the simplest possible English, but as clearly and precisely as possible. It pains and distresses me to find, especially today, even so-called educated Indians willing to murder the beautiful language that English is!...

With best wishes for the New Year,

Yours sincerely,
J.R.D. Tata

---

* A businessman friend from Bombay.

Guiding Principles

TO K.C. BHANSALI[*]

Bombay
13 September 1965

Dear Mr. Bhansali,

I thank you for your letter of the 6th August enquiring what have been the guiding principles which have kindled my path and my career. I do not consider myself to be an "illustrious personality" but only an ordinary businessman and citizen who has tried to make the best of his opportunities to advance the cause of India's industrial and economic development. Any such guiding principles I might unconsciously have had in my life can be summarised as follows:

That nothing worthwhile is ever achieved without deep thought and hard work;

That one must think for oneself and never accept at their face value slogans and catch phrases to which, unfortunately, our people are too easily susceptible;

That one must forever strive for excellence or even perfection, in any task however small and never be satisfied with second best;

That no success or achievement in material terms is worthwhile unless it serves the needs or interests of the country and its people and is achieved by fair and honest means;

---

[*] A school teacher from Calcutta.

That good human relations not only bring great personal rewards but are essential to the success of any enterprise.

Yours sincerely,
J.R.D. Tata

TO MISS V. YOGA JYOTSNA[*]

Bombay
7 September 1978

Dear Miss Jyotsna,

Thank you for your interesting letter of the 29th August. It makes me happy when I find any of our young generation of students taking a personal interest in public affairs and worrying when things go wrong in our country and for our people....

You ask me why I continue to live in this country. Isn't the answer obvious? It is my country, and I am an Indian.

Yes, of course, I believe in equality—not only in equality before the law and before God, but in equality for everyone, man or woman, in access to opportunities for employment and self-development.

Yes, I do believe in God, but not in the formalised and artificial God prescribed by organised religion. Therefore, while not an atheist or an agnostic, I do not believe in, or follow, man-made religious laws or prescriptions in the name of God. I believe, however, that there must be an ultimate and just purpose for our existence on earth, or for that of the earth itself, and that the purpose is the purpose of God.

I wish you luck and success, but remember that the degree of your success and happiness will depend largely on your own efforts and your adherence to the principles you set for yourself and the value you attach to those principles....

Yours sincerely,
J.R.D. Tata

---

[*]   A college student from Hyderabad.

TOWARDS FREEDOM AND AFTER

The War and the British

★

Industrial Mission, 1945

★

1947 and After

In one of the interviews with his biographer R.M. Lala, JRD said, "During my early years in India I had two personalities. I was an anti-British Indian and I was a Frenchman...." During the years before India gained Independence, his attitude to the British was like that of Pandit Jawaharlal Nehru. Like Nehru he supported the War against Hitler and at the same time he wanted to throw off the British yoke.

JRD played a leading role in encouraging support for Britain's war effort for the defence of India. At the time of the Battle of Britain in 1940 Tatas presented two Spitfires for the defence of the country. At the same time, JRD was concerned about the use of funds collected by Tata companies during the War. He wanted part of this amount to be spent on humanitarian work.

One of the occasions when JRD took a stand critical of the British was when he resigned from the Board of the Imperial Bank. He was annoyed at the discrimination against Indian officers which he perceived would continue even after the War.

JRD was keen that businessmen in this country should prepare themselves for what was to happen to India after Independence. They should work for its planned economic development. With this objective he took the initiative in 1944 to bring together five eminent industrialists and three technocrats in the country to draft the Bombay Plan—a 15-year development plan for the country. As JRD's biographer says, the Bombay Planners "were the first and the only capitalists in the world to draft an Economic Plan with a strong social concern for their country".

JRD's active participation in the visit of the Industrial Mission to England and the U.S.A. the following year, which was organised by the government, was also a step in the same direction.

JRD took every opportunity to bring his industrialist friends together to harness their energies to build a great future for this country.

The War and the British

TO SIR JEHANGIR GHANDY[*]

Bombay
18 February 1942

Dear Joe,

I have your letter of the 15th February, regarding your War Committee's wish to raise the sum of Rs. 1,40,000 for the purchase of another fighter plane, and your proposal that the Steel Company should donate Rs. 50,000 for that purpose.

I am sorry that I am not at all sympathetic towards this proposal. I have throughout held the view that, except for their sentimental value and for the enthusiasm that such appeals may arouse, the raising of funds in the shape of gifts for buying planes and other war weapons is wrong in principle and futile in fact. It seems to me that the various War Gifts Committees have, no doubt unconsciously, misled the public into believing that by giving their money for the purchase of war weapons they were actually helping in providing additional planes, armoured carriers, ships, & c. Actually such gifts do nothing of the sort. The manufacture and purchase of additional planes and other war weapons does not in the slightest degree depend on the provision of funds. The limiting factor in production is not money but industrial capacity and labour. Every plant and

---

[*] Sir Jehangir Ghandy (1896-1972), General Manager, TISCO (Tata Steel), 1938; Knighted, 1945; Director, Tata Steel, 1954; Director, Tata Sons, 1959.

every factory making armaments and munitions is working to full capacity and every plane, every tank and every gun that can physically be made is being made. By giving the Government Rs. 1,40,000 here or in England for a Spitfire, not a single extra bolt, nut or screw for a Spitfire will be made as a result, and the hope that at least one extra fighter plane will be allocated to the defence of Bihar or Bengal is equally fallacious.

All that money given for such purpose can buy is the privilege of having the name of the donors painted on a machine, and a letter or telegram of thanks from the Viceroy or Lord Beaverbrook,* while the only effective financial consequence of such gifts is an infinitesimal reduction in the ultimate burden of the taxpayer.

I therefore strongly hold the view that monies contributed by the generosity of the public should be used solely for humanitarian purposes and should be spent particularly on deserving objects which do not receive any support or adequate support from public funds. The relief of refugees from invaded countries and of bombed populations, amenities for troops—particularly wounded troops—the relief of families of killed or wounded soldiers, are some typical examples of such objects which would derive real benefits from donations. While there is so much war suffering in the world, which simply cries for help and which cannot get it in adequate measure from public funds, I think it is wrong to collect and give money merely for the privilege of having a name put on a plane.

For these reasons I am not in favour of the Steel Company making a donation of Rs. 50,000 as suggested by you....

Yours sincerely,
J.R.D. Tata

---

* Then Minister for Aircraft Production. Better known as owner/publisher of one of Britain's largest-selling newspapers, *The Daily Express.*

TO SIR WILLIAM LAMOND*

Bombay
2 April 1943

My dear Lamond,

With reference to the meeting recently held in your room, regarding the Indianisation of the officer staff of the Bank, at which you, Sir Rahimtoola Chinoy, Sir Vithal Chandavarkar and I were present, I wish to thank you for the information and explanations which you so readily gave me on the subject. I appreciate your helpful and courteous attitude in this matter, particularly as I am aware that this is a question of policy with which I, as a member of a Local Board, am not concerned.

From the information you were good enough to give me, it appears that the present officer cadre of the Bank consists of 150 Europeans and 43 Indians, and that there are no Indian officers in the first and second grades, every one of the higher appointments in the Bank being held exclusively by European officers. These facts fully support the complaint I made that after 22 years of the Bank's existence, the progress of Indianisation has been extremely disappointing, particularly at the top, where it has been entirely non-existent.

I therefore expressed the fear that unless concrete steps were taken to remedy the present situation, Indians would never occupy any of the senior posts in the Bank. You did not agree with this view and pointed out that between now and 1947, some 57 European officers were due to retire from the Bank, as a result of which a number of Indian officers would step into some of the vacated positions. While that may be

---

* Managing Director, Imperial Bank of India.

so, it is evident, considering the absence of Indian officers in the first and second grades, that such promotions will be mostly to junior posts and that all the key positions in the Bank will, for a great many years to come, remain in the hands of the European officers.

You pointed out that in 1935 the Central Board had laid down the policy that the recruitment of European and Indian officers should be so regulated as to result in due course in a 50/50 ratio in all grades between European and Indian officers. I believe I am right in saying that this policy was adopted as a result of considerable agitation by the shareholders of the Bank, and by Indian Chambers of Commerce in Bombay and Calcutta.

It appeared from the figures you were good enough to show me that, since 1935, a number of European officers have, under this policy, been recruited as probationary officers. I was glad to note that the number so recruited was relatively small, but this seems to have been due mainly to the war having made it impossible to recruit any at all during the last four years. It is, therefore, reasonable to assume that had it not been for the war, the number of probationary officers recruited from the United Kingdom since 1935 would have been much larger than it has actually been. On this subject I expressed the view, which I wish to repeat here, that there can in my opinion be no justification whatever for recruiting junior European clerks from British Banks as probationary officers, and that only when an expert with special qualifications and experience is required would the employment of a non-Indian be justified. Your answer, quite naturally, was that the recruitment had been strictly in accordance with the policy laid down by the Central Board and that it was for the Central Board to decide whether or not the Bank should in future continue to recruit European probationary officers.

If I remember right, you said that the proper time for the Central Board to consider the matter afresh would be after the war, as in practice, no staff could be recruited from Europe during the war. I submit, however, that there is no reason why the Board should not consider this question now. In fact, I believe, for the reasons mentioned verbally by me during our talk, that it will be very much in the interests of the Bank itself to be in a position, when the Constitutional changes promised after the war have taken place, to show that it has on its own initiative already taken effective steps to Indianise its officer cadre.

I made it clear and I wish to place it on record that my views on this subject are in no way derogatory to the officers concerned. I have the highest regard for the ability, integrity and loyalty to the Bank of its European personnel, and I have had nothing but the most courteous and friendly treatment from all those with whom I have come in contact. My attitude is based solely on the following considerations: If the Imperial Bank, whose shareholders, clients and employees are predominantly Indian is, as I believe it should be, considered an Indian Bank, it is desirable that its control and management should be in Indian hands. The complete exclusion of Indians in the past from all high positions in the Bank, and the insistence on reservation in the future of 50% of the senior posts for Europeans, can only be justified by the assumption that Indians are inferior in ability to Europeans, or, if they have the ability, that they cannot be trusted. As an Indian I cannot accept either of these assumptions, and unless, therefore, I felt that they no longer governed the policy of the Board and of the Management, it would be unfair to myself and to the other Directors if I were to continue as a Member of the Board.

I shall be much obliged by your letting me know whether you propose to have the matter considered by the Central Board in the reasonably near future; if you do, may I request that my letter be placed before them? I am postponing a decision until I hear from you.

With kind regards,

Yours sincerely,
J.R.D. Tata

TO R.S. PANDE[*]

Bombay
31 December 1973

Dear Pande,

I have only just seen your letter of the 5th/6th November regarding Wavell's *Viceroy's Journal*[**]....

I was rather amused at reading that Wavell had found me a "conceited, unhelpful, supercilious and tiresome young man", though I must say I was rather pleased with the "young" part, considering I was already a middle-aged 40 at the time!

My recollection of Wavell is that he carried the strong silent man characteristic to such a pitch that he never opened his mouth. I therefore found him as tiresome as he did me. I think he had reason, however, to dislike me because at the time, with the end of the war very near and no progress towards our Independence, I was pretty hostile to the British colonial government. I was offered one or two blandishments which I flatly turned down.

With best wishes for the New Year,

Yours sincerely,
J.R.D. Tata

---

[*]   Managing Director, Tata Steel.

[**] Lord Archibald Wavell was appointed Viceroy of India in 1943. His personality was not one that reached out to others. JRD's first meeting with him was not a happy one and he felt that the comments that Wavell wrote in his diary about him were coloured by this first encounter. Entries from Lord Wavell's *A Viceroy's Journal*—24th January 1944: I did not get on very well with young Tata, with whom I had a short chat after dinner, a pity as I think he is able and influential about Indian business, but he seemed to be conceited and unhelpful. I expect I did not take him in the right way. 21st April 1944: Young Tata came to lunch when I met him down at Bombay. I found him rather a supercilious and tiresome young man, but got on with him rather better today...

Industrial Mission, 1945

TO SIR AZIZUL HUQUE[*]

Bombay
26 April 1944

Dear Sir Azizul Huque,

I am sorry for the delay in answering your letter of the 14th April, inviting me to join a party of industrialists on a visit to the United Kingdom and the United States....

You were good enough to discuss this proposal verbally with me some time ago, and as you know, I should in principle be glad to take advantage of this offer. There are a few points, however, which require to be carefully considered before those invited can make a final decision...

I still feel that the nature of this mission and its objects need to be clarified. It is not even quite clear whether it is to be a mission at all, and from your letter it would seem that the intention is merely to give, informally, facilities to a group of industrialists and businessmen to visit Britain and, if possible, the U.S.A. If that is the intention, then I presume that except in so far as it would be more convenient for visits to factories, & c., to be undertaken by a group rather than by individuals, the members of the party would on arrival in England be independent of each other

---

[*] Member for Commerce, Industries and Civil Supplies, Government of India.

and would not necessarily have to move together or follow a common programme. So far as I am concerned that would be quite suitable. If, on the other hand, the party is to be more nearly in the nature of a mission, then its objects, leadership, & c., would have to be clearly defined and understood beforehand.

The number and composition of the party would also be of some consequence, particularly in the case of the second alternative mentioned above. I know of some people who have been asked to join the party, but I have no definite idea as to the number and names of all those who have been invited. It would be most useful and appreciated if you could see your way to communicate to us the names of the other persons invited.

Perhaps the most important consideration at this moment is the time of the visit. I note that it is proposed that it should start in June. My own feeling is that this is too early a date, and that it would be more suitable to fix a later time, say, the beginning of September at the earliest. My reason for holding this view is that from all one reads and hears about the war, it seems probable that the second front in Europe will be opened some time in May. If so, everyone's time, energy and thoughts in England will be so taken up with the war, which will then enter its most crucial stage, that it would seem to me most inopportune for us to arrive at such a time. In fact, I would imagine that a party of businessmen from India touring the country might during that period be in the way, and might even be considered a nuisance. By September or October, however, assuming that the war in Europe has not ended, the invasion of the Continent will have reached a stage where people in responsible positions, both in Government and in industry, will have a little more time, freedom of thought, and inclination to receive us, show us around factories and places of significance, and discuss matters of common interest with us....

Taking everything into consideration, therefore, and subject, of course, to the convenience and wishes of the other members, I would strongly urge that the visit be postponed to September at the earliest, and that the preliminary meeting at Delhi be held towards the middle of August. In the meantime, the Government could, I suggest, give us further information on the points raised earlier in this letter....

Yours sincerely,
J.R.D. Tata

TO H.M. PATEL[*]

Bombay
21 September 1944

Dear Mr. Patel,

I thank you for your two letters, regarding the visit of Indian industrialists to the U.K. and U.S.A.

Regarding the proposed press announcement, my own distinct recollection was that the communiqué was to be issued from Delhi, more or less as an official announcement and not by the members of the Mission. If the intention was that it was to be issued by ourselves, it would have been drafted somewhat on different lines.

As regards the possible date of the visit, here again my recollection of what was decided at the Delhi meeting in July differs a little from yours. The decision was that the departure should be tentatively fixed for the end of February, but that in the event of the European war ending very soon, the question of advancing the date would immediately be considered and the members would keep themselves in readiness to leave at a month's notice. The end of the war in Europe still appears to be uncertain, and I think that for practical purposes it is safer to assume that we shall not leave until February.

With reference to your suggestion that the Federation of British Industries and the Association of the British Chambers of Commerce should be informed of the names of any representative in the U.K. through whom the Indian industrialists could

---

[*] Secretary of Industries and Civil Supplies, Government of India, who later became one of the senior civil servants responsible for dividing the assets between India and Pakistan at the time of Partition. He went on to become Finance Minister and Home Minister in the Janata Government (1977-79)

severally be contacted, I am forwarding a copy to each of them, with the request that they should send you the information direct.

Yours sincerely,
J.R.D. Tata

TO G.D. BIRLA[*]

Bombay
28 September 1944

Dear Mr. Birla,

I was talking the other day to a highly placed friend who has just returned from England He confirmed that our proposed visit had aroused much interest in England and then said that he had gathered the impression that it would be to our advantage to go there, if not with orders in our pockets, at least with specific and clear ideas of what India would want in the way of machinery and equipment in the immediate post-war period. If we were found to have come merely on an exploratory and study mission, much less attention would be given to us and the usefulness of our work would be reduced. Although we shall obviously not be in a position to negotiate large purchases or contracts on behalf of India as a whole, I think there is some force in what he said.

In this connection you will have read in the papers of the formation in England, under the initiative of Sir George Schuster, of an industrial group comprising fifty industries from the Midlands, to prepare for our visit. It is clear from this and other things that have appeared in the press from time to time that when we get there we shall be faced by people and interests who will have taken the trouble to organise themselves to meet us, and ready to talk business. I feel, therefore, that it is important that we should also be prepared in advance, with facts and ideas, when we meet these gentlemen....

---

[*] Chairman, Birla Group of Industries.

Do you think it would be possible for us, before we leave India, by direct contact with individual industrial enterprises, and through Chambers of Commerce and Associations, such as the Jute, Textile, Coal and other Associations, to ascertain from them in a very approximate way what their requirements of machinery of various types would be during, say, the first five years after the war, assuming that prices were reasonable? This would necessitate a questionnaire and perhaps some press propaganda to arouse sufficient interest in the country. We would make it clear that the purpose of obtaining this information would not be to undertake any direct negotiations, but to be in a position to discuss practical possibilities with British and American industrialists. We would point out that this would be in the interests of all concerned, because, with the ground prepared by our visit, it would then be easier and quicker for individual interests to negotiate actual purchases. As we shall have a fairly elaborate secretariat, we could even offer to make preliminary enquiries for specific items of plant on behalf of purchasers in this country.

I believe that if we thus went armed with clear information of what India will need after the war, and the price level at which business might result, we would be treated more seriously by British and American industrialists and could achieve more useful results. I shall be interested to know what you think of the idea.

I am sending the same letter to Mr. Kasturbhai and Sir Padampat.

Yours sincerely,
J.R.D. Tata

Note: Following this communication G.D. Birla wrote an interesting letter to Sir Azizul Huque on 18 February 1945 as follows:

My dear Sir Azizul Huque,

I hear from my London Office that specially for vegetarians there is great difficulty about food and that it should be arranged beforehand. Myself, Mr. Kasturbhai, Mr. Krishnaraj and Sir Padampat, we four are strictly vegetarians. As one cannot live on vegetables alone or on bread, for protein food we need plenty of milk, sugar and butter. I think we shall need each of us about a quart of milk, about 3 to 4 oz. of butter and similar quantity of sugar per day. Besides this, we shall need vegetables and bread for which, of course, I understand there is no difficulty. The chief thing is milk, butter and sugar. I hope it will be arranged before we leave this country....

G.D. Birla

TO RADHAKISHAN KHAITAN*

Bombay
24 April 1945

Dear Mr. Khaitan,

With reference to your letter of the 23rd instant, the following are my answers to your five questions:

1) The delegation is neither on behalf of Government, nor on behalf of any association in the country. In fact, we are not going in a delegation at all, but as a group of industrialists and businessmen, to whom Government have extended facilities for travelling to England and to the U.S.A. Government have also, at our request, lent us the services of a secretary to assist the members of the group.

2) It is intended to visit both the U.K. and the U.S.A. No detailed programme has as yet been fixed.

3) The expenses of each of the members and of their respective Technical Advisers will be borne entirely by the members themselves.

4) There is no intention to enter into any arrangement committing the country in any way.

5) The aims and objects of the visit were set forth in the communiqué issued by Government in October last year, a copy of which I enclose for your convenience.

Yours sincerely,
J.R.D. Tata

---

* A lot of interest was generated amongst the general public in the country about the visit of the Industrial Mission to the U.K. and U.S.A. One Radhakishan Khaitan from Bombay wrote to JRD raising five questions about the trip which JRD answered. He was always punctilious about replying to letters, even when they were from unknown members of the public.

An artist's impression of J.R.D. Tata.

R.D. Tata – father of JRD.

JRD's parents, father RD, and mother Sooni.

RD and Sooni alongside her letter in French.

Sooni with her children –
Sylla, Jehangir, Rodabeh, Darab and Jimmy.

Sooni with her youngest son Jimmy.

Sylla, JRD's eldest sister.

Rodabeh Tata.

(top left and right):
A young JRD.

(centre):
JRD with his siblings.

JRD and Sylla in Japanese costume.

JRD with Sylla and Rodabeh.

With wife Thelly.

My dear Papa,

I am writing this letter to-day to ask you something. And this something is the biggest thing I ever asked for — and a thing which there are nine chances on ten you will refuse —. But as miracles do happen so happ... sometimes and that you don't consider me now as a child I take my courage in both my hands as we say in French, and ask you for a motorcycle!

JRD's letter to his father seeking permission to buy a motorcycle.

JRD with Nevill Vintcent on his left at the Juhu airstrip, Bombay, on October 15, 1932, after the first historic flight of the subcontinent landed from Karachi. The plane was piloted by JRD.

The postal peon with the mail bags which JRD carried from Karachi to Bombay on the inaugural flight on October 15, 1932.

Over 40 years of service.

J.R.D. Tata, Air-India's Chairman, inaugurated India's first air service on October 15, 1932, piloting this two passenger De Havilland "Puss Moth" from Karachi to Bombay.

Tata Airlines, founded by Mr. Tata, renamed AIR-INDIA in 1946, now operates a fleet of Boeing 747's and 707's serving five continents.

The De Havilland
Puss Moth DH.80A

Wing Span: 36 ft. 9 in.
Length: 25 ft.
Cruising Speed: 105 m.p.h.
Seating Capacity: 3 passengers

JRD in New York at the Air-India Fifth Avenue Ticket Office in January 1974 with models of the Puss Moth and Boeing 747B.

Re-enactment of the first airmail flight by JRD on the occasion of the golden jubilee of Indian civil aviation – October 15, 1982.

Hoarding by Air-India after the re-enactment of the flight in 1982.

The hoarding displayed by Amul after the re-enactment of the flight in 1982.

JRD with members of the crew in front of the Jumbo aircraft.

Commemorative Flight:
First Day Covers issued in 1982.

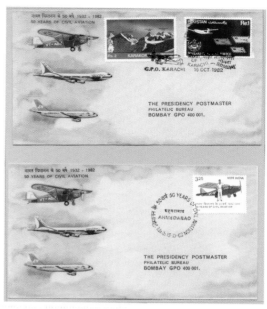

Stamps issued on the
first death anniversary
of JRD, 1994.

JRD in his office with a model of the Jumbo aircraft.

TO MAHATMA GANDHI

Bombay
9 May 1945

My dear Gandhiji,

You must have seen my statement to the Press on the communiqué* you issued a couple of days ago on the subject of our forthcoming visit to England and America.

I cannot tell you how hurt I was by the views you expressed about our trip and by the strong language you used.

What made it worse was that I, or some other member of the group, was not given an opportunity of removing the misapprehensions which you evidently entertained about the purpose of our trip. In the circumstances I was driven to issuing my statement to the Press in order to make my position clear.

---

* Gandhiji opposed the visit of the Industrial Mission to the U.K. and U.S.A. Issuing a statement to the press from Mahabaleshwar on 6 May, he said: "Ask them to wait till leaders are free. Freedom will come only after big business forego crumbs from Indo-British loot…All the big interests proclaim with one voice that India wants nothing less than her own elected National Government to shape her own destiny free of all control, British or other. This independence will not come for the asking. It will come only when the interests, big or small, are prepared to forego the crumbs that fall to them from partnership with the British in the loot which British rule takes from India. Verbal protests will count for nothing so long as the partnership continues unchecked. The so-called unofficial deputation which will go to England and America dare not proceed, whether for inspection or for entering into a shameful deal, so long as the moving spirits of the Congress Working Committee are being detained without any trial for the sole crime of sincerely striving for India's independence without shedding a drop of blood save their own." Source: *Bombay Chronicle*, May 7, 1945.

I am leaving on Friday morning and expect to return some time in August when I hope I shall have an opportunity of discussing the matter with you.

With kind regards and sincere wishes,

Yours sincerely,
J.R.D. Tata

FROM MAHATMA GANDHI

Mahabaleshwar
20 May 1945

Bhai Jehangirji,[*]

    I have your angry note, if you can ever write anything angry.

    If you have all gone not to commit yourselves to anything, my note protects you. My answer is to the hypothetical question. If the hypothesis is wrong, naturally the answer is wrong and is therefore protective of you all. There was no question of my referring to any of you, as I was dealing with an assumption. I hope I am clear.

                       M.K. Gandhi

---

[*]   In Gujarati.

1947 and After

TO PANDIT JAWAHARLAL NEHRU[*]

Bombay
14 August 1947

Dear Jawaharlal on this day my thoughts go to you whose steadfast and inspired leadership have brought India to her goal through these long years of struggle and suffering stop I rejoice that you who have always held so high the torch of freedom are the first Prime Minister of free India and I send you my heartfelt wishes for success in the heavy task of guiding her to her great destiny.

Jeh

---

* Regarding the friendship of Jawaharlal Nehru and JRD, R.M. Lala says in his biography of JRD that it went back to a time "when Nehru was a dashing thirty-six and JRD was only twenty." Their fathers—Motilal Nehru and R.D. Tata—were good friends and this friendship continued and grew in the next generation. On the eve of India's Independence JRD sent Prime Minister Nehru the above telegram.

TO MRS. VIJAYALAKSHMI PANDIT*

Bombay
21 August 1947

My dear Nan,

Thank you very much for your kind letter....
I was very happy to know that the flight to Moscow went off smoothly, and that you were satisfied with the manner in which Air-India carried it out. The pride and happiness at flying the first Ambassador of free India to the U.S.S.R. was really ours, and it was doubly so for me because you were that Ambassador....
Thelly joins me in sending you our sincerest wishes.

Yours affectionately,
Jeh

---

*   Next to Jawaharlal, JRD was close to his daughter Indira Gandhi and his sister Vijayalakshmi Pandit.
When India became independent JRD arranged for an Air-India plane to fly Vijayalakshmi to the Soviet Union as India's first Ambassador to that country.

TO G. D. BIRLA

Bombay
14 November 1947

Dear Mr. Birla,

As you may know, the Government of India have recently approved of a joint scheme* between themselves and Air-India, for the inauguration of an international service between India and the U.K. A similar scheme is under consideration in connection with the shipping industry. There are other projects which Government have in view, in some of which it would appear to be Government's present intention to set up industrial enterprises on their own, either managed wholly by themselves or in conjunction with private interests. All this raises large questions of policy and would have a profound influence on industrial development in the country.

I think it is essential, therefore, for a few of us to confer together with a view to arriving, if possible, at some uniform views on the general principles involved.

I am writing the same letter to Sir Shri Ram and Mr. Kasturbhai Lalbhai, and I am also verbally approaching Mr. Walchand Hirachand, Dharamsey Khatau, Krishnaraj Thackersey and Bhagwandas Mehta, the present Chairman of the Millowners' Association.

As all of us, except you and Sir Shri Ram are permanently in Bombay, and as Mr. Kasturbhai visits Bombay every week, I would like, if you agree with my suggestion, to arrange an early meeting in Bombay. I shall therefore appreciate it if you will let

---

* This is one of the earliest harbingers of the Government's policy of public sector undertakings, which is now, fifty years later, being dismantled.

me know when it would be convenient for you to meet in Bombay. It would be advantageous if you and Sir Shri Ram could agree between you as to a suitable date. I suggest it should be towards the end of this month or the beginning of December....

With kind regards,

Yours sincerely,
J.R.D. Tata

TO SIR ARDESHIR DALAL[*]

Switzerland
6 February 1948

My dear Ardeshir,[**]

The silence emanating from Bombay House (towards me) is well nigh deafening! While the resulting peace at this end is delightful its completeness is beginning to make me uneasy! That is the worst of having a restless nature like mine and yours. I think I would enjoy my rest and holiday better if I knew what was happening at headquarters....

I was horrified, as you must all have been, at the news of Gandhi's assassination. It is a World tragedy but who knows whether his paying the ultimate price may not in the end have done more for the cause of peace, tolerance and communal harmony for which he gave his life than he would have achieved by remaining alive. It may have, amongst other things, brought about greater solidarity and a tightening of the ranks in the cabinet and the Congress and healed, at least for the crucial time being, the differences and fissiparous tendencies which were beginning to make themselves conspicuous in government circles....I trembled to think what would happen if Jawaharlal met the same fate. I hope however, that the grief and anger caused by Gandhi's murder amongst the great mass of the people of India and the realisation of the

---

[*] Copy of a handwritten letter expressing anguish on hearing the shocking news of Mahatma Gandhi's death.

[**] Sir Ardeshir Dalal (1884–1949); Topped ICS examination 1907; Director, Tata Sons, 1931; Knighted, 1939; Member, Viceroy's Executive Council for Planning and Development, 1944; Vice-Chairman, Tata Steel, 1947.

righteousness and soundness of what he stood for, will keep the...extremists from further mischief: and wean away many from their fold. I wish the office had thought of sending me newspaper cuttings which would give me a better understanding of the feelings in the country than I can get from the Swiss and English papers here....

With affectionate wishes to you all.

Yours,
Jeh

AVIATION

The Beginnings

★

Management

★

Flight Notes

★

Major Events

★

Advice and Consent

JRD was the first Indian to qualify as a pilot. He received a pilot's licence on 10 February, 1929.

The proposal for Tatas to start an airline came the same year from Nevill Vintcent, a former officer of the R.A.F. who had come to India to give joy rides. It involved connecting the Imperial Airways main service to Karachi with Ahmedabad, Bombay and Bellary in 1929. The proposal was approved by the Chairman Sir Dorabji Tata at the instance of John Peterson, an ex-I.C.S. officer who was Director-in-charge of Tata Steel and JRD's mentor in Tatas. The decision to go ahead with it resulted in Tata Sons setting up the Aviation Department which was re-named Tata Air Lines in 1938. Eight years later it was converted into a public limited company and named Air-India Limited.

On 15 October, 1932 JRD piloted the inaugural flight of Tata Air Lines from Karachi to Bombay. This flight was re-enacted by him in 1962 and 1982.

In 1948 Air-India International (A.-I.I.) was set up as India's first joint sector project between the government and the private sector to start an overseas service.

In 1953 the government nationalised the aviation business. At JRD's suggestion two corporations were set up: one for the domestic operations, the other for their international counterpart. JRD agreed to chair the global airline which was offered to him by the government. He continued as Chairman till 1978 when his services were terminated by Prime Minister Morarji Desai. He was re-appointed to the Board of the airline by Mrs. Indira Gandhi in the early 1980s.

Over the years JRD had acquired considerable knowledge about different types of aircraft. He was also in touch with the latest developments in aeronautics the world over. At times people sought his advice in selecting aeroplanes for their organisations.

JRD would make firm plans before buying aeroplanes for Air-India. In his reply to a letter from the Earl of Kimberly, from England, he gave a detailed analysis of the company's policy of purchasing airships and the reason for not going in for Concordes which the former wanted Air-India to buy.

Correspondence in this section also gives an inkling of how efficiently the airline was run during JRD's stewardship for 46 years. He had a tough time running the airline against the background of its government ownership. He always kept the interest of the company paramount and fought uncompromisingly against the red-tapism of the ministers and bureaucrats to achieve his objective.

He would tolerate no compromise on operating and maintenance standards. On every flight he travelled, JRD kept detailed notes. On reaching his office he would send memos with his suggestions—criticisms and compliments—to the Head Office for immediate action. Some sample memos have been included in this section. To quote R.M. Lala, "He gave India pride of place in international air transport."

The Beginnings

TO DIRECTORS, TATA SONS

Bombay
16 December 1929

Directors, Tata Sons,

Air Mail Service between Karachi and Bombay

I called by appointment on Sir B.N. Mitra, Government Member for Industries and Labour, this afternoon and discussed with him the above scheme. I understand the present position to be this:

Government seem to think that an Air Mail Service between Karachi and Bombay to connect with the Imperial Airways Mail would be of no benefit to Bombay until night flying between Karachi and Bombay is made possible. Their reason is that the Imperial Airways Mail is expected in future to arrive regularly on Saturday evenings. The daylight service between Karachi and Bombay would not be able to start until next morning (i.e. Sunday) bringing the mails to Bombay in the afternoon. This would only be distributed Monday morning. The saving in time will, therefore, be small and the same result is going to be effected by the Government-run service between Karachi and Delhi....The theory, therefore, is that Bombay itself would derive no benefit by the special service between Karachi and Bombay, but Madras and southern India would, because mails brought to Bombay by air on Sunday afternoon could reach the Madras Mail on Sunday night....Sir B.N. Mitra told me that in spite of this view our scheme is being studied at present and will not be ditched purely on this account, because it may be advisable to gain experience from the daylight route before night flying is arranged for. I pointed out to Sir Bhupendra Nath that the Imperial Airways Mail may not always arrive on Saturday afternoons. It may, as often happens at present, arrive on Sundays or Mondays or if the service is speeded up, it may arrive on Friday evenings or Saturday mornings in either of which case Bombay and southern India would undoubtedly benefit by an independent Karachi-Bombay Service. I was told that the Imperial Airways Mails are expected regularly on Saturday evenings in future.

I was told that the main stumbling block is the question of finance, as they are entirely in the hands of the Finance Department who are expected to resist the grant of any funds for the Bombay route. Government seem to think that an Air Service to be run only during the dry season is not advisable and when the question of money is considered they include in their estimates the Rs. 10 lakhs necessary to render the Juhu Aerodrome fit all the year round. I pointed out that having at first a service during eight months only is better than having no service at all, apart from the valuable experience gained by running the preliminary service until the Bombay Aerodrome is ready for use in the rainy season. Sir Bhupendra Nath seemed to agree and said that it was possible that assuming they were satisfied with the scheme in its other aspects, they might obtain from the Finance Department only say Rs. 50,000 so as to be able to make a start next October, the question of raising money for continuing the service in 1931 being left over for the following financial year.

I explained to Sir Bhupendra Nath that frankly we thought our scheme based on one run a week in each direction was not commercially economical and that so as to render it more economically sound we would be quite prepared to run an extra weekly service if Government wished us to do so and if ordinary mail was available. Sir Bhupendra Nath at first objected to this as the subsidy asked for would be greatly increased. I showed him a copy of the expenditure statements in our application to Government and pointed out that there would be very little increase in the subsidy, and that only in the beginning and until mail increased, as the excess expenditure would only be for petrol, oil and an engine overhaul fund while the rates per pound could be greatly reduced. He said that this put a different aspect on the question as Government had thought that the heavy item of depreciation would have to be doubled if a bi-weekly service was run. I assured him that this was not so.

I urged that if a favourable decision was to be made, it should be made in time for us or anybody else who gets the contract to order equipment in time to start in October. I agreed that six months' notice would be desirable though at a pinch we could do with three to five months.

I understand that Government may have to consider the possibility of running such a service themselves as they propose to do in the case of the Karachi-Delhi Service. I pointed out that this was not done in the case of Air Services in any part of the world but was told that circumstances are partly different in India and public opinion which forced Government to take up Railways might make them to do so also in the case of Air Mail Services.

J.R.D. Tata

TO J.A.D. NAOROJI*

Bombay
28 December 1929

I met Col. Shelmerdine, Director General of Civil Aviation in India, at Delhi on the 20th instant and discussed our scheme with him. This interview confirmed the impression I had got from my conversation with Sir B.N. Mitra in Bombay that the Government are principally if not solely interested at present in the Trunk route across India from Karachi to Rangoon. They are committed to this policy and do not seem very keen at present to give much thought or time to any other internal route in India. I understand that preparations of their present Karachi-Delhi route to Calcutta are completed and they are now actually working on the preparation of the Calcutta-Rangoon extension which should come in operation about a year hence. It seems that the connection with Australia is already in active preparation through the efforts of the Australian and the Straits Government.

In spite of their apparent obsession over this route I understand that our scheme has not been shelved and is being seriously considered. I was again told that the main difficulty will be to get the necessary money from the Finance Department....

I gathered that as far as this route is concerned our scheme is at present the only one likely to be seriously considered although when and if Government decide to go ahead with this route they will most likely call for tenders.

Col. Shelmerdine seems to attach much importance to the Indianisation as far as pilots are concerned of any internal service in India at the same time saying that the passengers would not have much confidence in them at first. I said that as there

---

* Grandson of Dadabhai Naoroji, an officer in Tatas who looked after the airline business in JRD's absence; later became Managing Director, The Tata Oil Mills Company Limited (TOMCO).

are no Indian pilots at present of sufficient experience Indianisation could only be done by using Indian pilots holding "B" certificates as assistant pilots to the English pilots until they were capable of running safely fast and heavy machines. He said that would take a very long time.

J.R.D. Tata

TO NEVILL VINTCENT

Calcutta
28 August 1931

My dear Vintcent,

...Regarding your suggestion that if the Indian State Service is abandoned by Government we should consider making an offer for it ourselves, I personally think it unlikely that, in the present times, Tatas would want to take on the larger venture with the increased commitments which it would involve. We shall, however, be glad to consider any definite scheme you are able to put forward and we will certainly not turn it down without careful consideration. Times are getting from bad to worse in India and with all my personal enthusiasm I would be reluctant to recommend to the Firm the acceptance of proposals on a larger scale than our proposed West Coast line.

Yours sincerely,
Jehangir R.D. Tata

TO NEVILL VINTCENT

Bombay
16 *October 1931*

Dear Vintcent,

I am sorry to hear that you and Newall[*] have definitely parted as far as your business activities are concerned. I am writing this letter to you by Air Mail so that it reaches you before you leave, for two reasons; one of them is that I think that you and Newall should write to Tata Sons Limited jointly an official letter setting forth your relationship, or rather your lack of relationship, and your respective positions vis-à-vis Tata's future aerial activities. I am not sure I have made myself clear, but what I am driving at is this. You and Newall jointly put forward air mail proposals to us and it was verbally arranged that if and when our proposals to Government matured, we would enter into a pucca agreement. Until then we have naturally no claim whatsoever on you and you have no claim whatsoever on us. Now that you and Newall have terminated your partnership and that the latest proposals which we have forwarded to Government are based entirely on your work and investigations during your last visit to India, you have, in my opinion, a prior claim on us and it seems clear to me that if Government accept our scheme you will be our partner in the venture. It seems, therefore, only fair that Tata Sons should be protected against any future litigation which Newall may start against us. I do not think he would be so foolish as to do that in view of the fact that it has been made clear more than once that there is up to the present no legal connection whatsoever between us, but in view of what you

---

[*]   Captain J.S. Newall was Vintcent's partner in a firm which was involved in organising joy rides, aerial photography and survey work.

have told me about his "litigation complex" we want to avoid any possibility of trouble....

The second reason for which I want you to get this letter before you leave is that I am very keen that, if you can manage it, you should have a test flight in one of the new Italian machines, the "Breda 33". I have read in the Aeroplane Papers that these machines are now available in England, and there should be no difficulty, if you have the time to do so, to arrange for a test flight. I wrote a long letter to Bredas over six weeks ago, for full particulars, but have had no reply yet. Their cruising speed being around a hundred and twenty miles an hour, it occurred to me that if they are suitable in other ways, (they seem to have a fairly high wing loading between), they might do us very well as the extra 20 miles an hour cruising speed, as compared to the "Puss Moth", would practically ensure our being able to do the Karachi-Madras run in one day. They are Gipsy III engined.

Yours sincerely,
Jehangir R.D. Tata

TO FREDERICK TYMMS*

Bombay
28 *October* 1931

Dear Mr. Tymms,

In continuation of my letter from Jamshedpur of the 16th October, I have just received a telegram from Vintcent informing me that his post with Government has been retrenched and that he is, therefore, free to attend exclusively to our work. He strongly recommends that we should consider tendering for the Air Mail Service between Karachi, Delhi and Calcutta. He says that we should inform you, so that in case other offers have been received Government may defer their decision until we have had an opportunity of considering the proposal. Vintcent does not know of my letter to you of the 16th October in which I have already referred to the possibility of our taking an interest in this Service. I have no doubt that if Government are prepared to consider offers from private enterprises for this route, they will give Tatas an opportunity of bidding for the Service. I should be glad if you would kindly confirm this.

In order to save time and unnecessary correspondence, I think I should say straightaway that if Government were only prepared to consider a Service for passengers as well as for mails, my Firm would definitely not be interested.

There is no doubt in my mind that unless the country is prepared to subsidise Air Services very heavily, there is no chance for the operator to make both ends meet if he is to use large 3-engine machines indispensable for passenger work and has to lay down the extensive organisation which would be necessary for the purpose. I

---

*   He succeeded Col. Shelmerdine as Director General of Civil Aviation, Government of India.

understand that the Government of India are in favour of the Karachi-Delhi-Calcutta Service being State-controlled, and if they have gone to the length of cancelling the Indian State Service, for reasons of economy, it seems fairly obvious that they will not subsidise private enterprise sufficiently to make the running of a similar service a paying commercial proposition. The only alternative, therefore, is mails, and a fast and efficient Mail Service can be run at a small cost to the "Consumer".

Apart from that I think you will agree that it is wrong to combine passengers with mail and that it will be so for many years to come, until Passenger Services are so frequent that mails will not be delayed by being carried along with passengers.

Vintcent, I believe, has the same ideas as mine on Air Mail vs Passenger Services, and in his telegram he says that the proposal would be to carry mails between Karachi, Delhi and Calcutta with fast single-engined planes. As you are no doubt aware, Avros have recently brought out a mail plane with a cruising speed of about 145 mph and unless a faster or better machine is produced in the meantime, that is the machine we would propose to use.

I find that the approximate distances to be covered are about 680 miles from Karachi to Delhi and 820 miles from Delhi to Calcutta. With this machine there would be no difficulty in flying the mails from Karachi to Calcutta in one day. There would, therefore, be no need for lighting equipment, the number of machines required could be kept low, and those in use could as a result be worked economically.

I cannot, of course, give you any details of costs, etc., at this stage. They will have to be worked out and I would want to discuss the matter with Vintcent on his return.

I would be very glad to know as soon as possible whether you wish us to go further into the matter, and if so, I shall be much obliged if you would send me the latest figures of the weight of mails available on the route.

If it ultimately came to our running the Service, I am afraid it would affect our West Coast proposals, as I am sure that the Firm would not be prepared to start two important Services at the same time. We might however, possibly run a shuttle service between Jodhpur and Bombay in conjunction with the Karachi-Calcutta Service.

Yours sincerely,
Jehangir R.D. Tata

TO NEVILL VINTCENT

Bombay
9 December 1931

Dear Vintcent,

At present I am really more concerned with our first scheme. Tymms has told us that he has passed it as far as the technical part of it is concerned and that it has been sent on to the Post and Telegraph Department. They have been sitting on it since sometime in August, and we have heard nothing yet. I am getting fed up and I think that Government are treating us very shabbily over this. Though it may have had some advantages, I am sorry that all my correspondence with Tymms has been on a purely demi-official basis because it has practically muzzled us from agitating in the press, Chambers of Commerce, etc. about the delay. I am probably leaving for Europe at the end of this month or the beginning of the next and I may have to pay a flying visit to Delhi in the meantime to find out what is happening. I hope, however, that you will be able to save me this journey and to find out whether Government intend to say yes or no within the next 100 years!

Yours sincerely,
Jehangir R.D. Tata

Management

TO NEVILL VINTCENT

Bombay
14 September 1936

My dear Nevill,

I read in the papers about two passengers in a chartered Leopard who had a forced landing near Ahmedabad in a flight from Poona to Karachi and to whose rescue a relief plane was sent from Poona. I read also that they had reached too late to catch the Imperial Airways' machine which was the object of the flight. This was obviously one of our chartered jobs.

I shall be obliged if, whenever anything unusual or out of the ordinary happens in connection with our operations, you will kindly send me a few lines reporting the facts so that I may be kept informed. In this case I was asked by many people about the incident.

Yours sincerely,
Jeh

TO SIR G.V.B.[*]

Bombay
9 June 1950

Sir G.V.B.,

Filing System

Almost since 1932, I have endeavoured to inculcate in our staff modern ideas on filing. I have consistently failed. The attached File No.58, forwarded by Mr. Pavri, is a fine example of the absurdity of our filing system.

I am frankly surprised that we ever manage to get any papers or information with this kind of filing system, where papers on every conceivable subject are mixed up in one file. We are bound to get into a mess sooner or later if this goes on and I suggest that a drastic revision in our filing system be undertaken, if necessary in consultation with someone like Ibcons.

J.R.D. Tata

---

[*] Sir Gurunath Bewoor, ex-I.C.S. Officer, who joined Tatas as Managing Director of Air-India and Air-India International.

TO THE TRAFFIC MANAGER, AIR-INDIA*

Bombay
29 April 1953

Dear Sir,

I saw only yesterday the letter of the 14th April to you signed by 40 members of your Department.

I have been deeply touched by the kind sentiments expressed by the signatories towards me and by their appreciation of my solicitude for their welfare.

If I have been so distressed in recent years at the worsening position of Air-India it is not only because of my disappointment at seeing a concern which I had helped to create and nursed for over twenty years, fail to prosper and grow as it should have if given a fair chance, but also because it frustrated my desire to see it bring increasing prosperity and happiness to those for whom it had found employment, and for whose welfare I felt a personal sense of responsibility.

As regards the signatories' desire to present me with a souvenir, while I am deeply appreciative of this proposal I am sorry I am unable, on principle, to accept such a present however much I would like to respond to their kind thought. The sponsors have probably not realised that it might have undesirable repercussions and would place me in an embarrassing position. I am sure that they would not wish this to happen and I therefore request them to drop the proposal.

---

* After Air-India, along with the other airlines, was nationalised in 1953, several employees of Air-India, individually or in groups, expressed their good sentiments and gratitude to JRD for what he had done for the organisation.

It will be a wrench for me to see the end of Air-India as a valued part of the House of Tatas. It however gives me great comfort at this unhappy time to know that some at least of the employees share my regrets and have kindly feelings towards me. I sincerely hope that in the reorganisation of the industry under Government, their material prospects will improve, and I would like them and their colleagues to know that, if I remain connected with the industry, I shall always do whatever I can to safeguard their interests and those of all working for the new corporations....

Yours truly,
J.R.D. Tata

TO S.K.K.*

Bombay
22 *May* 1953

Thinking over all the posters and advertisements we have had in the past, I have come to the conclusion that they should be divided into two classes, one of a comic nature based on Umesh Rao's illustrations and the other of a serious nature, amongst the best of which was a previous poster of Paris with a very charming text by yourself.

Some of the posters and timetables made in Switzerland or Italy have been also of a good quality.

We must make a determined effort to raise the standard of our publicity material, particularly as we are in direct competition over most of our routes with TWA whose posters, etc. are exceptionally good.

I approve of the timetable stand.

J.R.D. Tata

---

* S.K. Kooka, who was Traffic Manager of Tata Air Lines, went on to become Commercial Director in charge of publicity of Air-India. During these years, he successfully planned Air-India's corporate branding strategy, reflected in everything from the décor of the aircraft and the appearance of the staff, to the advertisements, with the creation of the symbol of the "Maharajah".

TO CAPT. K.R. GUZDER*

Bombay
10 August 1953

My dear Guzder,

Your colleagues and other members of flying crews and ground staff stationed in London may have some apprehensions about the likely consequences of the nationalisation of Air-India International Limited, and such apprehensions may perhaps lead some to lose interest in their work and to seek employment elsewhere. While I hope that this is not the case, I wish, as Chairman of the new State Corporation, to assure you and them that any such doubts and fears are entirely unfounded....

The Government of India have publicly stated, and I have personally been given assurances to that effect, that it is their desire that the new Corporations should be run on business lines, with adequate freedom of action, and that the interests and prospects of their staff should be safeguarded.

All this and also the fact that I have remained as Chairman and shall continue to take the same close and personal interest in the affairs of our airline, should dispel any doubts in the minds of any of your staff. I hope, therefore, that, with renewed confidence, they will continue to work hard and loyally for the success of the enterprise and to maintain the high standards and prestige of Air-India International which they have done so much to build up....

Yours sincerely,
J.R.D. Tata

---

* A senior pilot who flew the aircraft on A.-I.I.'s inaugural Bombay-London service in 1948. He rose to become Operations Manager, London.

TO OPERATIONS MANAGER
(THROUGH GENERAL MANAGER)

Bombay
26 April 1954

Subject: Selection of Pilots

The selection of some of the pilots who have been transferred from I.A.C. to A.-I.I. would seem to indicate that the Selection Board base their recommendations exclusively on seniority backed no doubt by adequate flying ability, and ignore certain other qualities which, though less tangible, are highly important in international operations such as ours.

Every pilot transferred to A.-I.I. as a first officer under training should be considered as one who in due course will, or may, become a commander. While he should naturally have a high standard of professional ability as a pilot, it should be borne in mind that the degree of responsibility attached to the duties of a commander of heavy long-range aircraft operating on transcontinental routes, and the amount of technical, navigational and other specialised knowledge which he is required to assimilate and use, are much greater than in the case of the commander of smaller aircraft operating on short-range domestic routes. Furthermore, commanders on transcontinental air services, operated almost wholly out of India and at great distances from base, cannot be as closely and constantly supervised as the pilots on domestic services. Finally, apart from the ability of merely doing a good job, there are important public relations functions attached to an international commander, while on duty as well as when off duty, both as a senior representative of the Corporation and as an Indian abroad.

All these factors require that our pilots should possess certain human qualities of intelligence, personality, self-discipline, conscientiousness, leadership, etc., to a higher degree than strictly required in domestic commanders.

The management will therefore kindly note that in the recruitment of pilots and co-pilots, special attention should be paid to these factors and adequate weightage given to them in assessing the merits of a prospective recruit to the Air-India International cadre....

J.R.D. Tata

TO PROF. HUMAYUN KABIR[*]

Bombay
23 January 1958

Dear Professor Kabir,

I have written to you separately about the composition of the Board of this Corporation. I think I should at the same time let you know that ever since the formation of the two Corporations, I have been feeling increasingly worried at the enormous waste of time to all concerned involved in the Board Meetings of both Corporations and in the circulation of Board papers.

Whereas during the seven years' existence of the two predecessor Companies in the Tata group, papers were rarely circulated in advance and Board Meetings hardly ever lasted more than an hour, Government members of the Corporation have insisted on voluminous notes, with full enclosures, on every single item of the agenda even where the subject is of little importance. As a result, the agendas of both Corporations usually consist of between 100 and 150 pages, and sometimes more, and meetings last up to four hours. In some cases they have had to be adjourned to the next day. Every item is discussed at length and sometimes half of the meeting is taken in the discussion of a single item. Frequently minutes of the previous meeting are discussed to an extent that amounts to a repetition of the previous meeting's discussion. Quite frankly, if it was not for my desire to retain the friendliest relations with all Members and Government officials with whom we have to deal, and also my desire to avoid causing embarrassment or annoyance, I would have been unable to continue on the present basis upto now....

---

[*]   Prof. Humayun Kabir (1906-1969); Minister for Civil Aviation, Government of India.

I sincerely hope that as the Boards of the Corporations get "de-officialised" it will be possible gradually to reduce the amount of time and paper work required up to now for Board Meetings. It would be of great help if at the proper time you could put in a word in support of my views.

I shall always be willing to serve but not to waste my time. I feel that with the growth of the State sector in industry it is time that Government made up their minds as to whether they want State Companies or Corporations operated like Government departments or as commercial concerns. If the former, there is no room or need for men like myself. The Ministries concerned should take them over and run them departmentally. If Government want them run as commercial concerns, they should pick the best men they can get and let them get on with the job, subject only to general policy control....

Yours sincerely,
J.R.D. Tata

TO PROF. HUMAYUN KABIR

Bombay
7 March 1958

Dear Prof. Kabir,

Thank you for your letter of the 26th February.

I entirely agree with your statement that Government's exclusive responsibility to appoint members of the Board under the Act cannot be delegated. Not only have I never disputed this self-evident fact, but I have myself in my letter to you of the 19th referred to Government's right to make such appointments to the Board as they please.

I, however, stand by my view that Government should recognise the accepted convention under which the Chairman of a Board is extended the courtesy of being consulted before Government make a new appointment to a Board, although I would disagree. Government may consider that such courtesy is unnecessary in the case of Chairmen who happen to be Government servants, but if they want non-officials, such as myself, to undertake the task and responsibility of being the Chairman of a Government Corporation, they must, in fairness, treat them as any head of an organisation expects to be treated. I do not see what Government can lose by sounding a Corporation's Chairman before making an appointment when the final decision is wholly and indisputably theirs.

The convention I have proposed need not apply in the case of such nominees as the representatives of the Finance or other Ministries directly concerned with the operations of the Corporation, particularly when a new appointment is merely a replacement caused by the transfer of the previous nominee. We have in the last five years had many changes in the representation of the Finance Ministry on our Board, and I have, of course, never raised the slightest objection or suggested that I should have been consulted first. I hope you will agree that the stand I am taking in this matter is a sound and reasonable one and that this procedure should be followed in future....

Yours sincerely,
J.R.D. Tata

TO M.M. PHILIP*

Bombay

18 April 1958

Dear Shri Philip,

Re: Promotions to Posts exceeding Rs.1,500/-

On my return from abroad, I have seen your D.O. letter No.7CA(5)/58 of the 25th March, in which you request my views on a suggestion that every case of promotion within the Air Corporations involving a salary of Rs.1,500/- or more should require the prior approval of Government.

My views are entirely adverse to this proposal and I am frankly surprised that it should have been made at all. As it is, I consider that the Corporation is subjected to an excessive degree of financial control by Government.... I have urged at meetings of both the Air Corporations that Government having appointed high-power Boards should not intervene in such routine matters. The present proposal to subject even ordinary promotions to the prior approval of Government, would, without serving any useful purpose, increase bureaucratic control over day to day management and make a farce of the principle of autonomy in State Corporations. It would also amount to a declaration of "no confidence" in the Board and Executive Management of the Corporations. As Chairman of Air-India International, I consider this proposal totally unacceptable....

Yours sincerely,

J.R.D. Tata

---

* Secretary, Ministry of Transport and Communications, Government of India.

TO GEORGE WOODS*

Bombay
20 November 1959

My dear George,

I am glad you, like Gene Black, approve of Air-India's slumberettes. You may be surprised to learn that all the members of IATA, except Air-India, are in favour of banning both slumberettes and sleeping berths on the jets! We are up against the fact that most of the new big jets will be used in the first year over the Atlantic on which the big league fellows in the airline business want to cram the maximum number of passengers while the demand for seats in jets exceeds the supply! We think it is a damn silly idea and have resisted it up to now but we may not be able to hold out, being in a minority of one! The fact that the jets are faster does not mean that people are likely to spend less hours in them. For instance, some travellers between the U.S. and India, who used to break journey in Europe, may now travel straight through. Even in a jet, a flight from London to Sydney or London and Tokyo will still take around thirty hours, and thirty hours upright in a chair can be as uncomfortable in a jet as in a piston engined plane....

Yours ever,
Jeh

---

* President, First Boston Corporation, U.S.A. who later succeeded Eugene Black as the President of the World Bank. He helped Tatas in getting a loan from the Bank for the expansion of Tata Steel (from one million to two million tonnes).

TO SACHINDRA CHAUDHURI[*]

Bombay

19 October 1966

Dear Mr. Chaudhuri,

We have been recently informed by the Department of Aviation that the Government have decided in consultation with the Ministry of Finance that the facility of personal cars extended by the Corporation to some 10 senior officers, including senior Departmental Heads like the Commercial Director and Financial Controller who have enjoyed the facility for well over a decade, should be withdrawn with immediate effect. This has come as a complete surprise to me and to the Board of the Corporation and I am, therefore, constrained to bring the matter to your personal notice and to inform you that the decision is likely to cause utter frustration and loss of morale among the senior executives....

The question of withdrawal of personal cars from all officers except the Chief Executives of Public Sector Undertakings was first raised by the Ministry of Finance in November 1964. At that time the Board of the Corporation considered the matter carefully and the Management submitted a convincing case to the Government showing that the proposal, which was primarily intended to effect economy in expenditure, would actually result in additional expenditure in as much as a central pool of cars with drivers would in any case have to be maintained to provide essential transport facilities to the senior officers engaged in the running of the airline. Our representation was submitted in May 1965. We have now been advised after nearly 18 months that the Government, while agreeing to the continuance of the car facility

---

[*]   Finance Minister, Government of India.

to certain categories of officers, have nevertheless decided that cars should be withdrawn from 10 officers in Air-India.

I am extremely perturbed by this decision and I would earnestly request you to reconsider the decision. I can understand the necessity for effecting economy in expenditure but we have fully satisfied ourselves that the alternative of keeping a pool of cars with drivers would only add to the present expenditure while not fulfilling the requirement of quick movement of the officers as and when required and at the same time causing unnecessary resentment. The withdrawal of the cars from some of the officers at Headquarters who have enjoyed the facility for several years, while a large number of relatively junior officers in charge of our stations all over the world have necessarily to be given personal cars, is not a practicable proposition. We would indeed find it difficult to man the senior positions under these conditions....

With kind regards,

Yours sincerely,
J.R.D. Tata

TO DR. P. SUBBARAYAN[*]

Bombay
18 *January* 1962

Dear Dr. Subbarayan,

Many thanks for your kind D.O. of the 5th January regarding the proposed amendment of the Air Corporations Act. I am naturally disappointed to learn Government have not been able to accept our suggestions that the Act should be amended so as to leave the determination and conditions of terms of service of employees within the powers of the Boards of the Corporations.

We have, of course, no option but to bow to Government's decision, but as Chairman of Air-India, and also I hope as a friend with some experience of the management of industries in India, I feel it my duty to tell you that I consider that Government are making a serious mistake in retaining in the hands of the various Ministries concerned control over matters which, in the interests of effective management of Public Sector Undertakings, should be left to the Boards of the individual enterprises within, of course, the general framework of Government directives and policies and overall control.

Quite apart from the two Air Corporations, I have been feeling increasingly that with the rapid expansion of the State Sector of industry in India, both in the number and size of Government undertakings, the time has come when Government must make up its mind to free State enterprises from a large part of the control they exercise over them today. Having laid down certain norms and broad policies and having always the right to nominate and change at their will, the members of their Boards,

---

[*] Minister for Transport and Communications, Government of India.

the units should be given reasonable managerial scope which they definitely do not have today. There is not even any uniformity in the degree or nature of controls exercised over various enterprises....

I am firmly convinced that Government are frustrating their own oft-repeated desire that state-owned enterprises should be run efficiently as commercial concerns, and should make a profit, by the excessive degree of control they exercise directly or indirectly over the management of such enterprises....

From personal knowledge, I can assure you that the result of this state of affairs is that, with very rare exceptions, the first and foremost thought of all managers or administrators of State enterprises is to protect themselves against possible mistakes and criticism, thus avoiding responsibility and initiative. Only the brave or foolhardy are prepared to take commercial risks which would be considered normal in Private enterprise.

It is of course up to Government to decide on the form of management they want to impose on State Sector enterprises, but, with the greatest respect, I have no doubt at all in my mind that they are going about it in the wrong way and will never achieve thereby the degree of efficiency and the results I know they genuinely want....

With kindest regards,

Yours sincerely,
J.R.D. Tata

TO C.D.* (THROUGH H.O.)

Bombay
26 November 1969

Re: 1970 Calendar

I am sorry to express disappointment at our new calendar which, while no doubt extremely "arty", is in my view totally unsuitable for an airline calendar.

The pages of a commercial calendar must have two virtues, namely that of attracting the eye in the first place, and also remaining attractive, interesting and "viewable" for thirty days a month.

Except for its originality, the 1970 calendar does not pass either test. The February page, picturing a washed-out woman's mouth and nose plus large expanses of nothing, is a typical example. Can it be expected to draw pleasurable attention and a warm reaction from employees or visitors for thirty consecutive days in an office or shop?

I know that the Art Department and its controlling body CHO** have never liked the idea of consulting others. While I would not want to interfere with the artistic autonomy of the Department, I think it would be in the interests of the Corporation if occasionally they stepped off their high horse at least to discuss the concept of a calendar or of an advertising campaign. I am sure we shall be once again criticised, though for different reasons, about our 1970 calendar.

J.R.D. Tata

---

*   Commercial Director.
** Corporate Head Office.

TO A/M M.S.C.*

Bombay
i3 March 1970

I am worried about a matter affecting the safety of our operations, which we all agree must never be compromised. It concerns the extent to which our co-pilots are allowed to make landings and thus acquire and retain a degree of proficiency adequate to ensure absolute safety in the event of any of them having to take over from an incapacitated commander.

My understanding is that our co-pilots are put through a fairly brief but concentrated course once a year. There is however, I believe, no systematic scheme under which they are made to make a minimum number of landings spread out over a year. Theoretically at least therefore, it might happen that a co-pilot might do only one landing in a period of 12 months. If such a pilot had suddenly to take over an approach and landing into a crowded airport under adverse meteorological conditions, and if he "booped" and an accident resulted, I think we would come out badly from an enquiry if it was found that our co-pilots had such little practical experience.

I also understand that when our co-pilots are trained as co-pilots and in their refresher course, they are trained from the left-hand seat. This, in my view, is wrong, as they are obviously far more familiar with flying from the right-hand seat and in the event of an emergency they would almost surely have to operate from the latter.

The advent of the Jumbos has increased my concern in the matter and I frankly would not approve of our putting in an emergency these $30 million ships with their

---

*   Air Marshal M.S. Chaturvedi, Managing Director, Air-India.

precious load of up to 350 passengers and tons of cargo, in the hands of a co-pilot who might have done only one landing in the previous year or six months. I consider that something should be done about this and done quickly....

J.R.D. Tata

TO GM[*]

Bombay
25 June 1971

I have often in the past criticised our filing system, or at least some aspects of it, and suggested that we should consult some expert with a view to simplifying and streamlining it.

There are two main aspects involved:

Our files are unnecessarily cluttered up with every scrap of paper, however unimportant, that comes in, and in some cases with spare copies. The attached Publicity Department file is a typical example. Between pages 19 and 20 no less than 22 copies on thick paper of a now out-of-date and unimportant note from CD to RD/RMs re. the naming of our 747s, are placed in the file, and for good measure another copy appears on page 28! Such haphazard and extravagant use of a filing system naturally leads to an enormous waste of space....

There should be a continuous process of weeding out non-essential contents from files with a view both to taking up the least amount of available space and to making files more readable. Of all the companies' files I have dealt with I have found the Air-India files the most unreadable, as one often has to wade through masses of rubbish to get at the important letters or notes.

The second aspect that bothers me is the duplication of files on identical subjects kept in the offices of departmental heads and the GM's office. Where such duplication is unavoidable, as for instance between Bombay and Santa Cruz, the two sets should contain the duplicates of essential papers....

---

[*] General Manager.

One very good point about Air-India's filing system, for which I compliment whoever invented it, is the numbering of all pages from bottom to top, which makes it easy to call attention to any particular letter or memo; but this may be the very reason why no page is ever deleted from the file!

J.R.D. Tata

TO A/M M.S.C.

Bombay
9 May 1972

Re: Labour Relations

We must face the fact that our efforts at establishing good relations with our employees in Air-India have not met with full success upto now, at least in India. So far as employees abroad are concerned, including those under local unions, the situation is, I believe, excellent. In fact, I have been surprised at the extent of loyalty and devotion to the Airline that prevails amongst some of our foreign employees, particularly the senior ones.

Basically, Indians are sentimental and loyalty-inclined people, and we must therefore look for the causes of unrest and lack of loyalty and trust. The trouble in India lies partly in the fact that we have to deal with seven craft unions, each of which is led by Office Bearers who are employees of the Company, have no basic training and experience in trade unionism, and feel it their duty to their membership to show hostility towards the management as proof of their devotion to the members' interests. As a result, even in the intervals of wage negotiations every three years, the pot is kept boiling with endless correspondence and circulars, usually couched in acrimonious terms and spiked with charges of deceitfulness. The result is that Management-Union relations never seem to settle down to a state of mutual understanding and cooperation, and tempers remain frayed....

To the extent, however, that poor relations are due to mistrust and the existence of genuine grievances, it is up to the Management to do more than it has done in the past to remove the sources of such mistrust and sense of grievance. I have no doubt in my mind that while basically our Management means to be fair and honest, there is still far too much of a rigid, bureaucratic or legalistic approach and far too little of a human approach to our handling of staff matters. I have many times pointed out the lack of the human touch in our administrative offices in dealing with individual cases....

Dealing with thousands of employees obviously requires the establishment of rules and regulations, but they have to be interpreted in practice. In Air-India, when there is some doubt as to the correct interpretation of a rule, it is invariably interpreted against the employee, whereas the benefit of the doubt should be given to the employee and not to the Corporation.

It is a matter of great concern to me that year after year I have made no headway in instilling in our own officialdom, a realisation of the tremendous importance of morale. If Management would only take the trouble to find out what the rank and file of the employees feel about it, they would understand why it seems so easy for the Unions to create and sustain anti-management agitation whenever they want to. If, instead, we had created amongst the mass of individual employees and workers the belief that, apart from wage negotiations, Management deals with individual cases with sympathy and understanding, and shows genuine interest in their individual problems, I have no doubt whatever that the Unions would have found it far less easy to arouse and maintain anti-management feelings amongst the rank and file.

We seem far too inclined to fear that any sympathy in dealing with labour will be interpreted as a sign of weakness which will be exploited against us. This can be true only if weakness is shown in dealing with clear cases of misconduct, deliberate non-cooperation, laziness, insubordination, etc., or in meeting unreasonable demands on the part of the Unions. There is no such risk when dealing with individual cases of requests, applications or complaints in which there is no question of any such offence on the part of an employee.

There are two simple and yet significant requirements which, I have noticed more than once, we regularly fail to meet: one is to reply quickly to a letter or application from an employee, and the other is to couch a refusal to agree in sympathetic terms, and giving a reason for rejection.

While we must pursue our scheme for joint consultation, we must not forget that however well-conceived such machinery may be and however well-intentioned the Management, only a very small number of staff members will be directly involved in it. Unfortunately, they will inevitably consist largely of union office bearers who, as I have said earlier, have a vested interest in keeping up an atmosphere of agitation and dispute.

I am more and more convinced that we shall never create the right atmosphere and climate, or minimise mistrust or resentment, until we learn to deal in a human way with individual staff members as distinct from unions.

J.R.D. Tata

TO AIR MARSHAL Y.V. MALSE[*]

Bombay
3 January 1975

Dear Air Marshal Malse,

I have recently taken the trouble of spending some time at the Santa Cruz terminal, both in the early morning hours when a number of large aircraft, including our own, arrive from various parts of the world, and late at night at the departure end when, similarly, a number of aircraft leave Santa Cruz. I found the conditions indescribably bad at the arrival end, and only slightly less so on the departure side.

At the arrival end, the baggage delivery and Customs examination locations are appallingly congested, resulting in unacceptable inconvenience and delays, sometimes running into several hours, inflicted on passengers. Much of that delay is due to the totally inadequate arrangements for transferring baggage from luggage containers brought from the aircraft, placing it on the usually unserviceable conveyor belts, and lifting it off from the latter.

I am aware that you have a dispute with the supplier of the conveyor belts, the order for which you were not responsible, and that you have a court injunction against you; but the IAAI cannot on that ground plead helplessness as it seems to be doing, and thereby indefinitely fail to fulfil its primary and paramount responsibility to provide usable facilities at India's largest and busiest international airport. I am not aware of the details of the dispute with Dynacraft, but I cannot believe that there is no solution, including the deposit in court of whatever Dynacraft claim, so that immediate steps can be taken to remedy the situation.

---

[*]   Chairman, International Airports Authority of India.

It is clear that the two existing conveyor belts are such that they can never be made to give satisfactory service, and that even if they were, their capacity is totally inadequate. There is a need for at least four delivery belts of a different design and good quality. Whatever action is taken must involve the purchase of new conveyors. Have they been ordered? If not, why not?

Apart from the inadequacy or mechanical unreliability of the conveyor belts themselves, the baggage entry point is so congested and badly designed, that it is totally impossible to manoeuver the baggage containers and transfer their contents to the belts. This deficiency at the baggage unloading end has been brought to the attention of the IAAI more than once in the past year or two, and I would have expected that the urgent need for action would have been recognised and the situation remedied long ago. It is imperative that effective remedial action be taken immediately and not "in due course".

With due respect, the situation is nothing less than inexcusable for an international airport of a city like Bombay....

With all good wishes for the New Year,

Yours sincerely,
J.R.D. Tata

TO K.G. APPUSAMY[*]

Bombay
23 *October* 1978

Dear Appu,

Re: Staff Housing

One or two cases have recently come to my notice of employees of Air-India suffering great hardship due to lack of accommodation and having as a result to live in hutment dwellings under indescribably bad conditions. The housing situation in Bombay has gone completely out of hand and whereas I used to feel in the past that a company should not be expected to house more than a reasonably small proportion of their staff, it is clear that the present situation justifies a completely new policy, at least in the case of companies which are making a good profit. Apart from the humanitarian grounds, I have, as you know, always attached enormous importance to the morale of the members of any organisation, and it is clear that high morale cannot be maintained among those members of the staff of Air-India, as well as of some Tata Companies, who have to live with their families in single hutment rooms without toilet or water facilities in the appalling conditions prevailing in Bombay's hutment colonies. Shouldn't Air-India now consider a substantially new accretion to its staff housing? I am sure Government would support it.

I wonder whether the time has also not come to consider transferring out of Bombay some of the operations or activities which could be done equally well elsewhere, where housing and similar problems would not be so serious. If it is felt

---

[*]   Joined as an Engineer and rose to become Managing Director of Air-India.

that for the sake of efficiency and coordination the work should be as close to Bombay as possible, some of it could perhaps be transferred to places like Nasik or Pune....

I think we must face the fact that Bombay will continue to be the most congested city in India and increasingly so in the years to come, and it will be more and more difficult and costly for employees to find decent housing in it.

With all good wishes,

Yours sincerely,
J.R.D. Tata

TO I.D. SETHI*

Bombay
12 December 1978

My dear Inder,

Many thanks for your letter of the 2nd instant, confirming the good news I had heard in New York that Government had at last approved of your and Sharma's appointments as Deputy Managing Directors. I much appreciated the sentiments expressed by you...

It makes me happy to know that Government, whose way of dealing with public sector organisations is often unpredictable, have, in this case, recognised the importance of a dynamic enterprise like Air-India having at the top of their management young men chosen entirely on the basis of their merit, ability, competence and experience.

As you know, despite my special interest in aeroplanes and the technical aspects of operating them, I have always felt and said that the commercial department of an airline was the most important of all, if only because it is the only one that earns money while every other spends it!...

If, speaking as one who has helped to nurture most of the organisation including yourself since the airline's birth, I may offer a word of advice at this watershed of your career. I hope you will understand and not resent any natural feeling amongst senior executives, especially old-timers who have been with the airline for most or much of the thirty years of its existence, who may have some qualms about their fate now being in the hands of a young man junior in service to them. I am sure you have the tact and understanding to overcome any such feeling if indeed it does arise

---

* Deputy Managing Director, Air-India.

in the minds of some of your team, but I hope you will go further and make them feel that you recognise and appreciate loyalty and hard work even from men who have reached the limit of their abilities.

If I have learnt one thing about leading a team in my long career, it is the supreme importance of morale in any organisation whether an airline, an industry or for the matter of that of an army, and I would rather have a united team of average ability but of high loyalty, devotion to the company and morale than a group of outstanding prima donnas lacking in esprit-de-corps and working at cross purposes. If I was fortunate enough to earn so much support and loyalty, it was because I did my best to make all members of the Air-India organisation with whom I came into contact feel that their long service and personal dedication to the airline were recognised and appreciated so long as they did their best and were proud of the airline and devoted to it. You are fortunate in inheriting such a good and experienced team. I am sure they will serve you well and, in addition, give you their loyalty and friendship.

With my best wishes,

Yours sincerely,
J.R.D. Tata

TO B. VENKATARAMAN[*]

Bombay
7 January 1981

Dear Venkataraman,

I write on the subject of Government's decision for Air-India to participate in the setting up of a feeder airline in collaboration with Indian Airlines. The first news I, and presumably other members of the Board of Air-India, had of the decision was to read of it in the newspapers this morning and then being asked to attend an urgent Board Meeting in Delhi the day after tomorrow. I cannot but feel surprised that such an important decision should be taken by Government without extending to the Board of Directors the opportunity of expressing their views on a matter directly involving the airline. I regret that, apart from the personal feelings of responsible Board members at being treated with so little consideration, Government do not seem to realise, despite their own assurances, that if the large public sector they have created is to function efficiently and if the morale of its management is to be maintained, it *must* be given a minimum degree of autonomy. That minimum must surely include consultation before taking unilateral decisions on important matters of policy. Such a need was indeed recognised and acted upon for the first twenty years or so of Air-India's existence as a public sector enterprise, as a result of which the enthusiasm and morale of the organisation were kept high, and the airline not only became extremely profitable but also achieved a very high international reputation.

I do not contest the right of Government, as owners of the airline, as of all other public sector enterprises, to make any decision they like, nor do I want to appear

---

[*]   Secretary, Ministry of Tourism and Civil Aviation, Government of India.

difficult.... My remarks are from the point of view of all Board members of Government Corporations, whether they be Government officials or non-officials. Speaking for myself, however, while I shall always be willing to put at the disposal of Government all the time and thought that they seek from me, I do not think I could serve any useful purpose on the Board of Air-India if Government intend to treat it merely as an instrument to rubber-stamp their decisions....

I would be grateful if this letter were shown to the Minister.

Yours sincerely,
J.R.D. Tata

Flight Notes

TO G.M. (THROUGH H.O.)*

Bombay
30 *April 1951*

Flight 101 Bombay-Paris on VT-DAR on 8-9 April 1951
Flight 102 Geneva-Bombay on VT-DAS on 17-18 April 1951

The purpose of these notes containing comments and suggestions whenever I fly on Air-India and Air-India International is merely to help Management. They are *not* on any account to be treated as "complaints or instructions from the Chairman"....

As usual the standard of service, both operationally and passengerwise, was extremely high and I have no special suggestions to make in respect of the work of the crew, or cabin attendants.

Refreshments: A dark British beer is served on our planes. Few people, I think, prefer a heavy beer when flying and I suggest that a lighter brand of beer be stocked by us....

The tea served on board from Geneva is, without exaggeration, indistinguishable in colour from coffee. In fact, on my return flight confusion was caused amongst some passengers who thought that they were being offered coffee. I do not know whether the black colour of the tea is due to the quality used or to excessive brewing. I suggest that the Station Manager at Geneva be asked to look into the matter.

---

*   General Manager (Through Head Office). K.J. Bhore was G.M. of A.-I.I. from 1949 to 1951.

Magazines: As reported by me on previous occasions, the magazines issued to passengers are still excessively out of date....I can only repeat my previous suggestion that the London organisation should be made responsible for putting foreign magazines on board our planes and keeping them up to date....

Chairs: I found on VT-DAR, that some of the seats recline much more than others. As a result those seats are more comfortable. In view of the exceptional leg room in our planes as compared to the Constellations in competing airlines, I suggest that all our seats be adjusted to a maximum reclining angle except, of course, the rear-most seats which are limited by bulkheads....

Curtain: A curtain is badly wanted at the rear of the cabin just ahead of the lavatory doors, for two reasons. Firstly, it will shield the inside of the two lounges from the view of people in the cabin when the doors are opened and closed....Secondly, it will shield from the main part of the cabin the ceiling light which remains on all night and disturbs passengers occupying the rear seats.

Air Flow: On all my flights I have found, particularly at night, that the excessive downward draft of air from the overhead ducts makes the aisle seats uncomfortable.... The Engineering Department may please consider whether, in cruising flight conditions when the temperature of the cabin has reached a normal level, the velocity of the cabin air issuing from the main duct can be reduced....

J.R.D. Tata

TO K.C.B.*

Bombay
3 November 1952

I have not found the time up to now to dictate notes about my flight to London and back in September last.

Operation & Service: As usual, both flights were excellent operationally and from the point of view of service and courtesy to passengers. In fact, our standards compare very favourably with those of other airlines....

Cabins: I found that the interior of our Constellation cabins, particularly the upholstery of the seats, is beginning to look shabby. The original upholstery material being inferior in quality, seems to have suffered a lot. What plans do we have for gradual renewal, and in what material? It should be in a better quality material.

Library: On flight 105/199 on the 9th September, the book library on board consisted of six books in all, of which three were copies of the same book, namely, *Father Malachy's Miracle*! There is no doubt that the Cabin Service Department is the weakest link in the chain and this, to my mind, is a small but further example of it....

Flight Reports to Passengers: Most airlines give times of arrival and departure both in G.M.T. and local time. On long flights of this nature where time variation is very considerable, Captains should be asked to give the times both in G.M.T. and local time....

Menu: The dinner from Bombay to Cairo was particularly poor and tasteless on that day. However, this may have been an exception, as I have eaten good meals on board A-I.I. before and since....

---

* K.C. Bakhle, Managing Director, Air-India (1951-1953).

Cups and Saucers: Although I must have written a dozen times about introducing a rule that no cup should ever be served in a plate, but in a saucer, I find that coffee or tea is still being served on some flights with a cup floating about in a small plate. In fact, I was served that way, and as it was extremely bumpy at the time the cup slid to the edge of the plate and spilt on my clothes and on the seat. I saw it happen, though with less serious results, to another passenger. The hostesses seem to have a rooted objection to serving tea or coffee in the square saucer-cum-biscuit plates which go with the cups....

J.R.D. Tata

TO V.C. & G.M.*

Bombay
9 August 1955

Notes and Suggestions on my flights to Geneva and London on Flight 109 of 12/13 May, and back to Bombay on Flight 116 of 13/14 June, 1955.

Life Jacket Drill: Our life jacket drill needs to be revised. There is too much stress on "this is a normal procedure" which is repeated twice. The Pan American "patter" is much better than ours. I suggest we get a copy and more or less adopt it....

Coat Hangers: When A-I.I. started, decent coat hangers made of transparent plastic material were used exclusively. I find that these have now been replaced by cheap and nasty wooden hangers. Who is responsible for this change? I have previously said that no change in supplies to the cabin, including upholstery, curtains, crockery, colour schemes, etc., should be made without my express approval....

Hand Fans: The cardboard hand fans are another instance of cheap and unattractive articles being put on board for the use of passengers. Such articles should really be advertisements of A-I.I. Our fans compare very unfavourably with fans supplied by our competitors.

Playing Cards: On Flight 109 of the 12/13 May, I asked for playing cards and was handed, by the hostess...two worn and filthy packs. I was told they had not been replaced for over a year. I have on a previous occasion referred to the disgraceful condition of playing cards supplied to passengers....

Window Curtains: Something must be done about window curtains. The channel rails are bent, sliding holders jam and the curtains come off the holders. I suggest

---

*   Vice-Chairman and General Manager.

we gradually replace this hopeless arrangement by simple roller runners similar to doorway curtains....

Food and Meal Service: When the main dish consists of lamb chops and these are being cooked in the oven, the fat lets out fumes which fill the whole cabin. We should specifically order *lean* chops.

I think we should definitely consider one meal on a whole flight being a cold meal, tastily and appetisingly prepared and served, as, for instance, on Air France's Epicurean Services between Paris and London. In fact, I think it would be a good thing to have a few such ready prepared cold meals available for passengers who do not feel like having a full hot meal....

J.R.D. Tata

TO G.M.

Bombay
26 November 1955

Notes on my flight to London, flight 115 of 8/9 October, and my flight from Geneva to Bombay on Flight 102 on 15/16 November 1955.

Cabin Furnishing and Equipment: I found that the side panels of the tourist chairs are showing signs of distortion and crumpling as a result of points or edges of internal fixtures pushing through the rexine panel. We should put in stiff backing to these side panels otherwise the outward appearance of the seats will gradually worsen and the material will ultimately tear.

Slumberette Seats: These are undoubtedly a great success and much appreciated by passengers. Unfortunately...the design and construction of the attachments joining the leg rests to the seats is such that the leg rests are not held firmly to the seats. The slightest sideways motion pulls out the two metal prongs on the leg rests from the corresponding holes in the seat itself and the rest falls to the floor. This happened continuously to various passengers whilst sleeping and caused much inconvenience. The solution would seem to lie in (a) fixing the shaft or rod to which the prongs are fitted so that they cannot rotate, (b) ensuring that the size of the holes is only large enough for the prongs to fit in a reasonably tight fit, and (c) in having a ball or spring catch to hold the prongs in position. I understand that this is being done....

Sleepers: An immediate change needs to be made in the upper sleepers. These at present have a folding container for clothes hinged along the cabin wall and also an overhead strap with which the passenger helps himself to a sitting position. Both these are at present placed in a most inconvenient position much too near the passenger's head. As a result it is practically impossible to sit up and dress and undress in the berth without fouling both the container and the strap. These should be moved farther towards the feet. The folding container should be moved right up to the end of the berth, while the strap might be moved a foot or so towards the feet....

J.R.D. Tata

TO N.V.K.*

28 *September* 1960

Our announcements prior to take-off need to be revised. As on jets the time taken between engine start and take-off is much shorter than on Super-Constellations, and as announcements are made in three languages, they should be shortened by eliminating non-essential words. For instance, we may drop at once the sentence warning passengers about increase in engine noise after landing. Also "This is a normal procedure".

Apart from the announcements being too long, I find them tedious because they are repeated almost word for word at every stop. In fact, they must be a damn nuisance to passengers flying all the way from New York and hearing approximately the same announcements at New York, London, two stations on the Continent and one in the Middle East! Please put forward proposals urgently to me in the matter, attaching the present texts....

J.R.D. Tata

---

* N.V. Khote, Commercial Manager, Customer Service.

TO G.M.

Bombay
17 May 1966

FLIGHT NOTES

Flight 109/31 Bombay-Beirut-Frankfurt on 21/22 April 1966,
and Flight 102 Beirut-Bombay on 10 May 1966.

Sweets: The sweets we serve on take-off and just before landing taste like hair lotion and offer no choice....

Breakfast Service: I thought we had found a permanent solution to the problem of over-cooked omelettes. At my suggestion it had been arranged that the omelettes should be substantially under-cooked on the ground so that on re-heating on board they would turn out just right. This was done for a while, but now we seem to have reverted to the old state of affairs and the omelettes we serve are again grossly overcooked....

Fruit: I found that the choice of fruit we pick up in Europe and the Middle East is still not good enough. For instance, at this time of the year pears are freely available throughout the temperate zone, yet we only served apples, oranges and bananas.

Drink Service: I cannot understand why we do not use the trolley for drink service after take-off as is done by every other airline on which I have travelled. This is the only way we can give passengers a choice of brand of the liquor we serve them....

Foreign-speaking Hostesses: On both these flights although they were via Germany, there was no German-speaking hostess on board. This has been happening too often and too long. It is the policy of the Corporation which should be treated as a firm directive that we have French, German and Japanese-speaking hostesses on the relevant sectors, and there is no excuse for not providing the necessary recruitment to ensure that we do not fail to have them on all flights, except of course on rare unavoidable occasions....

J.R.D. Tata

TO CUSTOMER SERVICE DEPARTMENT

(For the attention of Mr. K.G.A.*)

Bombay
16 August 1967

On a recent flight from Delhi on the aircraft *Annapurna*, I noticed the following points:

The door between the First and Economy compartments has been replaced by a curtain but I found that the curtain was a white one which did not match the other curtains in the ship, and also that it was absurdly short, leaving about a two-foot gap from the floor to the bottom of the curtain. I don't know why this was done and who authorised it, but I must repeat that I do not want any changes made to the approved décor of our planes without my express approval. A full-length curtain should be fitted matching the other curtains in the ships.

The seat belt signs are totally invisible from the front seats as they are located on the aft side of the overhead service units. These are themselves located slightly to the rear of the front row passengers. They are naturally invisible from the seats. I believe that in some other airlines this minor problem has been solved by putting in a separate sign on the bulkhead facing the passengers. Has this been considered in our case?

J.R.D. Tata

---

* K.G. Appusamy.

TO C.M.-C.S.*

Bombay
21 February 1968

Hostesses' Duties: On a recent Swiss-Air flight from Bombay to Manila, I noticed that the hostesses invariably addressed passengers, at least in the first class, by their name. This, I think, is a good practice which our hostesses may be asked to adopt as a general rule.

Socks: I find that hostesses are inclined to be careless about issuing socks to passengers. Sometimes, men receive women's socks and women, men's socks. It has happened to me twice. To avoid this mistake, I suggest that the outer wrapper of the two types of socks should be in a different colour.

Time Announcements: In spite of there now being an accurate clock in every galley, hostesses apparently still announce the time taken from their wrist watches. On Flight No.105A/97, the time given on one occasion was incorrect by a full five minutes.

Make-up and Hair-do: As I have said before, while hostesses should be allowed a certain amount of leeway in regard to their hair-do, this should be within reasonable limits. One hostess on the London New York sector had an enormous hair bun at the back, larger than her whole head. She looked ridiculous. Some hostesses have either no make-up at all on their face or excessively heavy eye make-up....

Any public announcements apologising for delays, should have the word "unavoidable" deleted as most of the time it was due to some cause originally within our control. The word "unavoidable" should only be used if the delay is due to weather causes or to air traffic control....

---

* Commercial Manager, Customer Service.

Stationery: I have previously reported that envelopes do not match the writing paper when normally folded. In any case, it is time we change our stationery to a more attractive one. The Art Department may be asked to suggest a new colour and letter-head.

Wine Service: Cabin attendants still do not seem to have been properly briefed on the use of the wine carrier baskets. Once a passenger has chosen the wine he wants, the attendant must be allowed to place the carrier on the floor and to extract from it the selected bottle....

J.R.D. Tata

TO C.M.-C.S.

Bombay
6 January 1970

A number of reports have come to me that cabin attendants are seen smoking in the galley while on duty. This practice creates a very poor impression and must be firmly put down. I suggest that a note be sent to all cabin attendants, under your signature, reminding them that smoking in the cabin or in the galley while on duty is strictly prohibited. Cabin attendants should be allowed to smoke only when sitting in the crew rest compartment, preferably with the curtain drawn.

A small point about breakfast. I am told that while the scrambled eggs and omelettes we serve for breakfast in the first class are excellent, the bacon and tomatoes that go with them are often served stone cold. Presumably they are allowed to get cold while the eggs are being cooked or warmed up. I suggest that appropriate action be taken to ensure that bacon and tomatoes are served hot along with the eggs.

J.R.D. Tata

TO H.O.

Flight Al 131/41 of 23.5.70: Bombay-Beirut *Annapurna*

Departure was on time.

The breakfast on board was first class with, for the first time in my experience, a perfectly prepared omelette. My congratulations to the flight kitchen!

Galley: Unloading/loading: The used garbage bins and the new ones were taken out and brought in through the passenger steps and entrance! This is the second time I found garbage bins being either placed or handled in or through the passenger cabin. Strict orders must be issued to put a stop to this outrageous practice.

Drink and Meal Service: The wasteful practice of placing two packets of sugar in saucers along a cup of tea or coffee, where they get wet, may please be stopped and the sugar packets offered by the hostess or purser from a bowl. I have found that in some other airlines, and in all restaurants in America, saccharine packets are also included….We should adopt this practice….

Meal: The meal was from Bombay. The hors-d'oeuvres were uninspiring and tasteless. With amongst the best lobsters, prawns, shrimps, etc. in the world available in India, we should include them in every hors-d'oeuvres course. The hard-boiled half eggs were still deep frozen! The *bread sticks* were uneatable, hard and stale instead of crisp. The *pilaw* in the main course should have some fried onions and a few more almonds and raisins, which, in this case, had to be looked for with a magnifying glass! The *dessert* consisted of a small caramel pudding over a tiny scrap of some undefined cooked fruit. It was totally inadequate and the poorest dessert I have ever had on Air-India…

Coffee: The coffee was watery. In fact, it looked like tea and tasted like bean soup. Altogether a poor and depressing meal....

J.R.D. Tata

TO H.O.

Bombay
28 July 1972

I travelled on two consecutive Sundays to Delhi on our 747 Flight AI-101....

Earphones: I believe I have previously reported that the earphones we supply are quite useless. They are not only cheaper and shoddier looking than any earphones supplied on other airlines that I have travelled on, but because of their flimsy construction the rubber tubes that carry the sound to the ears gets crimped, thus interrupting the sound. We must definitely not order any more of this type....

Overhead Lights: The overhead lights, at least in Row 6, are fixed in such a way that they shine right on the head of the passenger instead of on the table, so that during dinner or when reading or writing on the table, the part that we want to illuminate is in the dark. Can something be done?...

Dinner: The dinner was identical on both flights. How long do we keep the same menu?...

Dessert: The dessert on both flights was Apple Charlotte. It is totally unacceptable, being both gooey, dry and under-cooked.

Cheese: The cheese served was O.K., but I think we should now always include one English cheese in our selection. As recommended earlier, we should and must serve cheese on a cheese board rather than on a plastic tray....

Coffee: On the 16th the coffee was undrinkable, being excessively watery. I examined the coffee maker in the galley and was shown the coffee bags or pads. As the coffee powder smelled good, and as the coffee maker is automatic, I must assume that the deficiency lay either in the coffee pads containing too little coffee powder, or in the machine being adjusted to provide too much water. This should be corrected without delay, as nothing ruins even a good dinner as much as a bad cup of coffee to end it. It is even worse when the dinner is as bad as this one was!

Butter: On both occasions the foil-wrapped Amul butter was completely soft and half melted. Orders may please be issued that butter packs should not be placed on the trays on the ground, but should be kept in the frigidaire on the plane, and placed on the trays by the hostess or purser only at the time of serving meals....

These two meals I have had on our 747s confirm that we now offer nothing better (except in the case of the hors-d'oeuvre) than a boarding-house meal, served as in a boarding-house....

J.R.D. Tata

TO CAPT. D. BOSE*

Bombay
28 November 1985

On my flights to New York and back earlier this month, I jotted the following minor points:

The table-cloths continue to be folded and ironed on a template made to suit the 707 first-class tables many years ago at my instance. The tables of the 747s are of a different size and the old template boards should have been replaced by new ones to fit the 747 tables. The system of folding and ironing on a template has worked extremely well as it keeps the table-cloth easily and accurately in position during the meal. I suggest that new templates be issued to the laundry units throughout the system.

On long flights on which plenty of time is available for meals and tables are laid, there is no reason why the cutlery should not be laid along with the crockery instead of being dumped on the table in plastic or polythene bags which passengers have to tear open themselves.

On those flights on which meal service is with trays, I think we should gradually switch to slightly bigger trays if there is enough room in our galley's trolley. The present ones while attractive, seem to be the same ones as served in Economy and are too small for the First Class tables.

On my return flight from London on AI-102 of November 12, the front left door leaked air, which produced a continuous and very loud whistle. I was told that the plane had just come from a major overhaul before proceeding to New York. I presume and hope that the problem has since been remedied.

J.R.D. Tata

---

* Managing Director, Air-India.

Major Events

TO SIR FREDERICK TYMMS

Bombay
27 *December* 1947

My dear Frederick,

I was delighted to receive your long letter of the 9th December, written from on board the *Queen Mary*. You need not apologise to me—of all people—for being a bad correspondent, as I can more than compete with you in this respect....

I have been wanting to be the first to let you know about the fruition, at last, of our scheme for Air-India International, but my nose has been kept so closely to the grindstone these last few months, that I have put off writing until now, by which time you have evidently heard the news. I had almost given up hope, and was getting ready finally to cancel our provisional order for the three Constellations when, at the last moment, the Government of India acted with unusual quickness of decision and accepted our scheme, almost in toto....We are now in the throes of preparing for inaugurating the service...and are all extremely excited about it.

We realise that a service of this type is a different proposition from running domestic services, and while I believe that our past experience and the tremendous keenness of our organisation to do a first-class job will give us a good start, I am keeping my fingers crossed. Fortunately, the poor service given by the American airlines serving India, and the obsolete equipment used by B.O.A.C., will greatly reduce our initial competition, in addition to which we have over these many years managed to create a reputation and passenger loyalty towards us which will be of great help...

Although, with your usual modesty, you will disclaim any credit for the final consummation of this long dreamed of and planned project, I want to take this opportunity of saying, once again, how much I appreciate all the valuable moral support, encouragement and advice which I received from you and which were of great help in the preparation and ultimate putting through of the scheme....

Goodbye for the present, my dear Frederick....

Yours very sincerely,
Jeh

TO T.P. BHALLA[*]

Bombay
23 September 1949

Dear Mr. Bhalla,

We have, as you know, been throughout opposed to the night air mail scheme as one which, although theoretically attractive, is in our opinion unsound and unjustified under present conditions. Recent developments have fully confirmed us in this view. For the last few months we have been suffering an alarming deterioration in the earnings of our Company which, coupled with rising costs, is causing us a heavy operating loss every month. This situation is now aggravated by the devaluation of the rupee which will substantially increase the cost of operating American aircraft and will probably also increase the cost of fuel and oil. I believe these unhappy conditions apply to the whole industry and I do not know how long, at this rate, it will be possible for it to survive.

In these circumstances I simply cannot understand and wish once again to record our protest against Government's insistence on re-starting the night air mail scheme. In return for only a minor saving in time to the mail-using public, this scheme will greatly aggravate the already parlous condition of the industry by depriving existing services of the bulk of their mail revenue, will waste public funds, burn large quantities of petrol and oil, and use up American equipment and spares and therefore, dollars, all of which is in complete conflict with the publicly announced policies of Government....

---

[*]   Director-General of Civil Aviation, Government of India.

We are satisfied that Government's policy with regard to the night air mail scheme is completely unsound and detrimental to the national interests as well as to those of the industry, and we cannot voluntarily be a party to it....

I therefore appeal to Government once again to give up their present scheme altogether, at least until they are prepared to meet its cost, or until the industry itself has attained a sufficiently healthy and financially strong position to enable it to bear the burden without endangering its very existence. It is, of course, quite possible that, as in the past, Government will find an operator prepared to commit slow suicide in a desperate attempt to expand his operations, and who will, therefore, be prepared to operate your scheme even at heavy loss. His fate will inevitably be the same as that which befell the previous night mail operators....

Yours sincerely,
J.R.D. Tata

TO RAFI AHMED KIDWAI[*]

Bombay
30 September 1949

Dear Mr. Kidwai,

Re: Night Air Mail Scheme

...If you will not mind my saying so, the trouble lies in the fact that Government view this matter mainly from a theoretical point of view and are unwilling to recognise the basic realities underlying it....

Under your scheme the air transport operators will suffer not only a direct loss on the night mail operations but also the loss of almost the whole of the present mail revenues on their day services. All you will have done in effect will have been merely to transfer the existing mail revenue from one set of services to a new service, the additional cost of which will have to be borne by the Industry.

Government choose to ignore the fact that most, if not the whole of their objective can be achieved by converting some of the present day services into night services, and that in the present economic and dollar crises facing the country, there is no excuse for wasting petrol and American spares when the purpose in view can be largely achieved in another way not involving such waste....

Government will not recognise the desperate plight in which the air transport industry is today, both in its immediate and long-range aspects, and the ruinous consequences to them of your scheme.

---

[*] Minister for Communications, Government of India.

Government still seem to consider air transport in general, and night air transport in particular, as an ordinary trading commodity, the procurement of which can be satisfactorily met by the simple process of obtaining bids from anybody. I am appalled to find from your letter that you apparently have no qualms in considering the possibility of entrusting night air mail operations, involving the life and safety of passengers, crews, mails and expensive equipment, to completely inexperienced operators who have never run scheduled services in their life and who wholly lack the technical organisation, skill and equipment essential for such a purpose. I have been a pilot myself and an airline operator long enough to know the tragic potentialities of such a perilous policy. The responsibility for any disaster involving loss of life and mail would squarely rest on Government's shoulders.

In spite of all these and many other points being repeatedly brought to their attention, Government continue to ignore them.

Yours sincerely,
J.R.D. Tata

TO PANDIT JAWAHARLAL NEHRU

Bombay
8 December 1949

My dear Jawaharlal,

I was most grateful for the opportunity you gave me at the end of last month to place before you our point of view in connection with the unfortunate controversy which had arisen over Civil Aviation.

In the light of your remarks and advice, I had hoped that the controversy would cease forthwith, and I certainly intended to take no further part in it myself. I did not, however, expect that Mr. Kidwai would make so unfair and unreasonable a speech in the Assembly. This speech, which I regret to say contains many incorrect statements and allegations, has naturally received a tremendous amount of publicity throughout the country.

If we give no reply at all, we shall stand doubly condemned in the eyes of the public, and much permanent damage will have been done to the good name and reputation of Air-India, and, for the matter of that, of Tatas. I have received innumerable enquiries from shareholders, employees, friends, etc., regarding Mr. Kidwai's charges, and in each case the hope is expressed that we shall at least state the facts where they have been incorrectly given by the Hon'ble Minister.

...By resorting to incorrect and unfair statements and allegations, he has convinced the majority of the members of the Assembly, who were naturally not in a position to differentiate between what was true and untrue in his remarks, that the airlines in general, and Air-India in particular, are dishonest and greedy, cannot be trusted, and fully deserve their present plight.

In the circumstances, we have had no option but to prepare a memorandum answering the more important statements and charges contained in Mr. Kidwai's speech....

I was heartened to learn from your statement in the Assembly that Government would, outside the context of the recent debate, consider submitting the case of the air transport industry to an impartial board of enquiry. I do hope that this will be done soon and that in view of the heat generated by the present controversy, the composition of the board will be entirely independent of the Ministry of Communication as well as of the air transport industry.

Yours sincerely,
J.R.D. Tata

FROM PANDIT JAWAHARLAL NEHRU

New Delhi
10 November 1952

My dear Jehangir,

I was very sorry to notice your distress of mind when you came to lunch with me the other day. You told me that you felt strongly that you or the Tatas, or at any rate your air companies had been treated shabbily by the Government of India. Indeed you appeared to think that all this was part of a set policy, pursued through years, just to do injury to your services in order to bring them to such a pass that Government could acquire them cheaply.

You were in such evident distress at the time that I did not think it proper to discuss this matter with you. Nor indeed am I writing to you today with any intention to carry on an argument. But I feel I must write to you and try, in so far as I can, to remove an impression from your mind which I think is totally wrong and is unjust to Government, to me as well as to you.

I cannot of course deal with any individual acts of discourtesy that might have occurred in the Secretariat here or any attitude adopted which was not becoming. That might well have happened. All I can say is that I regret that exceedingly and, whenever any such act has been brought to my notice, I have immediately taken steps. The machinery of Government functions in a peculiar way which is not to my liking. I have been six years here and still feel rather like a fish out of water. I have been impressing upon our officials and others that the old type of superior governmental behaviour is objectionable.

So far as the Tatas are concerned, you know my own high appreciation of the record of this outstanding firm in India which has pioneered so many projects. I think in this matter I reflect the general views of most of my colleagues. I have not heard at any time any adverse comments in regard to the Tatas, although there is plenty of criticism of others here. Of course, there may be disagreement in regard to policies and we may look in a somewhat different direction sometimes.

But the charge you made the other day which amounted to a planned conspiracy to suppress private civil aviation and, more particularly, Tata's air services, astounded me. I could not conceive of it and I am sure that nobody here could do it. This matter of air services in India has been discussed by us in Cabinet and outside on a very large number of occasions. As a matter of general policy, we have always thought that transport services of almost all kinds should be State-owned. Indeed, so far as the Congress is concerned, we laid down this general policy about twenty years ago. It is true that the policy could not be implemented for various reasons and we gave it no high priority. But the matter was discussed on many occasions. It was chiefly the lack of finances that prevented us from going ahead.

For a considerable period, Rafi Ahmed Kidwai was in charge of the Communications Ministry. Your grievance is that a large number of services were permitted to operate and these tended to eat each other up. I am not competent enough to judge of this policy. But obviously, all of us were anxious to develop air services in India. It may be that we went too far. It may be also that the Tatas were too cautious in some matters, such as the night air mail. I am not dealing here with the merits of the particular policy, but with your charge that a policy was pursued by the Government of India with the deliberate intention of injuring Tata's air services. That, I am quite sure, is completely unjustified. Rafi Ahmed Kidwai used to discuss air services with me frequently. He always had a good word for your air services, except for the fact that he thought you were too cautious and he did not like the idea of high fares. He may have been right or wrong. But I have no doubt in my mind that any desire to injure your air services was never present in his mind....

During the last few months, i.e. since Jagjivan Ram has been Communications Minister, this matter came up before the Cabinet on several occasions. We examined it thoroughly. We were driven to the conclusion that there was no other way out except to organise them together under the State. I remember that even then stress was laid on the excellence of your services and, more particularly, Air-India International. We did not wish to touch the Air-India International. We appointed a Committee of the Cabinet to go into this matter. Their report was that it would be difficult in the circumstances to isolate the Air-India International.

The purpose of my writing to you is to remove the impression from your mind that any policy has been pursued by us with the deliberate intention of acquiring them later after their value came down. Both from the civil and the defence point of view, we have naturally been anxious to develop aviation in this country. Our eagerness to do so may have gone too far. A situation arose ultimately when we were driven to a certain conclusion....

Yours sincerely,
Jawaharlal Nehru

TO PANDIT JAWAHARLAL NEHRU*

Bombay
12 November 1952

I deeply appreciate your letter of the 10th just received and am most grateful for the assurances of your regard for the organisation I represent stop I am sorry if you feel that in my distress I have done injustice to anyone but my only idea was to convey to you frankly my view of the policies and actions of Government which have brought about the present situation in the Air Transport Industry stop leaving aside the past however I am sincerely convinced that the Ministry's present nationalisation scheme is not sound and will not result in the creation of an efficient and self-supporting Air Transport system stop if as appears from your letter Government have already decided upon the adoption of this scheme I can only deplore that so vital a step should have been taken without giving us a proper hearing stop Mody and I were called by Mr. Jagjivan Ram only to be informed of Government's decision to nationalise the industry stop although I told him that I had prepared and brought with me an alternative scheme which in my humble judgement was better calculated to achieve Government's objective the minister sought our advice only on questions of compensation and the like stop....

I beg you to believe that I am motivated by no self interest in this matter stop my only anxiety is to see a strong and efficient Indian Air Transport System built up and at the same time to see justice done to investors and staff who have suffered heavily

J.R.D. Tata

---

* Telegram.

TO SIR FREDERICK JAMES*

Bombay
23 *December* 1952

My dear Jimmy,

Many thanks for your sympathetic letter of the 3rd instant regarding the nationalisation of the Indian air transport industry.

Even more than by the decision itself, I was upset by the manner in which nationalisation was introduced through the back door without any prior consultation of any kind with the industry. However, we have to reconcile ourselves to the fact that we are living in a political and bureaucratic age in which people like ourselves no longer count for much in the scheme of things.

I have been and am still much exercised, as you have guessed, over the question of chairmanship. My first inclination was to turn down the offer. I consulted my colleagues, the senior members of the staff of our various companies in Bombay House, and also some of our outside directors and friends. I came to the conclusion that if I was satisfied on the basis of the valuation in respect of compensation to the shareholders, on the fate of personnel and staff and on the most important point, of the structure and form of management of the new corporation and the scope I would be given for independent judgement and action, I should not shirk the opportunity of discharging a duty to the country and to Indian aviation. I am particularly anxious that the present high standards of A-I.I. should not be adversely affected by nationalisation....

---

* Sir Frederick James was earlier in charge of the Delhi office of Tatas. He retired as Vice-Chairman and Managing Director, Tata Ltd., London.

I have strongly advised Government, in order to avoid exposing the international operations to the difficulties, dislocation, loss of morale, etc. that are bound to arise for a couple of years during the process of integration, to have two separate corporations: one for long-range international operations, and the other for domestic and short-range operations (to adjacent countries), the Boards to be common. If Government accept my recommendation and if I am satisfied on the other points mentioned above, I have told Government I would be prepared to take the chairmanship of the international corporation. There the matter rests for the time being....

Thelly and I send you and Sarah our love and best wishes for Christmas and the New Year.

Yours sincerely,
Jeh

TO JAGJIVAN RAM*

Bombay
5 March 1953

Re: Air Corporations Bill

Dear Mr. Jagjivan Ram,

In the discussions with your good self and the Finance Minister and the Secretaries of the two Ministries last January, certain principles of valuation were enunciated by Government and we were told that these would be embodied in the Bill and that the Bill would provide for the constitution of a Tribunal to decide all disputes in connection with valuation. At these discussions, we urged that the Tribunal should consist of a High Court Judge, preferably from Bombay or Calcutta, with commercial experience; that another member should be a Government Officer of standing, with experience of Public accounts or finance; and that the third member of the Tribunal should be an independent Technical Expert who could be relied upon to make the detailed valuation in case of difference of opinion between Government and an air transport company.

Since then, we have been in touch with both the Communications and the Finance Ministries while the Bill was being drafted. Government have been good enough to show us the draft Bill and my colleague Mr. Choksi has made various suggestions which have received due attention. In fact, at least two drafts were prepared and these appear to accord with the decisions which your Ministry and the

---

*   Minister in Pandit Nehru's and Mrs. Indira Gandhi's cabinets—in charge of various portfolios— Minister of Communications when JRD wrote this letter to him.

Finance Ministry had taken and which were communicated to us at the time of the discussions. Although in drafting the Bill, Government had not accepted our proposal regarding the personnel of the Tribunal, still, in the drafts, which have hitherto been prepared, it was clear that all differences regarding valuation were to be decided by the Tribunal....

It has, therefore, come as a painful surprise to us on a perusal of the latest draft, which has been received by us today and which will be put before the Cabinet, that the underlying principle of investing the Tribunal with the power of fixing the valuation in case of a dispute has been largely undermined by two provisions in the Bill which had never been even remotely suggested either in the discussions at which I was present, or in the subsequent discussions when the preparation of the draft Bill was taken in hand.

These two provisions are in the form of explanations in the Schedule bearing on the valuation of aircraft and power plants and the valuation of stores respectively....

The effect of these explanations is really to remove from the sphere of the Tribunal any question regarding the service ability of aircraft or stores and to make the D.G.C.A. the sole judge of their service ability with the consequence that if he holds the view that they are not serviceable, even though they may be serviceable, the Companies will not be entitled to anything more than the scrap value. You will readily appreciate that this is a fundamental departure from the basis of valuation discussed at the meetings before yourself and the Finance Minister. What makes it most surprising is that it should be introduced in the latest draft without any consultation at all with the industry as a whole or with individual companies, such as ours.

In addition to these two matters, there has been a departure in the valuation basis in connection with buildings on leased land....

I cannot believe that these material changes in the Bill introduced at this very late stage could have had either your approval or that of the Finance Minister....If the Bill is proceeded with on this footing, we shall have completely failed in our duty to our shareholders to obtain a fair basis of valuation and I will have seriously to reconsider my position regarding my association with the two corporations which are to be created to take over the industry....

Yours very sincerely,
J.R.D. Tata

FROM COL. L. SAWHNY*

Bombay
16 October 1957

My dear Jeh,

It was only on reading the newspapers yesterday that I realised that it was the twenty-fifth anniversary of the flight which you made from Karachi to Bombay in 1932 to inaugurate Civil Aviation in India.

This is to write and tell you how very much I congratulate you on all that has happened since then and on the terrific part which you have played in developing the nation's airlines.

I personally was very fed up when your airline was nationalised, and at that time felt that you were making a mistake in accepting the Chairmanship of Air-India International. But now I am sure that you did the right and proper thing both by the airline and by India.

God bless, and all good fortune in the future.

Yours ever,
Duggie

---

* JRD's brother-in-law—husband of his sister, Rodabeh; was in charge of TOMCO and some other Tata companies.

FROM MRS. RODABEH SAWHNY*

Petit Hall
17 October 1957

Jeh darling,

It seems only yesterday that we were all waiting for you in a Juhu hangar, and you appeared as a little dot on the horizon, carrying the mail with the first Indian Air Line.

Twenty-five years have passed since and they seem to have flown by swiftly. Yet they have been full years for all of us, packed with happenings and changes in our lives and within ourselves.

You especially, have been a very busy bee during that time and your life has been full of achievements which you can look upon with pride.

The creation of a great airline is not one of the least.

I still remember when in 1929 you told me of your dream to start an airline, it seemed fantastic to me and it must have appeared as a most adventurous scheme to the old man at the helm of the Company then. But when I waited for you in the Juhu hangar I knew that through your tenacity and faith you had made your dream come true and that *your* airline would have a great future.

A few years later you spoke to me of starting an international airline. I knew that you would do it but nevertheless when the first Air-India International plane took off one night from Santa Cruz taking you on its first flight to London, Sylla and I held hands and shed a few tears of emotion and pride in our brother's achievement.

---

* JRD's sister, Rodabeh Sawhny.

Since then you have gone through much disillusion, heartache and maybe moments of loneliness, but one thing you must never forget is that millions of people in India and in many parts of the world are giving you freely and willingly their respect, trust and affection.

This the greatest of your achievements you can wear proudly as a crown, for you have not acquired it through meanness, deceit or false brilliance but through selflessness, integrity and hard, hard work.

And so darling the purpose of this letter was just to say, God bless you always and for many many years to come.

Love,

Dabeh

TO COL. L. SAWHNY

Bombay
19 October 1957

My dear Duggie,

Many thanks for your very nice letter of the 16th regarding the twenty-fifth anniversary of the birth of Indian air transport. Dabeh has written me a wonderfully sweet letter to which I have replied separately. These have been an eventful twenty-five years. I wish I was back in those early days!

Thanks again,

Yours ever,
Jeh

TO AIR VICE-MARSHAL A.M. ENGINEER*

Bombay
19 October 1957

My dear Aspy,

Of all the letters and messages I have received on the occasion of the twenty-fifth anniversary of the birth of India's first airline, none pleased me more or brought back more pleasant memories than yours. Those days were fun, weren't they? We were both so much younger, particularly yourself! Although you were only seventeen or eighteen at the time, I, at least, did not under-estimate you in the Aga Khan competition! Your flight to England with Chawla left me in no doubt about the capabilities of Parsee boys in Karachi. Maybe that was itself partly responsible for my defeat. I took you so seriously as a competitor that I spent at least a day more than I need have in checking everything on the plane and everything else connected with the trip.

Our friendship ever since has been much more worthwhile than winning the competition would have been.

I must say I enjoyed every moment of that adventure as I am sure you did too. Incidentally, one of the highlights that remains imprinted on my memory was my arrival at Karachi by Imperial Airways on my return to India when, to my embarrassment, you met me with a platoon of scouts and presented me with a medal. That was terribly nice of you and so undeserved....

With affectionate wishes to you and Ruby,

Yours ever,
Jeh

---

* JRD's friend from the days of his solo flight to London in 1930. He later became the Chief of Air Staff.

TO AIR COMMODORE NUR KHAN*

Bombay
18 October 1962

My dear Nur Khan,

I have been so snowed under the last two days that I have been unable to write to you earlier to thank you and Farhat for your kindness and hospitality to Thelly and me during our stay in Karachi and also for your kind message of congratulations. It made a great deal of difference being with such good friends as yourselves and we greatly enjoyed staying with you and also the cocktail and lunch parties you threw for us.

I am sorry I caused you some anxiety and inconvenience both on my arrival and departure. The causes on each occasion were most unexpected, although I suppose nothing should be considered as unexpected in the flying game, particularly with an old plane like the Leopard. Actually, the poor old lady was not at fault as the radio and power pack responsible for both delays were grafted on her long after she was born!...

Thelly joins me in sending you and Farhat our grateful thanks and very warm wishes,

Yours very sincerely,
Jeh

---

* Head of Pakistan International Airlines, Karachi.

TO SIR GEOFFREY DE HAVILLAND[*]

Bombay
22 October 1962

Dear Sir Geoffrey,

I was delighted to receive your cable on the occasion of my commemorative flight on the 15th October and thank you very much for it and for the kind sentiments expressed in it.

You will be glad to know that the Leopard Moth and its engine functioned perfectly throughout the flights to Karachi and back. I found her as delightful to fly after all these years as I did in the early thirties. I greatly appreciated the fact that De Havilland, at Air-India's request, sent out Mr. Brown to check on the overhaul and rebuilding work which had to be done on her in Calcutta. It is a pity we could not find a serviceable Puss Moth, but the Leopard was so close to it, both in construction, performance and outward appearance, that it did not really matter....

With kindest regards and good wishes to you and the Firm that bears your distinguished name,

Yours sincerely,
J.R.D. Tata

---

[*] Sir Geoffrey De Havilland (1882-1965); British aircraft designer and manufacturer; President, the De Havilland Aircraft Co., U.K., suppliers of aeroplanes to Air-India. A Leopard Moth was purchased from them for re-enacting the inaugural Tata Air Lines flight (1932) in 1962.

TO STAFF MEMBERS OF AIR-INDIA

Bombay
23 October 1962

If on the Thirtieth Anniversary of the birth of our Airline, I re-enacted our inaugural flight, it was not for sentimental reasons alone, or for the pleasure of doing it. I hoped that particularly to those of you who had never even seen a Leopard Moth, it would bring home the fact that the great airline which we all serve today, could be, and was actually built from the smallest beginnings, with little more to sustain it at first than the love, the sweat and the devotion of those who worked for it. If my flight helped to bring this message to you, its purpose has been fulfilled.

The flight was also for me a nostalgic but deeply satisfying journey into the past, which brought back bitter-sweet memories of aeroplanes, of events and people of long ago, and particularly of old friends and associates, some of whom, indestructible, are still in Air-India, others who are no longer with us. And as I flew from Karachi, my thoughts filled with memories of Nevill Vintcent who started it all, of others like Captain Jatar and his heroic crew, whose love of flying and devotion to the airline led them to the ultimate sacrifice. In my mind I dedicated the flight to their memory.

But this Thirtieth Anniversary is not merely an occasion to look back into the past, except to gather renewed strength from it and the will to achieve still greater things in the future. We have come a long way together these thirty years, we have accomplished much of which we can be proud, but there is even more to be done in the next thirty....

J.R.D. Tata

FROM MORARJI DESAI

New Delhi
4 February 1978

My dear JRD,

We have had under consideration the question of reconstitution of the Boards of Air-India and Indian Airlines. After taking into account various considerations which were relevant to the importance of securing efficient working of the two Airlines we came to the conclusion that there should be one Chairman of both the Undertakings. We have therefore, decided to appoint Air Chief Marshal P.C. Lal who is already part-time Chairman of Indian Airlines and who we thought could be spared by you, as the Chairman of both the Airlines. You know P.C. Lal very well and I do hope you will agree with our choice.

Let me assure you that we are very sorry to part with you as Chairman of Air-India. We are fully appreciative of the distinguished services you have rendered to Air-India during your long association with it and the great contribution you have made to its build-up. I have no doubt that it is your association which is responsible for its being able to hold its own among the airlines of the world despite certain disadvantages and drawbacks with which you had to contend. I am expressing these views particularly because I do not wish you to entertain any impression that we have in any way made this change because of any lack of appreciation of your conspicuous work.

With best wishes and regards,

Yours sincerely,
Morarji Desai

TO MORARJI DESAI

Bombay
13 February 1978

Dear Morarjibhai,

I write to acknowledge receipt of your letter dated February 4th and posted on the 6th, which I found on my return from Jamshedpur on the 9th February, informing me of your decision to replace me as Chairman of Air-India by Air Chief Marshal P.C. Lal. Since then I learnt from the morning newspapers of the 11th instant that this change has been made retrospectively effective from 1st February 1978, and also that I have been excluded from the reconstituted Boards of the two Corporations of which I have been a member since their inception.

As I told you in 1953, when Government, having nationalised Air-India, invited me to remain at its helm as Chairman, I informed Government that my services would always be at their disposal for as long as they felt I could serve a useful purpose. This holds good even today, and always will so long as I live and am able to work.

In the light of the work I performed for Government as a labour of love during the past twenty-five years, I hope you will not consider it presumptuous of me to have expected that when Government decided to terminate my services and my 45 years' association with Indian civil aviation, I would be informed of their decision directly and, if possible, in advance of the public, instead of the news being communicated to me by my successor who was good enough to telephone to me after you had informed him of his appointment and he had accepted it.

What pained me even more, in view of our long personal relationship over the past three decades, was the fact that when I paid a courtesy call on you in Delhi on the 24th of January, during the half hour or so of which you were particularly cordial and friendly towards me, you did not give me the slightest hint of your decision to bring my appointment to an end.

May I also express some surprise at the statement in your letter that the reason for my removal and the appointment of a common Chairman, was to secure efficient working of the two airlines, clearly implying that they had not been working as efficiently as Government would have wished in the past. Perhaps, busy as you are with more important national matters, you were not aware that at no time in its history has Air-India been so successful and so profitable as in the current year 1977-78, with the whole of its organisation at a peak of morale and enthusiasm, gearing itself for doubling the magnitude of its operations in the next five years, under a capital expenditure programme of about Rs. 500 crores which I presented to the Board only a few weeks ago. Our sister Corporation, Indian Airlines, has also done extremely well and is showing better results than ever before.

In closing, may I thank you for your kind words of appreciation of my services to Air-India and contribution to its development.

With kind regards,

Yours sincerely,
J.R.D. Tata

FROM MORARJI DESAI

New Delhi
26 February 1978

My dear JRD,

Please refer to your letter of the 13th February 1978 which has caused me some surprise and some distress.

I shall first clarify the point to which you refer in the penultimate paragraph of your letter. My reference to the efficient working of the two airlines obviously referred to the need for having a common Chairman for the two airlines. It had no reference to the past performance of the two airlines. I can only say that out of understandable sensitiveness over the manner in which the two Boards were reconstituted, you were not able to appreciate the reference in its true context. In fact, if I were not fully cognisant of the efficient management of Air-India under your Chairmanship, I would not have said what I did in the second paragraph of my letter of the 4th February.

From your letter I have not been able to judge whether you feel aggrieved about the termination of your Chairmanship of Air-India. Frankly speaking I thought that after so many years of useful services to the Corporation and the manner in which you had brought it up to its present stage of remarkable distinction, you would yourself offer to place the responsibilities on younger shoulders. You did not offer to do so which is why I did not broach the subject. We had felt, however, that it would be better to have the two airlines combined under one wholetime Chairman. There was, therefore, no alternative for us but to make the change. In doing so I naturally presumed that with your preoccupations and commitments it would not be possible for you to undertake the combined wholetime Chairmanship.

You have also made a grievance of the fact that you have been excluded from the reconstituted Boards of the two Corporations of which you have been a member since their inception. I think I am correct in saying that never in the history of the two Boards have the outgoing Chairmen been nominated as Members of the succeeding Boards. The reason is clear. The successor would be put in an embarrassing position in case he has to review any of the previous decisions or practices approved by his predecessor. Secondly, the staff of the organisation would also be overawed somewhat by his presence on the Board and may not be able to express themselves freely on matters in which the previous Chairman had taken a decision or any particular view. Moreover, I am sure you will agree that there is some advantage in bringing to bear on the affairs of an institution a fresh outlook uninfluenced by past associations. In the circumstance, I assumed that you yourself would find it embarrassing to continue on the Boards.

I do hope that in the light of what I have said you would appreciate better the reasons for which we made a change and in any case I can assure you that no extraneous consideration whatsoever was involved in bringing about this change.

With kind regards,

Yours sincerely,
Morarji Desai

TO MORARJI DESAI

Bombay
17 March 1978

My dear Morarjibhai,

I thank you for your letter of 26 February, received while I was out of India.

I do not wish to prolong this correspondence which I am sure is as distasteful to you as it is to me.

If I did feel somewhat hurt, it was on the two grounds mentioned in my letter of 13 February, to which I note you have avoided making any reference in your reply, namely the fact that you chose to give me no hint whatsoever of the impending change during our half hour's conversation on the 24th of January, only a week before it became effective, and that the first news of my removal was communicated to me not by Government but by my successor and through the Press.

My greatest regret is that the manner in which this matter has been handled has aroused so much dismay and heart-burning within Air-India's fine organisation whose high morale and dedication have been so largely responsible for the airline's outstanding progress and international reputation.

With kind regards,

Yours sincerely,
J.R.D. Tata

FROM MRS. INDIRA GANDHI[*]

In flight Gauhati-Calcutta
14 February 1978

Dear Jeh,

I am so sorry that you are no longer with Air-India. Air-India must be as sad at the parting as you yourself. You were not merely Chairman but the founder and nurturer who felt deep personal concern. It was this and the meticulous care you gave to the smallest detail, including the décor and the saris of the hostesses, which raised Air-India to the international level and indeed to the top of the list.

We were proud of you and of the Airline. No one can take this satisfaction from you nor belittle Govt.'s debt to you in this respect.

There was some misunderstanding between us but it was not possible for me to let you know of the pressures under which I had to function and the rivalries within the Ministry of Civil Aviation. I would not like to say more.

With all good wishes,

Sincerely,
Indira

---

[*]   Copy of handwritten letter.

TO MRS. INDIRA GANDHI

Bombay
28 February 1978

Dear Indira,

It was kind of you to have taken the trouble to write to me regarding the termination by Govt. of my association with Air-India. I was touched by your kind reference to the part I played in building up the airline. I was fortunate in the loyalty and enthusiasm of my colleagues and staff and the support I got from government without either of which I could have achieved little.

Hoping you are well and with all good wishes,

Yours very sincerely,
Jeh

TO RAGHU RAJ[*]

Bombay
11 June 1982

Dear Mr. Raghu Raj,

My re-enactment on the 15th October 1962 of my inaugural flight of 15th October 1932, which marked the beginning of Indian air transport, aroused considerable interest and gave good publicity to Air-India. The actual aircraft used for the commemorative flight hangs today, as you know, in the Customs Hall of the new terminal at Sahar.

I have, since last year, been toying with the idea of repeating the flight once again on 15th October 1982, which will mark the fiftieth anniversary of Indian air transport, if the same aircraft or one of the same type could be made flyable and available. As the Leopard Moth at the Sahar terminal must by now be over 40 years old and its fuselage and wings are made of wood, it would probably have to be very largely rebuilt. As there are no longer any engineers or mechanics experienced in the overhauling and repairing of wooden aircraft, the work would have to be done in England where there are one or two Clubs or Associations of enthusiasts who renovate and fly old aircraft or duplicate old ones going as far back as fighter aircraft of the First World War. If Air-India were to agree to sponsor this flight as a morale-building piece of public relations, the aircraft would have to be airfreighted to London. This would present little difficulty as it is quite small and can easily be dismantled and the fuselage, wings, under-carriage and other bits and pieces packed separately and carried in a 747 or our freighter.

---

[*]   Chairman, Air-India.

It may be that, on examination, the condition of the fuselage and wings will be found to be such that it would involve practically rebuilding the aircraft, in which case it might be cheaper to buy, hire or borrow a similar aircraft with a current certificate of airworthiness. When I was in England last month, I met and discussed the matter with the Secretary of the De Havilland Moth Club, and I enclose a copy of his letter to me of May 28, which indicates that such an aircraft will be available....

Before I pursue further discussions, I would like to know whether Air-India would support this proposed re-enactment of the 50-year-old flight. You might rightly question whether it would be wise or safe for such an undertaking, considering that I shall be 78 years old at the time. I am confident that it would be, in view of my present health and physical condition at the age of 77, apart from which, on this occasion, I would, if necessary, agree to be accompanied by a co-pilot. You may like to consult your colleagues before replying....

With kind regards,

Yours sincerely,
J.R.D. Tata

TO RAGHU RAJ

Bombay
17 August 1982

My dear Raghu Raj,

Thank you very much for your letter of the 12th. I am quite touched at the concern that you express on behalf of yourself and your colleagues about my undertaking the Karachi-Bombay commemorative flight solo, but I do feel that your and their worry in the matter is quite unnecessary.

Although I have reached an age at which most men are somewhat or seriously diminished physically, I have, as you know, maintained myself in a state of health and physical capability of a much younger man. Not only do I take fairly strenuous physical exercise every day in my house, but also continue to indulge every year in downhill skiing in Europe which, combined with the altitude and consequent lower oxygen content of the air, is quite a rigorous sport. I even tried my hand at hang-gliding on skis last winter! I drive high speed cars every year in Europe—a much more risky occupation than flying a plane like the Leopard, particularly on such an easy run as the Karachi-Bombay flight, which will involve no physical or mental strain but only a certain amount of boredom.

When I flew the Leopard at the Oxford airport the other day, I found myself totally at home in it and, in fact, except whilst taxiing, because of lack of brake power on one side and the loss of view straight ahead in the absence of a nose wheel, I found it easier than the school plane I flew with an instructor before test-flying the Leopard. The flights to and from Karachi will be over flat country with unlimited force-landing sites involving hardly any risk in a plane which lands at 45 mph or less in any wind. Even if I had a co-pilot, I would do the landing myself as the view from the rear seat is highly restricted. The only possible event in which a co-pilot would be useful that I can think of is if I suddenly decided to faint or die while at the controls!...

Satisfied as I am, therefore, that there is really no risk in what will be a very simple flight in a very simple and safe aeroplane now made like new, in which I have had considerable experience and feel extremely comfortable and at home, and having assured myself of such help at the ground stops and even en route, I have no doubt that there will be absolutely no difficulty or uncertainty on my re-enacting the commemorative flight by repeating it exactly as it was done 50 years ago, i.e. alone. The impact on the public, the prestige of the flight, the goodwill it would create— all would be largely lost if it was undertaken merely by an old gentleman flying with a professional pilot. I feel this so strongly that, as I have said in my previous letter, I would much prefer giving up the whole idea, which after all is of no real importance to the airline. So, however much I am grateful to you for your friendship and concern about my safety, please stop worrying about me all of you and let me have my fun!

Yours sincerely,
Jeh

TO MRS. INDIRA GANDHI*

Bombay
17 October 1982

My dear Indira,

I was greatly touched by your very kind message of congratulations which was handed to me as I stepped from the plane on the completion of my flight from Karachi. I deeply appreciated your thoughtful gesture and thank you warmly for it.

My pleasure was made all the greater on learning that I had been re-appointed to the Board of Air-India and would thus have a renewed opportunity to serve the Airline to which I have devoted so much of my working life. I thank you for that also, knowing the appointment could have been taken only at your instance or with your approval.

With affectionate wishes,

Yours very sincerely,
Jeh

---

* Copy of handwritten letter.

TO RAGHU RAJ

My dear Raghu Raj,

Although I did attempt in the course of my remarks at the reception at Juhu to express my deep appreciation of Air-India's sponsorship of my flight and of the help I received from its organisation, I feel I must write to thank you personally for your sustained interest in the project and for all the trouble you took from the start to ensure that every necessary step and every precaution was taken to ensure the success of the venture, starting with getting the plane sent to the U.K. for complete overhaul and deputing Mr. Baliwala to supervise the work.

I was touched by the over-kind words in which you referred to me and to my flight, and by the magnificent gift, both of which left me overwhelmed. I was also deeply touched, during the weeks before the flight, by your concern about my own safety and I am glad that I didn't let you down!...

My re-enactment flight could not have been the great success it was without the support and cooperation I received from Air-India, and I extend my thanks and gratitude to all those who participated to make it a memorable event.

With kind regards,

Yours sincerely,
J.R.D. Tata

Advice and Consent

TO GHULAM MOHAMMED[*]

Bombay
2 October 1947

My dear Ghulam Mohammed,

In continuation of my letter of the 5th September, I am sorry for the delay in sending you particulars about Executive types of aeroplanes....

There are, at present, only two suitable and well-tried types of aeroplanes available. One is the American Beechcraft "18-8" which is the post-war development of the "Expeditor", and the other is the British De Havilland "Dove"....I have flown the "Expeditor" quite a lot, and have also flown the "Dove" for about two hours in England....While the "Dove" engines are supercharged for normal cruising output at only 6,000 feet, the Beechcraft engines are supercharged for cruising at 9,000 to 10,000 feet, at which height the machine operates most efficiently and has a cruising speed of about 190 mph as compared to the 160 miles per hour of the "Dove" at 5,000 feet.

The "Dove" is a more modern machine in the sense that it has a tricycle undercarriage which gives the crew a better, and therefore, safer view on the ground,

---

[*]   A Director of Tatas in pre-Independence India; Liaqat Ali Khan requested Tatas to allow Ghulam Muhammed to be relieved of his directorship, in order that he may be appointed Finance Minister (and later Governor-General) of Pakistan.

and would enable shorter landings in an emergency. On the other hand, as stated by Bhore, its present engines are not as well proved as those of the Beech.

If the extra price is not a decisive objection, I would personally prefer the Beechcraft because of its better engines, and higher cruising altitude and speed....

If you decide on the "Beech" and wish us to place the order for you, we shall be glad to help.

I hope you are keeping well, and with best wishes,

Yours sincerely,
Jeh

TO GHULAM MOHAMMED

Bombay
20 May 1949

My dear Ghulam Mohammed,

I have your D.O.No.HM(F)-622/49 dated the 14th May 1949, enquiring about Executive planes.

For the use of Ministers and Senior Executives accompanied by their staff, I consider that the "Dakota" is still by far the best plane to select. The first cost is cheap, in fact cheaper than new planes half their size....On the other hand the cost of operation is naturally somewhat high owing to the horsepower used.

If the "Dakota" is considered too big and expensive to run for the purpose in view, I would recommend either the De Havilland "Dove" or the Beechcraft D.18.S (which is the successor to the Beechcraft Expeditor). These are small, twin-engine aircraft about one-third the size of the "Dakota". Although running costs will be much less than the Dakota, their first cost is high—for new machines being, I believe, in the neighbourhood of Rs. 3½ lakhs. Second-hand aircraft would be cheaper but may not be available....

Finally, if a still smaller type of aircraft is wanted, and particularly one for use from small fields, I cannot recommend anything better than the Beechcraft Bonanza, a single-engine, four-seater plane of 185 H.P., costing about Rs. 45,000/-, and having a remarkable performance for its size and horsepower. We have one at Jamshedpur....

You will appreciate that these three separate types, namely the "Dakota", the Beechcraft D.18.S. or the "Dove", and the Beechcraft Bonanza fill entirely separate needs, and the selection of the type or types for your Government must therefore depend on the specific purpose for which they are intended....

With best wishes,

Yours sincerely,

Jeh

TO SIR JEHANGIR GHANDY

Bombay
25 July 1952

My dear Joe,

Re: Purchase of a Twin Beechcraft D.18.S

There is no doubt that the post-war D.18.S is a much better aeroplane than the pre-war or war-time model such as ours. What is more important, it is a much safer aeroplane because of its feathering propellers which enable it to fly or even climb on one engine. It is because of its much improved single-engine performance that it has a higher all-up weight in the certificate of air-worthiness. This higher all-up weight in turn gives it a higher payload....

The first thing to do about the Gwalior offer is to have the aircraft thoroughly inspected. If you wish me to have it inspected by Air-India, I shall arrange for this to be done, otherwise Ghosh could go and inspect it himself. I am afraid, however, that the price asked for, unless it is a purely asking price, puts the aircraft out of our reach. Rs. 2½ lakhs is a very high price and in fact higher than the price of a fully equipped Dakota. I do not think anybody would pay such a price here and a counter-offer is therefore indicated. But the first thing is to have the aircraft inspected, particularly from the point of view of corrosion, if any, in the skin.

Yours sincerely,
Jeh

TO CAPT. H.K. GHOSH[*]

My dear Ghosh,

Re. Beagle B. 206

On the 7th November I was given a demonstration of the Beagle B. 206 and flew it myself from the left-hand seat. I must say I was extremely well-impressed by this aircraft. Its flying characteristics, finish, instrumentation, etc. were fully comparable to those of American aircraft in the same category, while the cabin was substantially more roomy. My only doubt was in regard to the cruising speed which seemed on the low side for a 1964 machine. As far as I could make out, it was approximately the same as that of the Beech 18.

Before the flight I had seen your letter T/AD/618/64 of the 14th July to the Head Office enclosing comparative data of the Beagle 206 and the Beech Baron. This comparison does not seem fair to the Beagle as it compares it with a smaller and lighter aircraft. I was told in the course of the demonstration that in fact the Beagle is substantially cheaper than any American aircraft of comparable size and performance. This needs to be checked.

I was particularly struck by two features of the B. 206. Although its stalling speed (unclean) is given as 76 mph, we musked along quite happily at 60 knots and the actual stall, a very mild one, was at 55 knots with four people on board. The recovery

---

[*] Company pilot of Tata Steel, Jamshedpur.

from the stall "hands off" showed no sign of dipping a wing. The other feature was its excellent short field performance.

I do not necessarily advocate TISCO buying one of these aircraft, but I think it should definitely be considered if and when we think of buying an aircraft of that particular size. I would like you therefore to prepare a detailed comparison between the B. 206 and American aircraft in the same category both in regard to specification and performance on the one hand, and price on the other. I believe that the most comparable aircraft would be the Queenair which I seem to remember was much more expensive.

Yours sincerely,
J.R.D. Tata

TO PETER MINGRONE*

Bombay

9 August 1974

Dear Peter,

Many thanks for your letter of 15 July. It is always a pleasure to meet you and to learn something, if not about aeroplanes, at least about Hi-Fi equipment!

I am afraid that I cannot accept your arguments against the 747 at their face value. You seem to forget that I have been intimately concerned with air transport for almost as long as you have been alive, so I am sufficiently clued up, at least to know when wool is being pulled over my eyes! It may be that the world's airlines did buy too many 747s, particularly of the first series, just as they would have been equally mistaken if DC-10s or 1011s had come first and they had bought too many of *them*!

I happen to know that the 747s that were grounded were the earlier series. Comparison with Delta is irrelevant, as they are a short/medium range airline. You conveniently ignore the fact that BA are buying more 747s, and that Qantas are standardising their fleet wholly on them....

Let me tell you that I retain the belief I have held all along, and which I think is one of the reasons for Air-India's success in the past, in standardisation of a fleet until an adequate number has been purchased. We bought the first 747 after we had a fleet of ten 707s. It would make just no sense, and I am sure you know it as well as I do, for us to buy one or two 1011s or DC-10s while we have only four 747s. In fact, the only justification would be if we were to sell the 747s which would be even more silly....

---

*   An executive of Lockheed-California Co., U.S.A.

Your argument in favour of Indian Airlines buying 1011s is about the only thing in your letter that makes any sense to me, provided that your claim, that the 1011 will be cheaper to buy and operate than A-300s, proves correct!

All the best, and keep firing!...

Yours ever,
Jeh

TO THE EARL OF KIMBERLEY

Bombay
20 *April* 1976

Dear Lord Kimberley,

Thank you for your letter of the 31st March, asking for my views on the Concorde*
generally....As Chairman of Air-India and its predecessor Tata Airlines, which I
founded as far back as 1932, I have throughout been extremely interested in the
development of new types of aircraft and, ever since it was announced, in the progress
of the Concorde project.

Realising, from the inception of our international operations in 1948, that we
could hold our own in the fiercely competitive international air transport market only
if we offered the highest possible standards of service with the most modern aircraft,
we operated, in turn, Lockheed Constellations, Super-Constellations, Boeing 707s,
and now Boeing 747s. However, being a relatively small airline, we have considered
it both prudent and sound to leave the introduction into service of the first generation
of any entirely new type of aircraft to the leaders of the industry who can better absorb
the costs and risks involved, and we have been content to purchase new types only
after they have been proved in regular airline use. This has had the additional
advantage of enabling us to get an improved model of the original one, usually
equipped with a more efficient and more economical engine. For instance, when the
Comet was first announced in the fifties, we reserved positions for the Comet II
(which later became the Comet III) and not the Comet I, and would probably have
bought it if, in the meantime, the 707 and DC-8 had not come on the scene. Even

---

*   Another prescient decision—Concorde was discontinued in 2003.

in their case, as more recently in that of the 747, we waited for the second generation of the type.

I am giving you this somewhat detailed explanation of our fleet equipment philosophy as background to our present views and attitude in regard to the Concorde.

In order to protect our competitive position in case the Concorde proved wholly successful as an economically viable aircraft, we booked, in 1964, two fairly late positions in the queue. At that time the aircraft was roughly estimated to cost 4.6 million, equivalent to US $13 million, jet fuel prices were about a third of what they are today, and there were no environmental and ecological objections which now threaten drastically to reduce the aircraft's one and only important advantage, namely, speed. It is true that first class fares have, in the meantime, gone up too, but by no means yet to an extent commensurate with cost increases.

The Concorde picture has thus turned out to be very different from what was visualised or hoped for twelve years ago. Not only has the dollar equivalent price of the Concorde gone up almost five-and-a-half times but, except over water and over some desert sectors of the world's international route systems, flying overland at supersonic speed has been, or is likely to be, banned by the governments of the countries to be served or overflown.

As if that were not enough, the US Government, who will no doubt be followed by other governments, have laid down noise control regulatory limitations which the present model of the Concorde cannot possibly meet.

In the circumstances, you will appreciate that, apart from our limited resources and prior commitment to mass air traffic which the 747 meets effectively, we cannot possibly contemplate the purchase of Concordes in their present form....

With kind regards,

Yours sincerely,
J.R.D. Tata

TO RAGHU RAJ*

Bombay
6 May 1981

Mr. Raghu Raj,

Now that I am once again a member of the Board, I propose to resume my practice of writing notes of impressions gathered on my flights on Air-India and other airlines which I feel might be of interest to the Management.

In the last few months I have made four long-range flights on Swissair, Lufthansa and BA, and three on Air-India. The point that struck me and worries me most is the continuing fact that whereas we hardly carry any first class passengers, their first class cabins are full, or nearly full, most of the time despite the fact that their first class cabins have more seats than ours. I have consistently pointed out the importance of our changing the policy we had wrongly followed in recent years of concentrating all our sales efforts on excursion and other promotional fare traffic, the yield from which is less than one-fifth of that of first class traffic. If we take also into account the fact that in addition to carrying five times the number of passengers we also have to carry five times the baggage and cabin service loads and proportionate additional cabin crew members and their baggage, the real yield ratio must be nearer to, or over, 6:1.

I am satisfied that our first class service has always been, and is today, as good as, if not better than, that of other airlines. In fact, a flight in first class on Air-India,

---

* Three years after JRD was sacked from the Chairmanship of Air-India by Morarji Desai in 1978, Mrs. Indira Gandhi appointed him as a member of the Board. Following this, he resumed his habit of sending suggestions for improvements in service to the Chairman, Raghu Raj. This is the first communication in the series.

ADVICE AND CONSENT **235**

with its outstandingly comfortable slumberette seats is far superior to one on Swissair, and yet Swissair's 22-seater first class cabin is always full. I could not get a seat on Swissair recently, *even as a paying passenger*.

I must once again urge that top management give firm instructions down the line that first priority must be given to securing first class traffic, and that the performance of our various sales offices will be judged not by the total number of bodies put on board but by the proportion of the total which consists of first class and executive class revenue passengers....

I am glad to say that our standards of food and service in first class continue to be fully comparable with those of our competitors....

J.R.D. Tata

TO RAGHU RAJ

Bombay
9 June 1982

...I flew to London on 29 April on AI-107, from London to New York on AI-111 on 1 May, from New York to London on 9/10 May, and London to Bombay on AI-110 on 15 May.

To me the most striking and regrettable fact on the first two flights was the almost total preponderance of staff and their families occupying seats in the first class. On AI-107 on the 29th April, 13 out of the 15 occupied seats were taken up by staff free-riders. A few days later on the London/New York flight, there was not a single paying passenger in the first class. Twelve were staff/family members, one interline and myself! Thus, on both these flights over 90% of the first class passengers were staff. I do feel it is time that this problem be faced and solved once and for all. I realise that any reduction of this amenity will be resisted by the staff and that it may be that such loss may have to be made up by some form of compensatory payment or alternative amenity; otherwise we shall never build up this important source of income, for everyone in the organisation, barring the few dedicated ones, has a vested interest in maintaining our first class as a staff amenity.

It is clear that the only practical and satisfactory solution is to give up the salary qualification for eligibility which was fixed some 30 years ago. As wage levels rise the number entitled to first class travel increases and has reached an absurd level where low ranking staff are entitled to first class travel. In no other airline in the world does such a situation exist. The right to travel first class, and always subject to load, should be allowed only to senior staff by designation so that increases in salaries do not add to the number. This is a matter that should be negotiated without delay with all staff unions, and the consequences faced....

J.R.D. Tata

MANAGING MEN

Managing Business
★
Colleagues
★
Employees and Shareholders
★
Nostalgia

When JRD became a Director of Tatas on the death of his father in 1926 he was only 22. Twelve years later, on the death of Sir Nowroji Saklatvala, he was appointed Chairman of the Group. JRD often said that his co-Directors appointed him Chairman of the Board of Tata Sons "in a moment of mental aberration".

When he became Chairman of Tatas in 1938 he was still by far the youngest member of the Board. Sir Homi Mody, Sir Ardeshir Dalal and others were all senior to him. Besides these, there were senior executives like Jehangir Ghandy (later Sir), K.A.D. Naoroji and P.A. Narielwala. While Naval Tata was of JRD's age, Col. Leslie Sawhny was younger than him. Amongst the important people whom JRD brought into Tatas, there were J.D. Choksi, Sumant Moolgaokar, A.D. Shroff, Nani Palkhivala and Darbari Seth.

The two previous Chairmen of Tata Sons were the Chairmen of all the companies which came under the group. JRD changed this. He gave some of the chairmanships, like the one of hydro-electric companies and that of textile firms, to his colleagues. This was a watershed in the life of the Group. In his operations as Group Chairman JRD was a consensus man. Regarding his style of functioning, he said, "If I have any merit, it is getting on with individuals according to their ways and characteristics. . . To be a leader you have got to lead human beings with affection."

JRD's relationship with shareholders and employees was also quite smooth. Annual General Meetings of the various Tata companies were generally held in a congenial atmosphere. Several of his colleagues and junior employees kept in touch with JRD even after their retirement. They wrote warm letters to him and he made it a point to answer most of them.

Managing Business

TO PANDIT JAWAHARLAL NEHRU

Bombay
10 August 1939

My dear Jawaharlal,

I feel I must write and tell you how appreciative I and all connected with the conduct of the Steel Company's affairs are, of the time, trouble and energy you gave to the recent arbitration proceedings* at Jamshedpur. In view of your heavy commitments in other directions and the short notice you were given I fear that this additional burden and the travelling it involved must have caused you much inconvenience and some physical strain. Your willingness in the circumstances to undertake this work is, I feel, an indication of your solicitude for the welfare of Indian industry and, particularly for that part of it which is represented by Labour. I sincerely hope that your and Babu Rajendra Prasad's efforts for a better understanding between the Steel Company and its workmen at Jamshedpur, will bring back some measure of harmony and co-operation between them. I wish to assure you, in all sincerity, that we are fully conscious of Labour's right to a fair deal, to the maintenance of

---

* Following a labour dispute in TISCO at Jamshedpur in 1939, Babu Rajendra Prasad and Pandit Jawaharlal Nehru were appointed as arbitrators. They visited Jamshedpur, studied the situation and submitted the report to the management.

their self-respect and to a steady enhancement of their material well being and that it is our earnest wish to do all we can on our side to achieve these objects....

With kind regards,

Yours sincerely,
J.R.D. Tata

TO SIR JEHANGIR GHANDY

Bombay
4 February 1941

My dear Joe,

Thanks for your letter No.193 of the 8/9th January sending me a copy of Sir Thomas Holland's* letter and your reply. I have asked Miss Cursetjee to collect documents regarding important events in the history of the Company and send them on to you for use and preservation. Proper arrangements should be made at Jamshedpur to have these indexed and preserved. There are some documents which are on our record and have to be maintained at Bombay, such as the original prospectus. We shall have a photograph taken of the original prospectus and send you a copy.

It would not be possible for anyone in the office here to go through *all* the old records in a search for items of possible interest, but the object in view will be kept in mind and the original documents or true copies of important events in the life of the Company will be passed on to you for record.

Yours sincerely,
J.R.D. Tata

---

* Ex-Director, Geological Survey of India.

TO K.A.D. NAOROJI[*]

Bombay
20 *May* 1946

My dear Kish,

In spite of my many requests, I find that you are still writing about a number of completely different subjects relating to different Companies in your letters to me.

I must, therefore, once again request you not to mix up different subjects in single letters, as this causes both inconvenience and annoyance at this end. If you find it difficult to remember these instructions when dictating letters, standing instructions to your secretary should do the trick!

I hope you won't drive me to returning your letters unanswered with the request that they be split up into separate letters pertaining to different subjects before they are considered at this end!

This letter is a private one, and not intended for the office files.

Yours,
Jeh

---

[*]   K.A.D. Naoroji (1893-1977), grandson of Dadabhai Naoroji, joined Tatas in 1922; worked in various capacities in Jamshedpur and Bombay; was appointed the first President of Tata Incorporated, New York, 1945; Resident Director of Tatas in Delhi, 1950; retired in 1962.

TO SIR JEHANGIR GHANDY

Bombay
13 October 1947

My dear Joe,

Will you please refer to your official letter No.AOC/465/47 dated 2/6th October 1947, regarding the advertisement about our Tool, Alloy and Special Steels.

While aware that there is no specific grammatical error in the advertisement, I wished to convey to you that its wording is not in keeping with the dignity and status of a concern like ours, and savours a little of "Babu English"....

I am surprised at your suggestion that the drafts of all advertisements should, in future, be sent to Bombay for approval. We have quite enough on our hands here. It is in the Sales Manager's office, where the advertisements are prepared, that a consistent attempt should be made to improve the quality of the text....

Yours sincerely,
Jeh

TO SIR JEHANGIR GHANDY

Bombay
15 June 1950

My dear Joe,

I have been thinking for over ten years that we should bring out an annual report to our employees in English and Hindi, and in simpler and more graphic form than our report to the shareholders and containing information of the type likely to interest the employees. Unfortunately, I have been so busy that each year this idea has been pushed into the background. I now feel that we should try and make a beginning with it, if not this year, at least next year for certain.

...I would appreciate your applying your mind to the question and letting me have your views and suggestions on the subject in due course.

I have asked Bhabha to write to Joshi for information regarding the number of our present employees with a period of service of over 35 years, in order that we may reproduce in the report to the employees the photographs of some of our workers and supervisors with long and valuable service to their credit.

Yours sincerely,
Jeh

TO T.T. KRISHNAMACHARI*

Bombay
28 November 1953

Dear Mr. Krishnamachari,

On behalf of the Tata Locomotive & Engineering Company, I submit herewith a scheme for the manufacture of diesel trucks in the Telco Works at Jamshedpur, with the collaboration of Messrs. Daimler-Benz A.G. of Stuttgart, West Germany, for which we seek the approval of the Government of India.

In view of the many and considerable advantages which the Tata Locomotive and Engineering Company already enjoys as a potential manufacturer of diesel trucks in the shape of available factory capacity, engineering facilities and technical resources, it is exceptionally well placed to undertake such a project.

The combination of truck manufacture with locomotive and boiler production will place this Company in a position to produce trucks on an economic basis despite the modest scale of 3,000 units per year which is contemplated in the initial stages....

With the help and advice of Messrs. Daimler-Benz A.G. we have framed a realistic and practical production programme to secure the fullest and quickest possible development of indigenous manufacture. The programme is so framed that by the end of the fourth year, the work to be done in the Telco Works will represent 75% of the value of the truck, involving the manufacture of a greater number and variety of parts and components within a single works than is normally the practice. I believe that the concentration of manufacture of the bulk of the parts and components of

---

* Minister for Commerce & Industry, Government of India.

the truck in a single factory will have many advantages, technically as well as financially, over the method of dispersing the work between a number of factories located at a considerable distance from each other.

By the end of the four-year development period not only will the Telco Works manufacture over 75% of the parts and components, but practically all the raw materials will be obtained from indigenous sources. We have arranged with Daimler-Benz to modify and adapt their specifications according to the availability of materials in India consistent with the maintenance of the highest standard of quality.

We hope also that by the end of the programme most of the bought-out items will also be obtainable from indigenous sources....A valuable consequence of such a high proportion of local manufacture will be that foreign exchange requirements will dwindle to a very small amount at the end of four years.

Messrs. Daimler-Benz have undertaken not only to provide all the technical information and assistance required for this scheme, but have displayed their confidence in the success of the project by undertaking to participate financially to the extent of about Rs. 80 lakhs.

In view of the valuable contribution they will make to the development of the Indian automotive industry by way both of their financial investment in the project and of the unsurpassed technical knowledge and experience which they will pass on to India, Messrs. Daimler-Benz propose to approach the Government of India for some assurance that the benefit of such contribution will not be lost to them through the compulsory acquisition of the factory during the period of the Agreement....

Even if Government were at any time to decide on nationalising locomotive manufacture, their policy could easily be implemented by the expansion of their own locomotive manufacturing facilities at Chittaranjan or elsewhere without acquiring the Telco factory.

I trust therefore that the Government of India will treat this request sympathetically and will give the desired assurance to Messrs. Daimler-Benz and to ourselves....

Yours sincerely,

J.R.D. Tata

TO GENERAL K.S. MASTER*

Bombay
7 March 1958

My dear General Master,

The Jubilee Park surpassed all my expectations and I would like most warmly to congratulate you and, through you, all those whose devoted work contributed so much to the wonderful final result....

My pleasure and pride in the Park are tempered by a good deal of anxiety in regard to its future at the hands of the three hundred thousand people of Jamshedpur. I feel it is imperative that the Park Committee should be set up immediately under your Chairmanship and should start functioning without a moment's delay. Until the people of Jamshedpur are fully educated to the fact that this is *their* Park and not a Company amenity and that *theirs* is the responsibility to keep it clean and safe from damage, we must, I think, divert a number of Town watch and ward personnel to the Park with instructions to stop such objectionable practices as riding bicycles on the lawns and the use by adults of children's equipment.

We should, I suggest, immediately put up a hundred or so litter baskets of metal mesh, with signboards in Hindi and English, requesting people not to throw litter on the ground but to place it in these receptacles.

We must also have quickly put up many more signs in Hindi and in English, particularly at points of special attraction, reminding the people that the Park is theirs and enjoining upon them to treat it with the care and love it deserves.

---

*   Director, Town Medical & Health, Tata Steel, Jamshedpur.

I hope that the fountains and jets will play and the coloured illuminations be switched on at least every Saturday and Sunday evening and on every holiday throughout the year, and on Founder's Day.

It has been suggested to me that the statue of Jamsetji Tata should be lighted up every evening. I think this is a good idea and may be considered by the Committee...

Yours sincerely,
J.R.D. Tata

TO J.D. CHOKSI*

Bombay
6 April 1959

Jehangir Dossabhoy Choksi, Esq.

    May I suggest that you instruct Rustom Furdoonji Sorabji Talyarkhan, Esq. to adopt a less grandiloquent description of Directors' names in Voltas Annual Reports as used in most Tata Company Reports, giving only the initials and also to drop the use of the absurd "Esq.", which I think should be used only when addressing British nationals in the U.K.

Jehangir Ratanji Dadabhoy Tata, Esq.

---

*   Joined Tatas in 1938 as legal advisor; appointed Director of Tata Sons in 1944.

TO M.D.s[*]

Bombay
28 July 1969

M.D.s

    The Chairman finds a continuing habit amongst various Companies and Departments in Bombay House to send for perusal/action a mass of papers every Friday afternoon. He appreciates the desire of officers to clear their desks before the weekend, but not the practice of compelling him to spend most of his weekend in clearing his! He has given his Secretariat orders, therefore, that all but the most urgent papers sent to his Office after 1 p.m. on Fridays are to be returned to sender.

    This is for your information and action, if required.

J.R.D. Tata

---

*   Managing Directors.

TO DR. S.D. TRIPATHI[*]

Bombay
31 *December 1973*

Dear Dr. Tripathi,

This is in reply to your letter dated 18th December regarding the project for case studies in Trusteeship Management sponsored by the Indian Council of Social Science Research.

While it is quite true that I have been deeply interested in the philosophy of Trusteeship enunciated by Gandhiji, and have from time to time taken part in discussions on the subject, Tatas have not undertaken a specific formalised experiment in Trusteeship Management as such. The Tata philosophy of management has always been, and is today more than ever, that corporate enterprises must be managed not merely in the interests of their owners, but equally in those of their employees, of the consumers of their products, of the local community, and finally of the country as a whole....

With best wishes,

Yours sincerely,
J.R.D. Tata

---

[*]   Project Director, Department of Commerce and Business Management, Punjab University, Chandigarh.

TO BIJU PATNAIK*

Bombay
8 January 1979

Dear Mr. Patnaik,

If I take the unusual step of writing this personal letter to you and other Members of the National Executive of the Janata Party, both as Chairman of the Tata Iron and Steel Company and as a citizen who has devoted over fifty years of his life to the industrial development of India, in the spirit of trusteeship advocated by Jamsetji Tata a hundred years ago, it is because recent events impel me to do so in what I sincerely consider the national interest. This move of nationalising Tisco involved basic issues of national policy transcending in importance the take-over of companies concerned.

While this important document (Statement of Economic Policy adopted by the Janata Party on 14 November 1977), states that "the Party is opposed to any economic system which allows individuals or groups freedom to exploit others", it also states: "At the same time it is not in favour of the State possessing unlimited power which will destroy all initiatives and freedom and result in the establishment of a totalitarian society."

The only argument said to have been advanced in support of the proposal to take over Tata Steel was that, as Tatas held only 3% (the real figure is a little over 4%)

---

* In December 1978, two cabinet ministers of the then Janata government proposed the nationalisation of Tata Steel. They were George Fernandes and Biju Patnaik—Ministers for Industry and Steel respectively. The Tata Workers' Union registered its protest by cable to Prime Minister Morarji Desai. The Workers said that nationalisation would be detrimental to all employees of the Company. Against this breakdown JRD wrote this letter to Biju Patnaik and other members of the National Executive of the Janata Party:

of the share capital of the Steel Company, there was no reason why they should retain control of its management. This argument is surprising for two reasons. Firstly, because it is incorrect. The Management control of the Company does not rest in the hands of Tatas but with a Board of Directors, the members of which, except for those directly appointed by Government or Government institutions, are elected by the shareholders, including Government. Secondly, because the ownership of the Company is spread amongst 80,000 shareholders, the argument is, therefore, in conflict with the view rightly held by the Janata Party that ownership should, as far as possible, be divorced from management and that the entire strategy of development must seek to achieve the widest possible dispersion in the ownership of property and the means of production.

Forty-five per cent of the voting power of the Company is, however, held, directly or indirectly, by Government, mainly through its financial institutions. Government, through its high voting power in the Company's capital and also in terms of the law, has the power to remove and replace every director on the Board. Four representatives of the Government, including the Secretary of the Ministry of Steel, the Vice-Chairman of the Steel Authority of India Limited and the Chairman of the Life Insurance Corporation of India, are members of its Board. Day-to-day management is in the hands of whole-time executive directors, all professional men who have risen from the ranks, three of whom also serve as Board members.

The Company's operations are fully integrated with those of the public sector plants.

Thus, apart from being totally irrelevant as a ground for taking over the Company, the low percentage of the Company's capital held by Tata Sons, their affiliates and their philanthropic trusts, is wholly in keeping with modern thinking and with the Janata Party's own philosophy and wishes, while Government exercises full control over its operations.

What then could be the grounds justifying nationalisation? Mismanagement? Undue concentration of economic power in private hands? Industrial sickness? Need for large funds for modernisation? Removal of disparities?

J.R.D. Tata

Colleagues

TO SIR JEHANGIR GHANDY

Bombay
5 August 1938

My dear Joe,

I thank you for your letter No.3168 of the 2nd August forwarding a copy of the proceedings of the public meeting held in the Town Hall to mourn the loss of our late Chairman.

I much appreciate the way in which you spoke at that meeting and also the kind sentiments expressed in your letter to me. I am feeling the loss of Nowroji* most acutely, particularly coming so soon after that of Jal.** The shock of losing both of them in one month—Chief and colleague and both most intimate and cherished friends—has been a terrible one indeed. With their loss have come greatly increased responsibilities which I should have preferred to see postponed for some years but now that they have come to me I shall of course do my best to do full justice to them and shall rely on the friendly co-operation and encouragement of yourself and all other responsible members of our great organisation.

Yours sincerely,
J.R.D. Tata

---

*&** 1938 was an important year for Tatas. Jal Naoroji, Director-in-Charge of TOMCO and Sir Nowroji Saklatvala, Chairman, Tata Sons, passed away during the year. JRD succeeded Sir Nowroji as Chairman of Tata Sons in the last week of July. This was one of the first letters written by him as Chairman of the Group to Sir Jehangir Ghandy who was then General Manager of Tata Steel.

TO A. D. SHROFF*

My dear Adi,**

I was surprised and upset at receiving your letter. I do not remember exactly the words I used during the somewhat heated discussion at the agents' meeting but my complaint to you was merely that an argument you used to score a debating point over me was not an honest one. That is surely a pretty far cry from questioning your honesty, and I am surprised you interpreted it in that way.

You have a right to resent my speaking angrily or showing you discourtesy as a result, and for that I sincerely apologise, but if friends and associates decided to part every time they had an argument life would become pretty difficult.

You refer to my firm. Except that I am personally a relatively minor shareholder, I don't think there is any difference on that account in any of us. We all work for it and I think we should think of it as *our* firm.

...The trouble with both of us is that we both have a hell of a temper!

Yours,
Jeh

---

* JRD and A.D. Shroff often used to have arguments at the agents' meetings. After one such incident Shroff sent an angry letter of resignation to which JRD replied as above. Courtesy *A.D. Shroff: Titan of Finance and Free Enterprise* by Sucheta Dalal (Viking [Penguin], New Delhi, 2000).

** Joined Tatas as Financial Advisor; was Director of Tata Sons from 1942 to 1960.

TO SIR HOMI MODY*

Bombay
26 December 1955

My dear Homi,

I have recovered from the "body-blow to my modesty and my kink about receiving presents", and I must say it is a delightful sensation. I trust you have taken note of the fact that my Golden Anniversary will be on 23rd December 1980!

I only wish you and my other colleagues had been a little less generous and had given me something a little more in tune with the natural humility of a dedicated Sampattidani. I find it, however, the most beautiful silver bowl I have ever seen. This proves, incidentally, how grossly untrue and unfair your remark is that I approve of nothing which is not modern and ugly. After all, I even approve of you and although quite handsome in your own way, you can hardly be considered modern!

Knowing where the initiative for this violation of my sentiments came from, it is to you that I want to send my first and foremost thanks and expression of gratitude. You have been a wonderful friend to me all along and in fact the rebuilt "Cairn"** is itself a monument of that thoughtfulness and kindness which you have always shown me.

Thelly and I thank you from the bottom of our hearts for your part in this most generous and undeserved gift.

Yours ever,
Jeh

---

* Joined Tatas as a Director in 1934 and remained a Senior Director until 1959 barring two interruptions in 1945 and 1949.

** The bungalow at Altamont Road in Bombay where JRD lived.

TO DR. JOHN MATTHAI[*]

Bombay

22 April 1957

My dear Matthai,

When we said goodbye at the aerodrome last month, I found it impossible to express my thoughts, but I think you knew or sensed that I was deeply moved at seeing you go and...come to an end our 17 years' association which had meant so much to me. Even though you abandoned me to my fate twice during these years, your absences were provisional; I could look forward to welcoming you back some day, and in the meantime you always seemed still to be one of us and close to me.

Throughout the years we have been together, you have been a wonderful source of strength and comfort to me. I always felt that I could turn to you when troubled or uncertain about any matter and get from you advice which would never compromise on fundamentals, particularly where the prestige of the Firm and the country was involved.

We all miss you here and I feel more alone, as a result of your going, than I can say....Homi is worried about what will become of you under the Communist influence in your part of the world. He fears that all the years it took him to save your soul will be wasted!

Hoping that you and Achamma are both well and with gratitude for your support and friendship all these years and warm wishes to you both,

Yours affectionately,

Jeh

---

[*] Dr. John Matthai joined Tatas in 1940 as Director-in-Charge of Tata Chemicals. Subsequently, he joined Government and left it in 1950. He was a Minister for Railways and later for Finance in the Nehru Cabinet. He rejoined Tatas as a Director in 1950 and left in 1957.

TO DR. F. KONECKE[*]

Bombay
13 December 1960

My dear Fritz,

I was most distressed to learn that you have decided to retire from the chairmanship of Daimler-Benz in the near future. This will be a great loss not only to Daimler-Benz, whose destinies you have so ably directed during the last eight years, but also to us here. If our joint enterprise has been so successful and the relations between our two firms so happy and cordial and based on so much mutual confidence and goodwill, it has been in large measure due to the part you have played in the project from its very inception. From the start of our joint negotiations in Geneva in February 1954, we have had ample and repeated evidence not only of your grasp of the intricate and delicate problems involved and of your resourcefulness in coping with them but also of your fairness and your readiness to identify yourself with your partners. It has been a privilege and a pleasure to be associated with you all these years and I deeply deplore the coming severance of our association....

We hope that this parting will not be a final one and that after a while your and Hansi's company will be available to your friends including ourselves.

With kindest regards and affectionate wishes to you both, in which Thelly joins me, for Xmas and the New Year.

Yours very sincerely,
Jeh

---

[*] JRD's friendship with Dr. Konecke, Chairman, Daimler-Benz, dated back to 1954 when TELCO signed a collaboration agreement to manufacture trucks in India.

TO N.H. TATA[*]

Bombay
24 August 1965

My dear Naval,

Even though we all knew that the end was to be expected any time during the past year in view of Navajbai's[**] age and state of health, her passing away last Friday still came as somewhat of a shock and I want to tell you how much it has meant to me both as a member of the family and as head of the Firm. She was a great lady in the best tradition of her era, who inspired both great respect and affection.

Although she had for some years taken no part in the Firm's affairs, her very presence meant something important to all of us, mainly I suppose, because she was the last surviving link with Jamsetji. To you, Simone, Ratan and Jimmy, of whom she was so fond, her death must be a great and grievous loss, particularly to yourself who owed so much to her. She will remain for us all a symbol of all that Tatas have stood for from the days of Jamsetji, from which we all derived strength and continued purpose. I know that you will carry on the ideals and traditions that she stood for....

In deep sympathy,

Yours ever,
Jeh

---

[*]   JRD's longest serving colleague on the Board of Tata Sons; adopted son of Lady Navajbai Tata (widow of J.N. Tata's son, Sir Ratan Tata). He joined Tatas and became a Director in 1941. He was later Chairman of the Electrical and the Textile Companies in the Group.

[**] Navajbai was Director of Tata Sons from 1918 to 1965.

TO SUMANT MOOLGAOKAR

Bombay
1 August 1974

My dear Sumant,

It was twenty-five years ago today that you joined Tatas after I had, with some difficulty, obtained your reluctant agreement to leave the ACC and come to us to make something of Telco. Considering the mess it was in at the time, your lack of enthusiasm was not too surprising! I remember, if my memory serves me right, that you accepted in the end only on condition that you would have a free hand, which I was of course only too glad to give you.

I bet, however, that during the next five years of struggle with the Railway Board, and until your friend dear Ashok* drove us into the arms of Daimler-Benz, you sometimes wished you were back making cement!

As I think of what you have achieved during this quarter of a century, I feel that if the only thing I had ever done for Tatas was to inveigle you into the Firm, I would have earned my salary for the whole of my career with them!...

Yours ever,
Jeh

---

* Daimler-Benz representatives had talks earlier with Ashok Motors of Madras. For some reason they fizzled out and they decided to collaborate with TELCO.

Employees and Shareholders

TO SIR FREDERICK JAMES*

Bombay
17 May 1957

My dear Jimmy,

Re. Staff Party

...I must say I am considerably upset at the realisation that the wives and husbands of our staff have been excluded from the dinner and theatre party....The idea of Tata Limited inviting its staff to celebrate such a unique occasion with a dinner and theatre entertainment and excluding the wives and husbands from the Firm's hospitality is most repugnant to me. The only possible reason in the minds of the staff will be that we do not want to spend the extra money on the wives and husbands. I can imagine the feelings of the latter as they are left at home that evening knowing that their spouses are enjoying themselves as guests of the Company. I hope it will still be possible for you to alter the programme and invite all wives and husbands. I would go so far as to say that if there are widows or widowers who have a grown son or daughter they should be allowed to bring them. If wives and

---

* Vice-President and Managing Director, Tata Ltd., London.

husbands are not invited, I do not think it would be worth bringing Thelly merely for the cocktail party, to which frankly I attach much less importance than to the staff party....

Sorry to be such a nuisance.

Yours sincerely,
Jeh

TO SIR JEHANGIR GHANDY

Bombay
11 November 1959

My dear Joe,

Re: Uniforms for Staff

Thanks for your letter No. AO/9299 of the 14th October.

When I first mentioned the subject, I did not have in mind the possibility of providing all the workers in the plant with coveralls or uniforms. I am sorry to find, therefore, that the idea has been turned down merely on the ground that it would cost an enormous amount to provide them for all workers. Even in Hindustan Aircraft, they have only introduced these coveralls experimentally and in a few selected departments. I do not see why we should not consider doing the same thing. There may be some departments in the plant which would lend themselves particularly well to such an experiment where, for instance, the men are not exposed to dirt, smoke and grease and where a high degree of cleanliness is desirable....I hope, therefore, that some further thought will be given to the above proposal.

Yours sincerely,
Jeh

TO M.A. MASCARENHAS*

Bombay
1 *July 1960*

My dear Mascarenhas,

I have just learned that this month you will complete forty-one years' service in the Indian Hotels Company. As Head of Tatas, I write to congratulate you on this achievement. The Firm owes much to men like you, who are a source of strength by virtue of their experience and the example they set to others, and I am happy to acknowledge that debt and to convey to you the Firm's and my appreciation of the valuable service which you have rendered to Tatas over this long period of time.

I would like to make special reference in this letter to the consistently high standard of cooking which one obtains at the Rendezvous. I think it is generally accepted that this Restaurant provides the best food in Bombay and this must be a matter of satisfaction and legitimate pride to you.

With best wishes,

Yours sincerely,
J.R.D. Tata

---

* Chef-de-Cuisine at the Taj Mahal Hotel, Bombay.

TO VIREN SHAH*

Bombay
30 August 1972

My dear Viren,

Thank you for your letter of the 25th August written after attending the Annual General Meeting of TISCO.

I have established, over the past thirty years, such a relationship with shareholders attending meetings that the conduct of meetings rarely presents any problem. I enjoy them only on the occasions, most unusual nowadays, when some shareholder makes intelligent criticism or asks difficult questions!...

With all good wishes,

Yours sincerely,
Jeh

---

* Former Chairman and Managing Director, Mukand Iron & Steel Company Limited, who became Governor of West Bengal.

TO MICHAEL JOHN*

Bombay
3 September 1975

Dear Mr. John,

Thank you so much for your letter of the 14th August, regarding the references in my Chairman's Statement to the unique industrial relations at Jamshedpur and the leading role played in achieving them by the Tata Workers' Union. It is good of you to thank me for my remarks which, as I am sure you know, were written with complete sincerity and conviction.

Apart from my personal esteem and friendship for you, I have always been conscious of your exceptional qualities of leadership in the trade union movement, and particularly the fact that you have never hesitated to take a stand for what is right and sound, even though it may not be popular at the time, and refused to let purely political considerations influence your decisions and policies. As an Indian, and as Chairman of the Company, I am proud of the unique labour situation and relationship between the Company and the Union that has prevailed for so long at Jamshedpur, and I am sure that we can and will remain a model to the rest of the country of what industrial relations should be in industry....

Yours sincerely,
J.R.D. Tata

---

* President, The Tata Workers' Union, Jamshedpur.

TO V.G. GOPAL[*]

Bombay
15 January 1979

Dear Mr. Gopal,

Thank you very much for your letter of the 8th instant, enclosing a copy of the resolution passed by the Executive Committee of the Union regarding the suggestions recently made by the Steel Minister to the National Executive of the Janata Party that Tisco should be taken over. I was touched by, and greatly appreciated, the action taken by the Union under your leadership....

I would be grateful if you would kindly convey to the members of your Committee my own and my colleagues' deep appreciation of their action, which, apart from its importance and timeliness in the context of the developments in Delhi, provides further proof of the mutual sincerity and understanding between the Company and its management on the one hand, and the workers and their representatives on the other, fostered in our long and unique management-labour relationship in which both sides have sincerely cooperated for the common good not only of the workers and the Company, but also of the nation.

Perhaps the greatest tragedy of the twentieth century, apart from its disastrous wars, has been the persisting lack of understanding and cooperation between management and workers throughout the world, resulting in wasteful, recurring conflict. Of the rare exceptions which have shown that such cooperation, based on sincere goodwill and mutual trust, can indeed be achieved with great benefits to all,

---

[*]   President, The Tata Workers' Union, Jamshedpur, who was shot dead in 1993 (see JRD's letter of condolence dated 15 October 1993 in *The Last Letters*.

none that I know of, in India or abroad, have been more strikingly successful than that which we have jointly achieved at Jamshedpur, despite the large size of the labour force there, the magnitude of our operations and the political and other pressures to which we have all been continuously subjected. I would like you to know that this unique achievement of ours is something of which I am immensely proud and for which I shall ever be grateful to the workers of Tisco and to their enlightened leadership.

With renewed thanks and all good wishes,

Yours very sincerely,
J.R.D. Tata

TO P.K. KAPADIA*

Bombay
25 August 1981

Dear Mr. Kapadia,

Thank you for your letter of the 12th instant, received in my office on the 19th. Since I became Chairman in 1938, I have presided over well over two hundred meetings, and this is the very first time that a shareholder has written to complain of rudeness or discourtesy on my part.

...If you felt that my manner seemed brusque and impatient towards the shareholders it is probably because, as a new shareholder attending a meeting of Tisco for the first time, you were not aware of the highly informal relationship I have established with them for the past forty-three years. Most of the shareholders who attended the Tisco meeting this year do so every year and also the other Tata shareholders' meetings. They have become old friends to whom I can show familiarity without offence....

Because of the exceptional importance this year of the three subjects of the issue of bonus shares and convertible bonds, and the conversion of preference shares into bonds, I was anxious that shareholders should have full opportunity to discuss those subjects....

---

* Annual General Meetings of Tata Companies presided over by JRD were generally liked by shareholders who used to eagerly look forward to attending them. Rarely, if ever, did people complain. Here JRD answers a letter from one such shareholder who, probably being new, was not in tune with him at the meeting.

I welcome you as a new shareholder of the Company, and look forward to listening to you with patience and respect for your views at the annual meeting next year.

Yours sincerely,
J.R.D. Tata

TO DR. C. MALANI[*]

Bombay
26 September 1983

Dear Dr. Malani,

I refer to your letter of 25 August, 1983, in which you advise me to "refrain from unfair and unjustified negative comments on the profitability and dividend of TISCO" ... My remarks to the shareholders, whether in my printed Chairman's Statement, or at the Press conference I hold each year immediately after the Board meeting declaring the dividend, or finally at the Annual General Meeting, are for the sole, and in my view wholly necessary purpose, of ensuring that the shareholders are correctly informed and are not misled by interested speculators. I do not express personal views or expectations but give facts as they have occurred or as they are known unavoidably to occur, e.g. wage increases, interest charges, provision for depreciation.

As you say that there are other ways and means of achieving this objective, you may if you wish communicate them to me, but I shall certainly continue to make correct information available to *all* shareholders.

Yours sincerely,
J.R.D. Tata

---

[*] A shareholder of Tata Steel.

TO MRS. MARION HAWGOOD[*]

Bombay
1 September 1984

Dear Mrs. Hawgood,

...I would, normally, have written to you in a few days to felicitate you on your completing a full 38 years of continuous service with Tatas, of which 30 have been with Tata Steel. It is with deep regret that I must at the same time bid you farewell on your retirement.

During those 38 years, you have not only rendered admirable services to Tatas but, by your unstinted devotion to the Firm, your total honesty of mind and purpose, and your human qualities which earned you the respect and esteem of all your colleagues, you have been a model employee and officer whom any company would deem it a privilege to have in its organisation. You have been, in fact, a true member of the Tata family.

For virtually the whole of your association with Tatas, it has been my good fortune to have you assigned entirely to my secretariat and to me personally. The exemplary quality of your work, and the patience, understanding and uncomplaining acceptance of long and sometimes arduous hours of work you displayed throughout, were of immense help to me and have earned my lasting appreciation and gratitude....

With my warm and grateful wishes,

Yours ever sincerely,
J.R.D. Tata

---

[*]   JRD's secretary at Bombay House.

A thoughtful JRD.

JRD (above left and below) in his office at Bombay House; and (above right) at his intercom.

JRD with Dr. Homi Bhabha.

JRD at a reception at the
Indian Institute of Science.

Waving to crowds in Jamshedpur.

Photograph of JRD by Gautam Rajadhyaksha.

JRD standing before the statue of Jamsetji at Jamshedpur.

JRD in the Bombay House boardroom with the bust of Jamsetji Tata in the background.

JRD at Chowpatty Beach, Bombay.

Nostalgia

TO JOHN PETERSON*

Bombay
7 June 1935

Dear Peterson,

....You will perhaps be glad to know that our Air Mail business in the formation of which you took such an interest is doing quite well. The loads have gone up about 600 per cent since the start and there is no doubt that we have got the most profitable route in India. We have recouped our losses and have laid the foundation of a very valuable business for the future. In spite of your previous disclaimers I maintain that nothing would have been done if you had not bearded the lion in his den in 1929 and influenced Sir Dorab in favour of taking the risk!

I hope Mrs. Peterson and you are in the best of health....

With best wishes,

Yours sincerely,
Jeh R.D. Tata

---

* Ex-I.C.S. Officer who joined Tatas as Director-in-Charge, TISCO in Bombay. He retired and left India in 1931. JRD had started his professional career in Tatas under him.

TO JOHN PETERSON

Bombay
1 December 1949

My dear Peterson,

Many thanks for your letter of the 25th October just received, together with the two copies of your son's book which I look forward to reading. I shall be glad to send one copy to Jamshedpur, as suggested.

It is nice to hear from you again. You have been in my thoughts often lately, particularly since the death of Ardeshir Dalal. You are now the only remaining link with the past and I often think nostalgically of the old days when I got my training in business and administration from you, and then, while in the thick of all the exciting things that happened, I could enjoy the fun without carrying the burden and anxiety of responsibility. Today most of the fun has gone from work while the anxieties remain. Living in these revolutionary times may be an interesting and exciting experience, but it is also a strain sometimes, particularly in our business. Industrialists and managing agents are not particularly popular as a body these days. I do not know whether it is because of this or because I am getting old, but hopes and dreams seem to come harder, and a sense of duty and service rather than a zest for achievement and for new fields to conquer, provides the driving force to keep one going. Sometimes when the going gets a bit tough, I look at that fine photograph of yours on the wall of my room and think of the ease and sense of humour with which you faced and dealt with the problems of those days and I derive some comfort and strength from the memory....

I hope that you and Mrs. Peterson are both well....

Yours sincerely,
Jeh

TO MRS. E. ALTON*

Bombay
2 *February* 1979

Dear Mrs. Alton,

I was very sorry indeed to learn from your letter of 12 January, which arrived in my absence from India, that Ath Alton had passed away, and Mrs. Tata and I extend to you our sincere sympathy and condolences.

Your letter brought back happy memories of the days of early 1929 when I learned to fly, and just before that when aviation in Bombay consisted entirely of Ath Alton and his plane. I had been enthused about flying since my very young days, and his appearance on the Juhu mud flat was the precursor of the first chance I would have to learn to fly. He gave me my final dual test before my first solo.

Ath marked the very beginning of aviation in India which, as you say, has gone a long way since then. He and the Bombay Flying Club gave me my first chance, which led to the creation of an airline which, as you may know, I founded in 1932.... I gave up my flying licence three or four years ago, having passed the age of 70, but I still retain my love and enthusiasm for aviation....

With kind regards,

Yours sincerely,
J.R.D. Tata

---

*   Wife of Ath Alton, who was one of the first flying instructors of JRD.

TO TEMPLE TUTWILER II*

Bombay
2 February 1979

Dear Mr. Tutwiler,

Thank you so much for your letter of the 5th January which reached my office on the 20th while I was out of India. I was happy to know that you enjoyed your stay in India, particularly in Jamshedpur; and that you were well looked after there. As you must have found yourself, the Tutwiler legend lingers on at Jamshedpur, and old-timers like myself who knew him well will always retain the memory of the outstanding and warm-hearted man that he was, however hard he tried to hide his warmth at times behind a forbidding demeanour and lurid language which failed to fool anybody!

Your and your party's visit revived memories of those difficult but freer days, and everyone was, I know, most happy to greet you and appreciated your visit.

I was touched by your letter and by its warm sentiments. It seems that Alabamans, if such a word exists, are just as sentimental as we Indians!...

With all good wishes to you, Mrs. Tutwiler and to your son and Miss Chappell.

Yours very sincerely,
J.R.D. Tata

---

* Temple Tutwiler was general manager of Tata Steel in Jamshedpur in the 1920s. There were some stories in circulation in Jamshedpur regarding his lurid language.

TO A.D.C. PETERSON*

Bombay
6 February 1980

Dear Peterson,

I apologise for the delay in replying to your letter of the 17th December 1979. First of all, let me say that not only do I remember your father, but there is perhaps no single person in my long business career, now spanning some 55 years, for whom I have had greater regard, esteem and affection. When I joined the Firm in 1925, my father took me to your father, who was then Managing Director of The Tata Iron and Steel Company, and asked him to "look after this young man". To my astonishment, your father had a small desk put alongside his own for me, and from then on until his retirement from Tatas in 1931, he not only deprived himself of the privacy which any high executive should have, but took immense personal trouble in my training and development. I learned a lot from him and shall ever be grateful to him. I was immensely impressed by his outstanding ability and intellectual gifts, including his beautiful command of the English language which he wrote so well and so lucidly. Your letter brought back fond memories of him and of those early, and in many ways better, days....

With kind regards,

Yours sincerely,
J.R.D. Tata

---

*   John Peterson's son.

TO SIR FREDERICK TYMMS

Bombay
27 September 1982

Dear Frederick,

I was very happy indeed to receive your letter of August 23rd as I often thought of you and wondered where and how you were.

We all get old, my dear friend, but the disabilities of age do not matter much in late life so long as the mind remains unaffected, as obviously yours is. So is mine, in case you have any doubt about it! In fact, perhaps through taking regular exercise and working as long hours as ever, though not as efficiently, I am keeping physically well and mentally active. I still ski every winter and fly a plane when I can....

Now, however, I have a chance to indulge once again in the kind of flying I did fifty years ago and if everything goes well, I shall undertake on the 15th of October this year a re-enactment of my 1932 flight which I already repeated in 1962 when you and Milly did me the honour of being present on my arrival from Karachi. I would love to have you come again and am asking Maneck Dalal to enquire whether, in spite of your age and low opinion of your state of health, you would care and be able to respond to an invitation. I shall be flying the same Leopard Moth you saw me land in at Juhu in 1962. After keeping it unused for the next twenty years, the last two of which it spent suspended from the ceiling of the Customs Hall of the new terminal building at Santa Cruz, it was sent to the U.K. for complete reconditioning and fitted with a radio and ADF avionics. I went to England in July and flew it there. It all seemed so natural and I found no difficulty or feeling of strangeness, except that it had no brakes on one side and fierce braking on the other. I managed to avoid trouble on that account, but the local instructor, at the end of a test flight, veered off the runway and charged into a high standing wheat or some other crop field into which he disappeared for a while, fortunately with no harm to the plane or to himself! The plane has been brought back to Bombay, re-assembled, and I am flying it from time to time during monsoon breaks....

With warm and affectionate wishes,

Yours ever,
Jeh

P.S. I held back sending this letter to you in order to wait for Maneck Dalal's reply which I have now received, giving me the latest news on your health and informing me that you did not feel up to undertaking the trip. I quite understand this, and in fact would not have suggested it if I had realised you were over 90 years old. It seems impossible that it should be so long ago that you used to stride ramrod straight and with ringing steps through the corridors of Bombay House in 1942. Those indeed were better days, except of course for the loss of Nevill.

J.

FROM SIR WILLIAM HILDRED*

Surrey
14 July 1985

Dear JRD,

I was delighted to learn from Freddy Tymms who is in a place for elderly fit people a few miles from here that you were fighting fit; and this sparked off my desire to write to you....

As a treasury man I have served on many committees but never had a better one than IATA's Executive Committee long ago.

I was glad and proud when I persuaded you to join that Committee to its great benefit and which led to the AGM in New Delhi, an occasion no one will ever forget....

I hope you may find time, to let me know how things stand with you. A letter would give me great pleasure.

With kindest regards,

Yours sincerely,
Dick

---

* Former Director-General, International Air Transport Association (IATA) at whose invitation JRD had become a member of the Executive Committee of IATA for 17 years and became President of IATA for the year 1958-59. In this capacity he organised an IATA conference in New Delhi.

TO SIR WILLIAM HILDRED

Bombay
14 August 1985

Dear Dick,

Thank you so much for your most welcome letter of the 14th July, which brought back happy memories of the exciting days of my membership of IATA's Executive Committee. Those years were amongst the most interesting and rewarding ones of my career in aviation, not only because of the interest I found in the deliberations of our Committee and the fun of attending the annual meetings as for the opportunities they gave me to meet and develop a heart-warming friendship with so many fine men. ... I do not forget that it was you who gave me those opportunities when you invited me to join the Committee in those still early days of post-war IATA....

I continue to be active, as Group Chairman of Tatas, but although I have passed on most of my administrative responsibilities, I seem to remain as busy as ever....

I was impressed to learn from your letter that you were 92 and Freddy Tymms 96, for it gave me greater confidence in planning my own future!...

Thank you again for remembering me. It would be wonderful to meet you and Freddy again one day....

With kindest regards and warm wishes,

Yours very sincerely,
Jeh

CITY, NATION AND BEYOND

A Citizen's Concerns

★

Economic and Industrial Scenario

★

The Political Scene

★

Family Planning

★

Business Ethics

JRD was always concerned about the deteriorating condition of the civic life of Bombay (now Mumbai) where the Tata headquarters are located. He was continuously aware of the woes of the people of this metropolis which is the commercial capital of the country. He discussed various issues in person and through correspondence with various government officials on a regular basis, in order to motivate them to take action in respect of citizens' grievances.

He was concerned about the economic and industrial problems of the nation more as an Indian than as a businessman. From time to time he wrote letters to various Prime Ministers and other ministers, bureaucrats and intellectuals on issues of vital interest.

JRD was the first Indian of note to suggest a Presidential system of Government for India in the late 1960s. He was also one of the first to warn the country about the dangers of the population explosion. In 1970 he was actively involved in setting up the Family Planning Foundation of India, in association with the Ford Foundation. His idea was to launch a private initiative to supplement the government's effort in the field of population control. For this pioneering work he was awarded the U.N. Population Award in 1992.

Besides social issues, if there was one area in his professional life he was concerned about, it was business ethics. He once defined the house of Tata as a group of individually managed companies united by two factors. First, a feeling that they are part of a larger group which carries the name and prestige of Tatas and public recognition of honesty and reliability. The other is more metaphysical. There is an innate loyalty, a sharing of certain beliefs, a certain pride in being somewhat different from others.

JRD actively associated himself and backed every effort made by fellow industrialists to cleanse the business system and eliminate the black sheep in the industry.

A Citizen's Concerns

TO P.M. AGERWALA*

Bombay
4 April 1957

Dear Mr. Agerwala,

For some years now I have watched with a mixture of puzzlement, amusement and annoyance a sort of a ritual that seems to form part of the way of life of your Department and the Bombay Municipality jointly. This consists, at regular intervals, of the digging of a big hole in the road at the corner of Altamont and Anstey Roads near my house. After a few days of some mysterious work underground, the hole is roughly filled, leaving an irregular surface which, for some weeks, takes its toll of tyres round this corner. In due course a municipal roller turns up and re-establishes a decent surface. Your people evidently keep a close watch for this, for, as soon as the road is finally repaired, they pounce on the same spot and dig it up again and the process starts all over again!

As, apart from the inconvenience to the neighbourhood as well as danger to motor traffic, some considerable expense is being repeatedly incurred, I have been wondering why, if regular work has to be undertaken on underground telephone cables at or near that spot, a permanent junction box cannot be established there once and for all.

---

* General Manager, Bombay Telephones.

If it has to be underground, the hole might be kept open as a manhole, and covered with the usual cast-iron plate....

With best wishes,

Yours sincerely,
J.R.D. Tata

TO N. PILLAI*

Bombay
4 July 1959

My dear Pillai,

I find that according to the present practice, passports issued to Indians, including my own, show the christian or given name first and the surname or family name last.

To the best of my knowledge, in most other countries of the world the surname is written first in capital letters followed by the christian or given names. The Government authorities in those countries therefore assume that the same practice is followed in India and I have repeatedly met with difficulty in foreign countries as a result of the authorities there insisting that I was Mr. Jehangir and not Mr. Tata.

I know that in India the use of surnames is a comparatively recent development, yet all people who travel abroad on a passport have of necessity adopted the practice and it would, I suggest, be helpful and the right thing to do if the Government of India, when issuing passports, adopted the practice of showing the surname first in capital letters or at least give such prominence to the surname that no mistake can be made about the correct name of the bearer.

If you agree, you will, I hope, arrange for appropriate instructions to be issued in the proper quarters.

Please do not bother to reply to this letter.

Yours sincerely,
J.R.D. Tata

---

* Secretary-General, Ministry of External Affairs, Government of India.

TO A. GHOSH[*]

Bombay

27 April 1961

Dear Shri Ghosh,

It has been brought to my notice that the Monastery Wing of the Jesuit Church in the old Portuguese Fort, north of Bassein, incorporates a carved stone doorway which experts consider to be exceptionally beautiful and the only surviving example of pure Renaissance art in India and, as such, of great artistic and historical value. The door has on each side two small carved windows which are also of great artistic merit.

In the centre of the Bassein Fort, there is also a beautifully arcaded Senate building of the time and style of the Renaissance. This building and the Monastery Wing of the Jesuit Church with the above mentioned door and windows, are already partly in ruins and decaying rapidly and may be totally lost during the next monsoon, and it would be a great pity if these two monuments were allowed to crumble and disappear owing to neglect.

In case the matter has not been brought to your notice, I write to urge that protective work be undertaken at an early date and that temporary roofs be put up over these fine art monuments to protect them from the coming rains.

...If the Archaeological Department of the Government of India do not feel inclined to undertake this task, would Government permit Tatas to do so at their cost?

I would greatly appreciate an early reply.

Yours sincerely,

J.R.D. Tata

---

[*]   Director-General of Archaeology, Government of India.

TO S.E. SUKTHANKER*

Bombay
18 August 1965

My dear Sukthanker,

You will remember that on one or two occasions when we met at parties, we discussed the terrible problem of the squatters' shanty towns which disfigured so much of Bombay and its suburbs, created appalling social problems and endangered the health of the city. The news in the papers yesterday of an epidemic of typhoid is a reminder of the dangers of such unhygienic colonies, wallowing in dirty and stagnant water.

You will also remember that I had strongly recommended that quite apart from finding a solution to the problem of the existing colonies, it was, in my view, imperative to prevent its further growth by ensuring that no new squatters' colonies are allowed to start anywhere. This, I suggest, could easily be achieved by the Municipality and the Police jointly forming a few motorised patrols consisting of a jeep with a couple of policemen aboard, and a lorry with a few mazdoors. Such patrols could move about the various parts of the city every day and wherever they find anyone starting a hutment with stones, gunny sacking or scrap galvanised sheets, remove the materials on the spot. We have done that very successfully at Jamshedpur where the same problem would have arisen if we had allowed it. Once people know that they are not going to be allowed to put up any new structures, they will soon stop trying it. After all, no attempt has as yet been made to build such hutments, say, in the Military Area at Colaba, or on the Oval or in the Government House

---

* Municipal Commissioner, Bombay.

grounds and many other places where people know full well that some counter action would be resorted to within a matter of hours.

My purpose in writing to you today is to draw your attention to the situation that has started developing on the road leading from the big circle at the beginning of Hornby Vellard towards Mahalakshmi; within a few yards of the circle a dozen such hutments have appeared only in the last few days and are being extended every day. Already quite a number of families have started living there. Unless immediate action is taken, you will have another serious problem on your hands. I would therefore urge their immediate removal before the number of occupants gets too large and creates trouble.

Yours sincerely,
J.R.D. Tata

TO J.H. PATWARDHAN*

Bombay
20 December 1966

Dear Mr. Patwardhan,

I am writing to you in connection with a matter concerning the construction of buildings on Juhu Beach as I understand that Juhu now forms part of Greater Bombay and comes under your control....

The area abutting on Juhu Beach is recognised as a major resort attraction for Bombay as a whole and I submit that it is the responsibility of the authorities to ensure that building developments are in keeping with an appropriate master plan which will see to it that the beauty of this area is not spoilt and also that no risk is undertaken in connection with flying operations from the Juhu and Santa Cruz airports. The construction of multi-storeyed buildings at Juhu will be subject to many objections. It will create congestion, cause excessive demand on roads, electricity, water supply, fire-fighting services; result in slummy conditions; endanger the safety of flying operations and destroy the beauty and attractiveness of the area as a whole.

I strongly urge, therefore, that the Municipal authorities should give serious consideration to this problem and adopt a firm and permanent policy of protecting the area from indiscriminate multi-storeyed construction and to limit all such construction to a ground and upper floor at the most....

I am writing also to the Director General of Civil Aviation, New Delhi, in regard to the safety aspects of multi-storeyed construction at Juhu...

---

* Municipal Commissioner, Bombay.

Thanking you in advance for whatever you may be able to do in the matter in the interests of all concerned,

Yours sincerely,
J.R.D. Tata

TO DEPUTY COMMISSIONER OF POLICE*

Bombay
20 *August* 1968

Dear Sir,

Re: Traffic Lights and Traffic Control

I do not know whether it has been reported to you that the traffic lights controlling the flow of north-bound traffic from Churchgate Street into Marine Drive remain green for only about twelve seconds at a time. As in the evening most of the traffic from the Fort area towards North Bombay flows through that point, it is severely impeded by this maladjustment of the traffic lights and backs up all the way to the Eros and even beyond. I have myself had to wait for as many as five or six traffic light cycles to pass through the point. I urge that immediate action be taken to have the lights properly adjusted so as to speed up traffic.

While on the subject, may I say that whereas in all foreign cities I have known and driven in, traffic lights never seem to fail and their timing is also kept properly adjusted, in Bombay traffic lights seem to be out of action as often as they are operative, and many of them are poorly adjusted, sometimes in a dangerous way. It would seem that once installed, no action is taken to check on their proper timing and to adjust them according to traffic needs....

I do not know whether the installation, maintenance and adjustment of traffic lights are the responsibility of the Police Department or the Municipality. Whichever it is, I suggest that one officer be assigned the specific duty of constant checking

---

*   In charge of the Traffic Control Department, Bombay.

on the proper functioning of traffic lights in the city, their timing, and re-timing where necessary, in the interests of traffic flow and safety.

Finally, may I take this opportunity of urging that some action be taken to enforce motor driving laws and regulations in this city?...For instance, the ban on blowing horns is totally ignored and no action ever taken, even when horns are blown under the very noses of our traffic policemen. Half the cars in Bombay have defective lights, front and rear, and there is not an evening or night when one does not see cars driven without any lights at all past policemen who seem totally oblivious of such infringement. Parking regulations are totally ignored and hundreds of cars illegally parked in every conceivable non-parking area. Never does one see in Bombay, as one does in other cities abroad, traffic officers enforcing parking and driving regulations.

The worst offenders by far are taxi drivers who are a law unto themselves and break every traffic regulation in the book, impeding traffic by slow cruising in the middle of the road, parking at corners, weaving from one traffic lane to another, cutting across the path of other cars, and stopping to drop or pick up passengers, all without signalling either by hand or electric trafficators and with complete impunity....

I am sending a copy of this letter to the Municipal Commissioner and to the Traffic Advisory Committee.

Yours truly,
J.R.D. Tata

TO DR. NAGENDRA SINGH*

Bombay
13 December 1968

Dear Dr. Nagendra Singh,

   ...While I have you at the end of my pen, so to speak, may I draw your attention to the painting on the left at the entrance of Rashtrapati Bhavan, showing Dr. Rajendra Prasad being sworn in as first President of India. The scene as described on the brass plate at the bottom of the picture says, as far as I recollect, "Dr. Rajendra Prasad *Swearing at* Ceremony...", or words to that effect! I am sure that Dr. Rajendra Prasad never swore at anybody! I would suggest that this descriptive plate on the painting be corrected.

Yours sincerely,
J.R.D. Tata

---

*   Secretary to the President of India, New Delhi.

TO M.S. MUTHANNA[*]

Bombay
1 July 1974

Dear Mr. Muthanna,

This morning, when I tried to check the time by dialling 174, the automatic time recorder must have been out of order, for I was very politely answered by a girl whose accent was so unintelligible that I had to dial three times before I understood what she said, and then discovered that she was wrong by a full five minutes. Perhaps this was because, as sometimes happens on Air-India, the girl gives the time from her own wrist-watch which may not always be correct.

May I suggest that whenever the time recording machine is not working, an English-speaking girl with an intelligible accent should answer 174 and should check the time from an accurate clock?...

Yours sincerely,
J.R.D. Tata

---

[*] General Manager, Bombay Telephones.

TO M.M. KINI*

Bombay
27 March 1978

Dear Mr. Kini,

    As a businessman I well appreciate the desire of the Telephone Department to add to their revenues through the inclusion of advertisements in their telephone directory. I do feel, however, that some consideration should be given to the convenience of the public. The Bombay Telephone Directory already has 850 pages of subscriber numbers to which, in the latest directory, have been added 465 pages of advertisements. As a result, the directory has become most unwieldy and difficult to handle, especially by women. Its soft binding makes it all the more vulnerable to falling apart. I hope you will kindly consider deleting this feature from future directories or, if the inclusion of advertisements enables the cost of the directory to be reduced, you might consider dividing it into two volumes as is usually done in cities of the world with a very large number of telephone connections. Even in that event, I do feel that the advertisement pages should not exceed, say, 15% of the total number.

    With kind regards,

Yours sincerely,
J.R.D. Tata

---

*   General Manager, Bombay Telephones.

TO B.K. CHOUGULE*

Bombay
16 May 1979

Dear Shri Chougule,

I was very surprised and concerned about the news item, accompanied by a picture, on page 5 of today's issue of *The Times of India*, regarding the felling of trees on Linking Road, Santa Cruz.

Since coming to the office I have also received calls of distress about this destruction by a department of the Municipal Corporation of these beautiful full-grown trees which must have taken many decades to reach their present shape and size.

...I am addressing this letter to you, with three points in mind, for your consideration.

Firstly, if a decision has been taken to widen a certain road, it would be advisable not to leave to the Roads Department the action to be taken regarding the removal of trees that come in the way of road widening. We know from past experience that this department would view the matter exclusively from the angle of its set target of widening the road and from no other angle. If the decisions regarding the particular trees which actually come in the way of widening the road were to be left to a representative of the Tree Authority or to the head of your Parks and Gardens Department, at least there would be a hope of some of the trees being saved by a painstaking realignment of the road and only those which had unavoidably to be removed could be marked for removal.

---

*   Municipal Commissioner, Bombay.

Secondly, in view of the large-scale destruction of trees that has been going on for decades in urban environments, it will no longer satisfy public opinion for the Corporation to announce that for every tree cut down it will plant so many more saplings, because for those saplings to grow to any height and size will take so many years, that many, at least, of its citizens, including myself, may no longer be in this world to see the result of the tree-planting.

Thirdly, I feel it is very important, in view of the growing feeling of unhappiness among the citizens of Bombay at the developments in the city over the last decade, for the Municipal Corporation to do everything possible to enlist public support and sympathy for its actions....

With kind regards,

Yours sincerely,
J.R.D. Tata

TO P.S. PASRICHA[*]

Bombay
13 December 1979

Dear Mr. Pasricha,

As you are aware, at important traffic intersections involving a number of traffic lights, a device has been provided for the police to overpower the lights and to operate them manually when traffic is exceptionally heavy or when there is a traffic jam. Kemp's Corner is one such intersection. While the use of this facility can be understood when traffic conditions are such as to demand manual intervention in order to ensure the proper flow of traffic, I find that it has become a regular practice for the constable on duty in the morning at Kemp's Corner to fiddle with the manual control, as a result of which long lines of traffic build up beyond sight and the normal alternative flow is impeded rather than facilitated, and much inconvenience and delay are caused.

I would therefore urge that at Kemp's Corner or at any other intersection where the same problem may arise, only officers and not traffic constables should be permitted to use the manual control of the traffic lights except in emergencies....

Yours sincerely,
J.R.D. Tata

---

[*] Deputy Commissioner of Police (Traffic Control Branch), Bombay.

TO KISAN MEHTA*

Bombay
7 August 1981

Dear Mr. Mehta,

Re: Bombay Mainland Link Project

Thank you for your letter of July 13th, from the penultimate paragraph of which I am happy to note your acceptance of the inevitable continuous growth of Bombay. My colleagues and I on the Steering Group share your and your Committee's view that growth must be spread throughout the metropolitan region, much of which lies across the harbour East of the Thane Creek.

Whatever priorities are given in the long-term development of the BMR, the decongestion of the island city must obviously be in the forefront and this itself, in our view, can only be achieved by transferring as large a part as possible of the industrial and commercial activities at present centred in the city, and particularly in South Bombay.

At the same time it is inevitable, as has happened in virtually all other great maritime cities of the world, that the present Bombay will remain India's main commercial and financial capital, a major international business centre, a great maritime gateway of the country, and a tourist centre. If this is accepted, as I believe it must be, it is clear that whatever the exact nature, scope and speed of the development of the new areas of the Bombay Metropolitan Region, there will be an imperative need for quick communication at least during working hours between the old city and the new areas under development.

---

* President, Save Bombay Committee.

If economic and industrial activities are to be induced to move away from the old city, it is essential that easy and quick access is available between it and the new centres, most of which will be across the harbour. I have visited most of the megalopolises of the world in Europe, in North and South America, and in the Far East, and I find it difficult to agree with your Committee's claim that the world over road links aggravate problems of a city and add to congestion. That roads themselves are congested at peak hours is an indication of their inadequate size and the need for people to travel from one part of the city to another.

I agree, however, that the main links cannot and should not be only road links. Rail or other forms of rapid transit means are necessary, particularly during peak hours. In its consideration of the link project across the harbour the Steering Group has already included the possibility of a quick rail or other form of mechanised mass transport in addition to the road link, and it will be included in the terms of reference of the international consultants. Whether or not a rail link will be established as part of the bridge, causeway or tunnel complex which will ultimately be adopted for this project, there can be no question that in any case a road link is essential for buses, trucks, delivery vans, cars, scooters, and bicycles, though hopefully not hand or bullock carts!

One of the main reasons why in the past twenty or thirty years new business, industrial and other economic activities, and the labour population which has grown with them, concentrated so much of their location on the island city, has in fact been the lack of quick and convenient links across the harbour with the areas on the mainland, which Government hoped to see develop and absorb such growth. People and business would seem to prefer to suffer congestion than long and tedious travel....

While I agree that road links cannot be considered in isolation from other vital factors, they are an essential element of the process of decongestion and helping the transfer of activities to the outer areas of the metropolitan region. I do feel, therefore, that instead of opposing the proposed and badly needed link, which as I have said earlier may well be a road-cum-rail link, I believe that your Committee, and other citizens' organisations interested in the rehabilitation and future orderly and sound development of Bombay, should concentrate their efforts on urging the State and

Central Governments on means to facilitate the transfer of industries out of the city, a costly and difficult process which cannot be tackled or afforded on their own by the private sector companies concerned....

With best wishes,

Yours sincerely,
J.R.D. Tata

TO P.C. JAUHARI[*]

Bombay
19 November 1981

Dear Mr. Jauhari,

You may remember that earlier this year at about the time when you took up your present assignment, we had a conversation over the phone about some of the problems of Bombay Telephones' international service, and you said you would call on me after a while. I have not had the pleasure of meeting you yet, and I would be happy if you would come and have a cup of tea with me at around 4.30 or 5 p.m. on any day convenient to you next week.

In the meantime I would like to mention one small matter concerning a recent rule introduced in international bookings which I feel has aggravated an already unsatisfactory situation—the rule which, as far as I know, is unique in the world, that any international call from India must be to a particular person. As it is, the present procedure is an unnecessarily time-consuming one in which the calling party has to repeat to the operator, usually more than once, the number and name of the calling party and the foreign number, is given a ticket number, and later on repeat the same information when enquiring about his call for which he is issued another ticket number. The additional compulsory requirement of naming the foreign party usually results in a considerable waste of time because the local operators, with their poor knowledge of English, find great difficulty in correctly recording the name and pronunciation of foreign PPs, and therefore require the names to be spelt out in coded language.

---

[*]   General Manager, Bombay Telephones.

You can imagine the fun I had with the following call for which I needed only a station to station call, but for which the operator insisted on the PP's name:

Prof. Dr. Gritli von Mitterwallner in Munich!

I had, as a result, to dictate the words: gold, raja, India, table, lady, etc.

Irrespective of what else you can do to improve the situation, I do urge that you withdraw forthwith this requirement of naming the PP when the calling party does not need to have it recorded.

With kind regards,

Yours sincerely,
J.R.D. Tata

TO SAM PITRODA[*]

Bombay
28 March 1990

Dear Mr. Pitroda,

As a regular and frequent user of the ISD telephone facility, I have been increasingly concerned at the apparently growing shortage of circuits available to India for foreign telephone communications as a result of which any attempt to communicate by telephone with foreign countries, particularly countries of Europe, merely leads to being informed by a recorded female voice advising that "all the lines on this route are busy; please dial after some time" or words to that effect. This occurrence has become so frequent in the past year, not only during the busy hours of the day but recently even at night, and on Saturdays and Sundays, that the situation has become almost intolerable at times.

International telephone communications have become so much a part of modern business life that one wonders why of all countries of the world India should be about the only one in the world to be made or allowed to suffer from this serious deficiency. My purpose in troubling you with this letter is simply to ask if you would kindly let me know what action, if any and when, your Department or Government is likely to take to ensure that a sufficient number of satellite or cable channels are made available to India to enable it to enjoy the same freedom of use of international telephone facilities as seems to prevail in every country but ours....

With many thanks and kindest regards,

Yours sincerely,
J.R.D. Tata

---

[*] Worked as the Chief Technology Advisor to Prime Minister Rajiv Gandhi.

Economic and Industrial Scenario

TO S.N. CHIB*

Bombay
5 March 1953

Dear Mr. Chib,

Thanks for your D/O letter No.6-TT(16)/52 of the 25th January, which I found on my return to Bombay.

I am glad to note that the formalities imposed upon foreign visitors to our country have been relaxed to the extent that they are no longer required to report their movements within India to the police. They still have, however, to go through the annoying formality of calling at the police office of the port of entry and spending hours there answering questions and filling in forms to obtain a registration certificate or a residential permit.

No other democratic country known to me enforces such a procedure on foreign visitors and I hope that the Central Tourist Traffic Advisory Committee will strongly recommend to Government the abolition of this objectionable and, to my mind, quite unnecessary formality. The Government of India has two opportunities to check on the desirability or otherwise of letting in a foreigner: first when granting him or her a visa and second at the port of entry.

---

* Deputy Secretary, Ministry of Transport, Government of India.

If Government really want foreigners to visit, and spend money in, our country, the least they should do is abolish bureaucratic formalities which are an obvious source of annoyance and resentment amongst them. I am sure that Indians travelling abroad would feel very sore if, for instance, the French or the Swiss authorities imposed the same humiliating formalities as are inflicted on foreigners visiting India....

Yours sincerely,
J.R.D. Tata

TO SRI PRAKASA[*]

Bombay
11 July 1953

Dear Mr. Sri Prakasa,

Your kind and interesting letter of the 25th June reached me on the 30th....

I am glad that you liked what I said in my farewell speech to the shareholders of Air-India Limited which, in a way, was my swan song. I am glad too that it has touched some responsive chords....

I could not agree more with all that you say in your letter about the trends in our country. Three features of our economic life are particularly worrying to me and I am sure to many others.

The first is the folly, to use your own word, of so many members of our merchant and industrial community who have been largely responsible for the present widespread prejudice against private enterprise, and who are still unmindful of the grave they are busily digging for themselves.

The second is the trend towards socialism. No one with any social conscience can disagree with the ideals of socialism but world events of the last thirty-five years or so have made thinking people in most countries pause and take stock of its practical aspects and consequences. They have come to realise that the dream of a classless society organised on the basis of cooperative endeavour is one thing, but that the concomitant reality of the rule of an all-powerful bureaucracy under a ruthless dictatorship is another. In our country political immaturity and economic illiteracy aggravate the tendency of our people to avoid thinking through problems that face

---

[*] Governor of Tamil Nadu, Madras.

ECONOMIC AND INDUSTRIAL SCENARIO 311

them. Slogans and over-simplification provide easy and glib solutions requiring no mental strain. Thus socialism, to most of them, boils down merely to state ownership of all the means of production and it is rarely understood that full-scale socialism or state capitalism is inherently incompatible with democracy. The concentration of all economic power and patronage into the hands of a few at the top of a pyramid must ultimately lead to a similar concentration of political power and therefore to totalitarianism....

Few seem to realise that capitalism is the most democratic form of economic organisation as it is based on wide diffusion of economic power....

The third matter which worries me is the refusal of all those in authority squarely to face the problem of our increasing population which, unless tackled and solved, will inevitably nullify all our economic plans....

With kind regards and renewed thanks for your letter.

Yours very sincerely,
J.R.D. Tata

TO KHANDUBHAI DESAI[*]

Bombay
17 December 1954

Dear Shri Khandubhai,

Re. Rationalisation

Thank you very much for your letter of the 6th December commenting upon my remarks on the above subject at the annual meeting of the shareholders of the Tata Iron and Steel Company....

I quite appreciate that Government cannot allow the unemployment situation to be further aggravated but I am sure they realise that the lack of modernisation in equipment and methods can itself be the creator of unemployment by destroying the earning and competitive power of a concern or industry.

Unemployment in our country is of course due far more to our growing population coupled with the existing over-employment in agriculture than to temporary recession in any particular industry or to rationalisation. With total industrial employment (in factories) at not much more than three million, forming barely 3% of the total male employable population and much less than that if women are included, and with an annual addition of a million and a quarter employable males, it is clear that rationalisation or lack of it is a negligible factor in the overall problem of unemployment in the country.

There are to my mind only two ways of solving this problem: one is to find a means of arresting the growth of our population for the next twenty-five or fifty years

---

[*]   Minister for Labour, Government of India.

so that every advance in economic activity will bring about a real improvement in the living standards of the people, and the other is to stimulate to the maximum industrial employment both in large-scale industries and in small-scale and cottage industries....

Yours sincerely,
J.R.D. Tata

TO PANDIT JAWAHARLAL NEHRU

Bombay
31 December 1954

My dear Jawaharlal,

I have been thinking for a long time now of writing to invite your personal interest in the need for doing something to remedy the unfortunate impression which foreign visitors get of India the moment they set foot on our soil through the rigid and cumbersome formalities imposed upon them. The need for action in this direction has been brought home to me repeatedly both as Chairman of Air-India International and personally through bitter complaints made by visitors to our country of the highest standing....

The troubles of the intending visitor to India commence when he seeks to obtain a visa. To start with, I understand that the number of Embassies and Legations which are permitted to issue tourist visas is very limited. Even those which have this authority do not exercise it freely but go in for careful screening to determine whether the purpose of the proposed visit to India is for tourism. Businessmen who desire to combine tourism with business are not considered to be eligible for a tourist visa. There have been one or two cases to my knowledge where people of the highest standing in their own walks of life were asked to furnish letters of guarantee from Indians against their becoming dependent on the Indian revenues and in respect of their repatriation. I have myself had to give such guarantees for people whose income is considerably larger than mine!

Quite apart from the long delay and the plethora of forms which a non-tourist visitor has to fill in before he can get a visa to India, it is a rude shock to him, with his belief in the traditional hospitality of this country, to find on arriving in India, that unlike his experience in other countries, it was merely a foretaste of the red tape which is about to enmesh him. Having gone through the normal immigration and other formalities at the port of entry, the visitor finds that he has to put up with the indignity of having to spend hours at a police office registering himself and filling up forms in triplicate....

It is difficult to understand why in peace time, and ten years after the last war ended, a foreigner, who has been granted a visa and has passed through immigration and other formalities at the port or airport of entry and who therefore has presumably been accepted as fit to enter the country, should be subjected to such irksome and time-consuming formalities which were obviously necessitated by the wartime conditions of 1939. Foreign visitors have often privately remarked to me that rules of this nature may be expected in a police state but are unheard of in modern democratic countries of the West. It seems to me that to treat foreigners visiting this country on legitimate business—many of them consultants, representatives of manufacturers and others including those who come to India at the invitation of Indian authorities—as if they were suspects, or potential criminals not only creates a fund of ill-will for our country but is hardly consistent with Government's oft-expressed desire to encourage tourist traffic and foreign investment and to obtain for our country the benefits accruing from such traffic and investment. I therefore would earnestly urge that the wartime formalities and harassing procedures still in force should be abolished altogether or considerably relaxed....

I apologise for troubling you in this matter but I am convinced that only your personal interest in it will bring about results. May I suggest that you should ask for a complete picture to be placed before you of every formality which a visitor to India has to go through and every form he has to sign before, during and at the end of his visit, covering immigration, customs, currency, income-tax and health regulations. I think you will be appalled, as he is!

With my very best wishes for the New Year,

Yours very sincerely,
Jeh

TO D.P. KARMARKAR*

Bombay
8 January 1959

Dear Shri Karmarkar,

I am approaching you as Chairman of Air-India for your kind support to a request made by the Director General of Tourism, to the Director General of Health Services, for the discontinuance of an existing practice under which all passengers departing from India are required to undergo a health check at the point of embarkation. This requirement, which probably goes back a hundred years, was enforced by the British presumably for the protection of their own and other countries against diseases carried by travellers from India, a country then renowned for the frequency and variety of its epidemics. Times have changed since then, and this regulation, whatever useful purpose it may have served in the old days, serves none today except to act as an irritant to embarking passengers. It is also wholly out of tune with air travel.

Furthermore, most of the other countries for whose sole benefit we undergo this expense and trouble themselves do not want it or do not ask for it. In fact, most countries in Europe have now given up health checks even for incoming passengers. Apart from this, the check itself is necessarily somewhat perfunctory, if not farcical, as obviously a doctor processing in a hurry a long queue of embarking passengers, cannot do more than glance at each and feel his hand to see if he has any fever. If the intention were to ensure that any passenger leaving India was not suffering from anything serious with which he could contaminate the country of destination, the medical check would have to be a very thorough and time-consuming one....

---

*   Minister for Health, Government of India.

I am sure that by doing away with this purposeless and troublesome check-up at airports, Government would not only save themselves unnecessary expense, but also inconvenience to passengers. I hope that we may rely on your kind support. With best wishes for the New Year,

Yours sincerely,
J.R.D. Tata

TO DR. V.K.R.V. RAO[*]

Bombay
4 May 1961

My dear Rao,

I am sorry I have been so long in replying to your cyclostyled circular letter of February 28, enclosing a copy of the lecture you had delivered in November last to the Leeds University on "International Aid for Economic Development"...

I have read your lecture with the interest which it deserves and congratulate you on a very lucid and convincing exposé of the needs and possibilities of international aid to developing economies such as ours.

While it would naturally be wonderful for India and similarly placed countries if international aid could be organised on the scale and on the lines visualised by you, I fear your scheme does not take sufficient account of the grim realities of the international scene, particularly the cold war which will continue, I fear for many years to come, to influence the actions of most Governments. Be that as it may, we and other underdeveloped nations have much to be thankful for in regard to international aid granted, mainly by the U.S.A., since the war. We only have to look back to the pre-war days to realise the immensity of the revolution that has taken place in international thinking in this regard. One point on which I wholly agree with you is where you deplore the fact that so much of this aid has been linked to military effort and based on military alliances. I have myself always argued with American friends that this was, from the donor's own point of view, a silly thing to do and of

---

[*] Chairman, Board of Governors, Institute of Economic Growth, Delhi. An eminent economist, Dr. Rao was later Union Minister for several years.

course a dangerous one from the point of view of world peace. Most of the non-European recipients of military aid from the U.S., other than Japan, have been and are still economically and politically so weak and unstable that they would be worthless as allies in any serious international emergency let alone a world war. The only worthwhile ally is one who is economically and politically strong and stable. Thus economic aid is much more potent in strengthening an ally or a potential ally than military aid....

Incidentally, two minor errors have crept into your quotation. The author of *Soviet Economic Aid* is J.S. Berliner, and not J.G. Bertiser. While in your lecture the Berliner figures are shown as Soviet aid, Mr. Berliner in his book has made it clear that they represent aid from the entire Soviet Bloc, including Eastern European countries and China, and not from the Soviet Union alone....

Thanks again for sending me your most interesting paper. Hoping you are well,

Yours sincerely,
J.R.D. Tata

TO PROF. HUMAYUN KABIR*

Bombay
24 March 1964

Dear Professor Kabir,

I have read in the *New Republic*, a local Bihar paper, that in the course of a speech at the symposium held at the National Metallurgical Laboratory at Jamshedpur on March 10th, you strongly criticised concerns in the Private Sector for luring away technicians and scientists from the Public Sector. You are reported to have said also that such action was "not only anti-national but a mischievous design to starve the Public Sector of qualified manpower". From bitter personal experience, I treat with suspicion any report in the papers, but in case you did say something on the lines mentioned, I would like to bring two aspects of the question to your attention.

First, while it may be a fact that some staff from the Public Sector has transferred to the Private Sector, the reverse has happened on a much larger scale. In fact, both the Steel Company and TELCO at Jamshedpur, have lost a considerable number of men to Public Sector enterprises like the Heavy Engineering Corporation at Ranchi. In neither case, however, can it be fairly suggested that the purpose of "stealing" the other party's staff is deliberately to starve it and thus sabotage the opposite Sector. If you did really express that view at Jamshedpur, I do feel you have been wrongly informed or advised.

The second point I want to make is that it is a good thing and not a bad thing that staff should move from one sector to the other for it must result in increasing experience and a better understanding and appreciation by each of the problems and conditions existing in the other, to the mutual advantage of both.

---

* Minister for Petroleum & Chemicals, Government of India.

Furthermore, in a democracy people have the freedom to choose their employers and to better their prospects by switching jobs irrespective of whether such jobs are in the Public or the Private Sector. In fact, I do not think that a question of Public vs Private Sector should arise at all...

Hoping you are well and with best regards,

Yours sincerely,
J.R.D. Tata

TO AIR MARSHAL ASPY ENGINEER*

Bombay
3 April 1964

My dear Aspy,

Re: Photography at airports

The ban on taking photographs of "installations, buildings, air strips, or any landmark in the vicinity of the airport" is tantamount to allowing only photographs aimed towards the sky to be taken. Incidentally, I am surprised that the banned items do not include aircraft!

You can imagine the reaction of foreign transiting travellers who, having taken one or two exposures out of a multiple picture film, would be ordered to send their film to Delhi for vetting by Headquarters! I blush in advance at the language likely to be heard on such occasions!

All this, in practice, is equivalent to a total ban on taking photographs on the *ground* at *civil airports*, where there is nothing of any militarily secret significance. It is, to the best of my knowledge, unheard of anywhere else in the world in peace time outside communist and other totalitarian countries, and achieves nothing except to cause irritation and annoyance and to bring us into ridicule in the eyes of travellers from more enlightened countries. In fact, the only possible justification I can see for such a ban is that it prevents a photographic record being kept by anyone of the backwardness and inadequacy of our airport installations!

I do not believe that the present situation is insisted on by Air Headquarters, but in case it did initially originate there during the war and it is felt by some senior

---

* Chief of Air Staff, Delhi.

officers that even now the restrictions serve some useful purpose, I hope it will be realised that if they are right in this matter the military authorities of every other democratic country in the world must be wrong. This would be a bit hard to swallow!

My concern in the matter is from the point of view of tourism in which I am deeply interested both as Chairman of Air-India and as an Indian citizen alive to the need for earning the maximum foreign exchange, of which tourism is a major source. Photography has become a part of modern civilisation and is universally adopted and enjoyed by tourists all over the world, and anything which irritates tourists is a deterrent to tourism and therefore bad for our country. If the taking of photographs from the ground at civil airports was, in fact, a source of danger to our security, the adverse effects would have to be accepted in the greater national interest, but in this case no question of security can really arise and there is no excuse for continuing such purposeless and annoying restrictions.

I would be grateful if you would give this matter your personal attention, and let me have your views which, if you so wish, I will keep entirely to myself.

Yours sincerely,
Jeh

TO DR. V.K.R.V. RAO

Bombay
16 November 1964

My dear Rao,

Thanks for your letter of the 22nd October inviting me to participate in a roundtable discussion on Economic Growth and Social Justice to be held in Delhi on February 24th, 25th, and 26th.

I am afraid I shall be abroad at that time and it will therefore not be possible for me to be one of the leaders on Topic III: Industrial Growth.

The subject of social justice in the context of economic growth is no doubt an important one but it has been so prominently kept in the forefront since Independence, as evidenced by our labour laws and penal taxation on individuals amongst others, that I would have thought there would be no need for such a high-power international discussion on the subject as you propose. The innumerable restrictive laws and ordinances, endless and all-pervasive controls and an ever-proliferating bureaucracy to administer them have discouraged, harassed and hampered good and honest entrepreneurs, large and small, and driven most of the rest underground. In the name of social justice we have sought to regulate our economic activities to protect everyone against everyone else including himself! As a result, instead of prosperity combined with social justice, we have today acute shortages and inflation coupled with rampant tax evasion and black markets.

Probably no country in the world has so many intractable and urgent problems to deal with and has devoted so many words, written and spoken, to discussing them. As an old friend of yours, I hope you will not mind my saying that if instead of interminably discussing our problems in committees, councils, conferences and seminars, we devoted more of our time and energies on action, free from dogma, ideology, fads and prejudices, we would make better progress than we have made upto now and are likely to make in future. I sometimes feel that we have so hopelessly confused ourselves with words, slogans and clichés that we have lost sight of the simple truths, the simple objectives and the simple means of attaining them.

For instance, we hear incessantly nowadays from Government spokesmen and others that our goal is Socialism, a sentiment to which you no doubt heartily subscribe! Yet, quite obviously, it is the welfare of the people which is or should be our main goal, not an idealistic, ill-defined social philosophy which at best can only be a means of achieving the objective, not the objective itself....

After reading this letter, you may well feel that it was for the best that I couldn't come to your Conference, for the success of which I however send you my best wishes.

Yours sincerely,
J.R.D. Tata

TO JAYAPRAKASH NARAYAN*

Bombay
21 December 1964

My dear Shri Jayaprakash,

Many thanks for your letter of November 5th regarding your press statement on profiteering and on the need for business and industry to adopt a code of conduct. I could not be more in sympathy with the views you have expressed and I hope that the various associations you have addressed will follow up your suggestions for a code of conduct....

It is a tragic but real fact that, owing perhaps to some lacuna in our family and school educational processes, we have on the average woefully low ethical and civic standards in our country. We have not, it seems, been educated or indoctrinated to understand that profiteering, black-marketing and tax-evading are offences as criminal in nature and social implication as theft or violence. In fact, I have been told in all seriousness by a member of a certain well-known community that it is their duty, taught to them since childhood, to ensure the safety, health, and material prosperity of the family ahead of any other duty. Thus, he claimed, there was nothing wrong in hoarding food or gold and in evading taxes in the interest of one's family, even if it is to the detriment of the community as a whole...

There is one major aspect of this problem of corruption, black-marketing, tax evasion, etc. which is to my mind not adequately appreciated, and that is the fact that our Government have themselves, during the last seventeen years, created

---

* Jayaprakash Narayan (1902-1979); Sarvodaya leader, popularly known as Loknayak; social reformer; instrumental in forming the Janata Party; Bharat Ratna recipient.

conditions which foster and encourage such malpractices. On the one hand, widespread and continuing shortages combined with the all-pervading system of licences, permits and controls imposed on the country encourage hoarding and profiteering, while on the other, expropriatory taxation unheard of in other countries, including Russia, has created a climate in which to remain honest results in impoverishment for one's self and one's family, while tax evasion brings immense rewards....

While, therefore, the pleas you have made and the steps you have advocated are to be unhesitatingly supported, I hope you will give some thought to the other aspects of the problem I have outlined in this letter and use your immense prestige and influence in the country in bringing about a better understanding of the root causes of this frightful problem which is destroying the soul of the nation.

With warm regards,

Yours sincerely,
J.R.D. Tata

TO H.V.R. IENGAR[*]

Bombay
6 September 1968

Dear H.V.R.,

Thanks for your letter of the 2nd instant.

I note that the P.M. has expressed...great concern at the loss of momentum of our economy, at the feeling of despondency and frustration in the country, and is anxious to know what should be done to get it moving again. I am glad that you have been asked to prepare a paper.

In my view, much of the loss of momentum and frustration stems from the P.M.'s own Cabinet from whom it has now become virtually impossible to get any decision at all on any business or industrial matter. I am sure you know as well as I do how heartbreaking it is and how long it takes nowadays to get our Government's approval or decision on any matter....

If the P.M. is looking for ways and means of getting the economy moving again and reducing the "frustration and despondency" in the country, she couldn't do better than to start with getting the machinery of Government itself moving again. This would no doubt necessitate a number of steps.

First of all, the P.M. should herself initiate a sense of urgency in the various Ministries and in her own Cabinet on economic matters, which is clearly non-existent today. As P.M., she should order the Cabinet Secretariat to ensure that economic matters are accordingly given a high degree of priority at Cabinet meetings. Today the very opposite is the case.

---

[*]   Former Governor of the Reserve Bank of India; Chairman, the E.I.D. Parry Group, Madras.

Secondly, she should entrust economic portfolios to Ministers who understand something of economics, business and industry, and who devote the whole of their time to the matters with which they are entrusted....

Thirdly, let the Government remove all controls on price and distribution in industries in which there are no shortages of supply. There is no excuse, except political expediency, for maintaining controls, for instance, over the steel, cotton textile and cement industries. Let them also do away with licensing of new industries or of additional capacity in existing industries, except in cases where foreign collaboration or foreign exchange of some magnitude is involved. They should remove all other controls except in respect of foreign exchange.

While these appear to be, in form, largely negative steps, they are essential steps to remove obstacles and open bottlenecks. On the purely positive side, to the extent that the current recession, which was sparked by the stoppage or reduction in Government orders—e.g. railway wagons—from engineering industries, a programme of resuming orders would obviously be helpful, even if it involves some additional temporary deficit financing.

Let Government realise that with the marked change in terms of trade in the last year or two, as shown by the fact that as much as 60% of any rise in the national income now goes to the rural areas, there is going to be an explosion of demand for consumer goods from the rural sector. Let Government therefore free consumer goods from all shackles. While encouraging small industries because of their employment potential, they should free the organised sector of industry from the largely misconceived restrictions imposed on them allegedly for the protection of small-scale industries....

Finally, let the P.M. and her Cabinet make up their minds whether they want a socialist economy or a mixed economy to which up to now they have paid only lip service. A mixed economy can work satisfactorily only if both the Private and Public Sectors are allowed to function....

These are some ideas which I have no doubt you have thought of yourself and which you might use when advising the P.M.

Yours sincerely,
J.R.D. Tata

TO P.L. TANDON[*]

Bombay
29 January 1970

Dear Prakash,

Thank you very much for your letter of January 20.

I usually find it difficult to disagree with you, but I feel I must in this case! In my view, Indian private industry's poor, or in places downright bad, public image is due far more to the depredations and unethical practices of some of its members than to its deficiencies in the use of its resources.

While I share your views on the importance of efficiency and the full use of resources, I seem to go further than you in my interpretation of the social obligations of Industry. That is why I consider that even those of our companies like Telco, Tomco and Tata Chemicals, which are efficient producers and progressive employers, and which therefore fully meet your criteria, should in addition accept some responsibility towards the welfare of the communities in the midst of which they are established.

Yours sincerely,
Jeh

---

[*] Prakash Tandon (b.1911) – Chairman, Hindustan Lever (1961-1968); State Trading Corporation (1962-1968); Director, Hindustan Steel (1962-1971); Chairman, Punjab National Bank (1972-1975); Director General and subsequently President, Board of Governors, National Council of Applied Economic Research.

TO KESHUB MAHINDRA*

Bombay
13 July 1970

Dear Keshub,

Thanks for your letter of June 26, enclosing a copy of your inaugural address on the occasion of the 75th anniversary of the Indian Paper Makers' Association, which I have read not only with great interest but with much pleasure.

I naturally agree with almost every word you said and am glad that you too are now being forthright and outspoken in regard to the economic policies of Government, which have become steadily worse during the last two years....

We all know that, apart from confirmed Marxists and other members hostile to private enterprise and with totally closed minds on the subject, there are quite a few Members of Parliament and State Assemblies who, while believing in socialism, do not agree with the extreme Leftist economic policies of Government. Most of them, however, lack the necessary knowledge to understand the full implications of those policies, nor are they aware of the compatibility of capitalist enterprise with modern socialist aims. I have been feeling that some effort should be made to establish a dialogue with them in an attempt to bring them around to a more rational point of view than dogmatic socialist brainwashing has left them with....

With kind regards,

Yours sincerely,
Jeh

---

* Chairman, Mahindra & Mahindra Limited, Bombay.

TO JUSTICE ALWAR N. ALAGIRISWAMI*

Bombay
6 December 1971

Dear Mr. Alagiriswami,

I was very sorry to learn from my colleague, Mr. Moolgaokar, that you had been upset at the reference to the Monopolies Commission which I had made in the Chairman's Statement attached to the Directors' Annual Report to the shareholders of Tata Chemicals....

Throughout my career I have felt deeply about the appalling poverty of the vast majority of our people and the duty it imposes on every Indian fortunate enough to be free from that tragic burden and in a position to do something about it for others, to dedicate himself to the task of raising living standards by creating industries for the country and employment for its people. For over forty years I have worked hard and long to discharge that duty and at the same time to ensure that the Firm's actions, policies and practices always upheld the prestigious example and high ideals and traditions of Jamsetji Tata.

For most of my career, and until recently, I had reason to believe that Tatas' services, motives and ethical standards were widely recognised, and that in particular our Government knew and appreciated the fact that our companies, and my colleagues and I individually, were always unreservedly at their disposal in any manner in which we could be of service to them and to the country.

You will appreciate, therefore, the dismay with which realisation came to me in the last couple of years, that while Tatas' public reputation and prestige seemed to

---

* Chairman, Monopolies Commission.

remain as high as ever, they were being increasingly denied the freedom and opportunities to contribute to the full extent of their considerable potential to the economic development of the country. In an obsessive anxiety to prevent concentration of economic power, and influenced by the misdeeds of some elements in the Private Sector, Government used their formidable armoury of powers, controls and restrictions not only against the guilty ones who had misused their economic power to the public detriment, but also against those, including Tatas, with an irreproachable past record.

Prevention of the concentration of economic power in private hands became the sole objective, whether used for the common good or to the common detriment.... No distinction was drawn between one firm and another, and Tatas' century-old record of dedicated service, their vast potential for further service, and the fact that they provided perhaps the most outstanding and respected group of professional managers and administrators in the country, were totally ignored, and every effort of Tatas to accelerate industrial development, by undertaking new projects or expanding existing capacity, was treated with suspicion and either indefinitely delayed, as in the case of the Tata fertiliser and acrylic projects, or turned down from the start on the ground that it came from one of the larger houses.

We, along with others, were made to understand in effect that we were not wanted any more and had no further role to play except in a most difficult and restricted field and subject to highly onerous conditions.

Then came the M.R.T.P. Act and the Monopolies Commission. I personally welcomed the creation of the Monopolies Commission and felt, as stated in my Statement to the shareholders of Tata Chemicals, that "by setting forth sound and reasonable criteria or guidelines, a Monopolies Commission could, if anything, help to simplify and expedite existing procedures"...

I was, therefore, shocked to the point of disbelief, as well as deeply distressed, by the procedures adopted by the Commission towards us which compelled a large number of companies, having nothing whatever to do with Telco's application, to spend hundreds of hours on answering a host of questions, many of them on trivial matters, and subjected the whole of the Tata organisation to a form of investigation akin to a police or Enforcement Branch examination of a suspected criminal. This was pretty hard to bear for a Firm which, throughout its 100-year history, had earned universal respect for its integrity and spirit of service and had always been treated with consideration by Government....

I apologise for the length of this letter, but felt it necessary to explain in full the background to my decision to comment publicly on a matter which I considered of public importance....

With kind regards,

Yours sincerely,
J.R.D. Tata

TO DR. V.K.R.V. RAO

Bombay
20 August 1980

My dear V.K.R.V.,

I am sorry for the delay in replying to your letter of May 14, with which you enclosed the text of your Dr. Zakir Husain Memorial Lecture, which I have gone through with interest.

You have raised a pertinent question: With such a high savings ratio and a high rate of capital formation, why is it that our GNP growth rate is still stagnating at a mere 3.5% per annum?

I personally have little doubt that one of the causes lies in the industrial policies adopted all these years, in a misguided interpretation of socialism, by all our governments since Independence. It is disheartening to find that, even after seeing the dismal results obtained after twenty-five years of the same medicine, an expenditure of over a hundred thousand crores on development, and the strikingly different results obtained in other developing countries which have followed a different path, we still persist with barren and outmoded ideas and our obsessional fears of concentration of economic power in private hands after virtually all economic powers are in the hands of the politicians and the bureaucracy. For that state of affairs, my dear VKRV, notwithstanding my high regard for you, and others like yourself, I must blame those who, having imbibed Britain's impractical socialist concepts of fifty years ago, from which the British economy is still suffering today, insisted on building an authoritarian economy within a political democracy, and who, not surprisingly, fell in the process between two stools.

Is it not time that you and other economic thinkers, with the added background that you have of Government administration, should look to the events and developments of the past thirty years in Western Europe, Japan, Korea and other developing countries, and ponder on the reasons for the great contrast between their achievements and ours?...

With all good wishes,

Yours sincerely,
Jeh

TO R. VENKATARAMAN[*]

Bombay
17 September 1981

Dear Shri Venkataraman,

In recent months Government spokesmen have complained that the private sector has not adequately responded to the several concessions and policy relaxations extended to them by Government, and a hint was even given of a possible withdrawal of such concessions and other helpful measures....

I have been concerned at this charge against the private sector because I do feel it is not justified. While I agree that fresh industrial investment should be much greater than it is, the private sector, or at least the larger houses as represented by M.R.T.P. companies, deserves greater recognition of their efforts to expand existing ventures or to promote new ones....

You have also called upon the private sector to reduce their claims on Government's financial institutions and to rely more on self-generated funds and the private investment market. Here again, you will pardon me for feeling that you are not being entirely fair to the private sector so far as M.R.T.P. companies are concerned, in view of the realities and consequent constraints they face in the task of expanding existing industries and creating new ones. On the one hand they are mainly restricted by Government to the development of core industries which happen, unavoidably, to be the most capital-intensive industries. On the other hand, the Government of India as a matter of national policy has virtually monopolised all sources of finance other than retained earnings and the share market.

---

[*] Minister for Finance, Government of India and later President of India.

I am sure you will agree that it is impossible for capital expenditure on capital-intensive projects to be financed mainly, let alone wholly, out of equity. In fact Government and the financial institutions have always recognised that new projects or the expansion of existing ones have to be financed out of a combination of equity and term loans on the basis of an approved debt equity ratio. If resort to Government's financial institutions and banks—the only available source of rupee term loans—is to be denied or substantially restricted, to whom is the private sector to turn to for the debt element of the above combination?...

With kind regards,

Yours sincerely,
J.R.D. Tata

TO PROF. S. SITARAM[*]

Bombay
21 October 1981

Dear Professor Sitaram,

I am sorry for the long delay in replying to your letter of September 14, written after reading an extract from a convocation address I delivered to the Bombay University, in which you ask for my reaction to the views you have expressed....

That corruption is gnawing at the vitals of the nation is undoubted, and increasingly so. The basic causes, as I see them, lie largely in the economic policies adopted for the last thirty years by successive governments and Parliaments in the pursuit of a misconceived interpretation of socialism, which have placed enormous economic powers in the hands of a grossly swollen and underpaid bureaucracy....

The remuneration levels on which they cannot make both ends meet, combined with powers of approval of a host of licences and permits, has naturally led to an unprecedented growth of bribery and corruption. As, additionally, Government's policies all these years have resulted in serious shortages of all kinds of goods and services, which automatically lead to black marketing, is it surprising that a growing part of the total money in circulation today consists of black money, which itself increases the opportunities and rewards for corruption and illegal profit? Until there is a fundamental change in Government's approach to the management of the country's economy, which will discourage bribery and corruption instead of encouraging them

---

[*] Executive-Director, All India Manufacturers' Organisation, Bombay.

as it does today, I see little hope of any real and lasting improvement in the present dismal situation in which we are wallowing and the growing loss of character and moral values so prevalent today....

With best wishes,

Yours sincerely,
J.R.D. Tata

TO ASHWINI KUMAR[*]

Bombay
23 November 1981

Dear Mr. Kumar,

I am sorry that your letter of October 5, received in my office while I was abroad, got temporarily lost in the accumulation of arrears with which I had to deal on my return. I was glad to read from it that you had found of interest the Convocation Address I delivered to the Bombay University earlier this year, particularly in regard to my views and recommendations in connection with the population problem.

I am sorry to note, however, that you are one of those who are averse to the influx of foreign seed capital into India to accelerate the pace of our economic development on the ground that foreign capital brings foreign influence. As things are today, about 500 foreign companies have invested in the capital of Indian companies a total of around Rs. 2,000 crores. The majority of them have today a minority holding in the capital of the Indian companies, mostly below 40%. About one-third have a holding higher than the FERA 40% cut-off point. Nevertheless they have to operate under the strict conditions and regulations imposed on all FERA companies. In none of these is there, that I can see, any political or economic influence that could be considered harmful to India....

As it is, no country in the world has imposed such draconian restrictions on foreign investments as we have, which in fact is the reason why there is so little inducement for foreigners to invest in India. In fact, Indians like myself who travel a lot around the world and talk frankly to business friends abroad invariably meet

---

[*]   Member, Rajya Sabha from Patna.

with the view expressed that India is the least attractive country for any foreign investment because of the irritating and burdensome controls and delays imposed by our restrictive laws and regulations.

I personally hold the view that the basic infrastructural needs of our country such as those of rail and road transport, power, steel, fertilisers, irrigation, afforestation, roads, schools, hospitals, etc., and the general development of our rural areas, are so great that if they are to be met, there will just not be enough resources left to develop industries. That is why I am convinced that substantial foreign investments will be essential to the rapid economic growth we must achieve if we are to ensure adequate standards of living of our people within a reasonable time....

With kind regards,

.Yours sincerely,
J.R.D. Tata

TO P.N. HAKSAR[*]

Bombay
26 September 1984

My dear P.N. Haksar,

I am sorry for the long delay in writing to thank you for your charming letter of August 1, and for your good wishes on the occasion of my 80th birthday....

You have asked me whether it is not time for me to reflect creatively and constructively on the state of our country. I have done so, and for a long time. In fact, my published views over the past many years have shown the extent to which I have not only reflected on, but worried about, what has been happening to our country after Independence, but having resolutely refused to enter into politics, the only way I could try to be creative and constructive was necessarily in the industrial and business field.

I was a little puzzled by your own puzzlement at what you consider the failure of leading members of the Indian bourgeoisie to measure up to their counterparts in Europe and Japan. I don't know by what criteria you compared us, the Indian bourgeois, with our European and Japanese counterparts, and what you would expect from them, but if it is initiative and creativeness in their field of activity, I would imagine that, particularly in the light of the limitations to which Indians were subjected in our colonial days, men like Jamsetji Tata and his sons fully measured up to their counterparts elsewhere in the world, including America....

I think you will agree that in India, in the hundred years or so prior to Independence, such opportunities created by the industrial revolution were pretty well denied to

---

[*] P.N. Haksar (b.1913) – Held various diplomatic positions (1947-1967); Secretary, Prime Minister's Secretariat (1967-1971); Principal Secretary to Prime Minister (1972-1973); Deputy Chairman, Planning Commission, Govt. of India (1975-1977).

Indian merchants, financiers and other affluent members of the bourgeoisie. The advent of Independence brought a dramatic change in the situation which would normally have provided the same vital base, as in other countries, for great projects, ventures and adventures by Indians. An essential pre-requisite, however, would have been a freedom of choice, of investment and of action which it took no time at all for our politicians and our burgeoning bureaucracy to block or stifle in the process of concentrating all economic power in the Government. Instead of releasing energies and enterprise, the system of licences and all-pervasive controls imposed on the private sector in the country, combined with confiscatory personal taxation, not only discouraged and penalised honest free enterprise but encouraged, and brought success and wealth to, a new breed of bribers, tax evaders and black-marketeers. In a single generation, great fortunes, largely transferred abroad, were built at a time when personal incomes in excess of Rs. 1 lakh per year were being taxed at 98%.

The nationalisation, on expropriatory terms, of insurance and banks conveniently created a virtual state monopoly of investible and lendable funds, while fiscal policies, combined with the use made of the Companies Act, the Industries (Development & Regulations) Act, the Monopolies and Restrictive Trade Practices Act and innumerable other enactments, regulations and administrative decisions, effectively concentrated all real economic power in the hands of the politicians in power and the bureaucracy. Under such conditions, efforts at promoting and bringing to fruition large projects, however desirable, became a nightmarish and time-consuming one, or ended in outright rejection....

I am sorry to inflict this tirade on you, for which my excuse is that you, albeit innocently, provoked it yourself by your question! I began my 55-year career as an angry young man because I couldn't stomach the foreign domination of our country. I end it as an angry old man, certainly not because I didn't grow wealthy or powerful like the great industrial and philanthropic bourgeois of other countries; not even because Tatas were prevented from serving the country and enriching its economy to the full extent of their capacity and will; but because it simply breaks my heart to see the continuing miserable fate of the vast majority of our people, for much of which I blame the 35 years of ill-conceived economic policies of our Government.

With warm regards,

Yours sincerely,
Jeh

TO DR. MALCOLM ADISESHIA[*]

Bombay
February 21, 1985

Dear Malcolm,

Many thanks for sending me a copy of your John Matthai Memorial Lecture on the "Role of Private Corporate Sector in the Seventh Five Year Plan"...which I have now read with great interest.

After thirty-five years or so of hearing the role of the private sector in the economic development of the country devalued or denigrated by most members of official economic academia, it has warmed the cockles of this old heart to find in your lecture a refreshing and heartening appreciation of the importance of, and need for, the private sector in the country's development. I hope that some if not all of your recommendations find their way into government policies and actions, but I must confess I have become somewhat pessimistic, if not cynical, in my old age!

I personally believe that the main need of both the private and public sectors is to be freed from most of the controls which have delayed and obstructed its growth and freedom of decision and action all these years and that the Government and the bureaucracy will at long last stop referring to the examples of what Japan, Hongkong, Taiwan, Singapore and Germany in the years following World War II, and America today, have achieved, as having no relevance to India.

I do believe that Rajiv intends to free industrial management from many of the shackles which have restricted its growth, but it will need tremendous determination

---

[*] Noted educationist and economist who was Deputy Director General of UNESCO; founded the Madras Institute of Development Studies; Vice-Chancellor of Madras University (1975-1978); Member of Parliament (1978-1984).

on his part to break down the fierce resistance that I am sure the bureaucracy will put up to the loss of any of their powers and privileges. Still, having foolishly remained an optimistic despite all evidence to the contrary all these years, I shall continue to look for the rainbow in the sky, if not any pot of gold at the end of it, and your lecture encourages me to continue in that foolishness!

With best wishes,

Yours sincerely,
J.R.D. Tata

TO P.N. HAKSAR

My dear P.N.,

On my return from a fairly prolonged absence from India, I saw your letter of September 20, which I read with interest, and apologise for the delay in replying to you.

I agree that there is, perhaps, lacking today a commonly shared vision of the kind you have in mind amongst business people in our country. The main reason, in my view (which I do not expect you to share!), is that during the last 30 years or so virtually the whole of the Indian industrial community has been mainly engaged in its struggle to overcome or minimise the constraints, limitations and unending delays imposed on it by the Government's economic policies.

Those in Government who sat on the other side of what unfortunately proved to be a high fence instead of a channel for dialogue and consultation have begun to realise only in the last two or three years the extent to which the type of socialism they sought to bring about crippled the economy's progress and made it the high cost and un-competitive one it is today. During that long and frustrating period, meetings were regularly held every year between Government and Chambers of Commerce and similar bodies but invariably led to a monotonous repetition of the same pleas and the same negative replies. The only exception, I can remember, is the brief era of T.T. Krishnamachari who, though an impossible man to deal with, received full credit for cutting through the fog and red tape and getting things done, in fact often ordering them to be done the MITI way as in the case of Tata Steel's expansion and Telco's conversion from rail road rolling stocks to trucks.

The clouds have lifted and the winds of change are still blowing. The clogged channels of purposeful communication have been cleared and new ones created. For the first time since Independence have I become young again with reviving hopes and confidence in the country's future! There is still resistance to be overcome and clear thinking to be done, but there is a clear surge of hope visible amongst those who now feel they can do something to help speed the country forward....

With warm regards,

Yours sincerely,
Jeh

TO RAJIV GANDHI

Bombay
24 November 1986

Dear Rajiv,

I am most grateful to you for giving me some time last week to speak to you on some matters of public interest which have caused me concern and on which I felt my views were worth bringing to your attention.

Amongst the subjects I brought up was the very unhappy reaction in industry circles to the decision of the Government of India to blacklist all companies which have outstanding Central excise claims in excess of Rs. 5 crores each.

There could be no question, I said, of condoning attempts by dishonest business houses or companies to evade excise dues or to secure long delays in their payment by exploiting the lengthy process of court action unfortunately prevailing in India. The Government would be fully justified in taking stern action in such cases. But, surely, it has adequate means of differentiating between such reprehensible resorts to courts and genuine cases in which responsible and honest companies, having failed to convince the tax authorities of the correctness of their objections to the latter's tax assessment, have sought relief from a High Court and abide by its ruling.

For the Government to treat all writ petitions to courts alike as dishonestly motivated and, in virtual defiance of a court order, to resort to the blacklist device to put pressure on assessee companies by depriving them of rightful claims in entirely different and unrelated matters such as in regard to share issues or industrial or import licences, is, I submit, unfair and unworthy of a democratic government and, according to some eminent lawyers, also unconstitutional and possibly in contempt of court.

Apart from its legal and moral aspects, the blacklist scheme will, if continued, cause great harm to the economy by eroding the confidence and support which the Government's new approach to industrial and fiscal policies had evolved in the business world in the past two years, and delaying important projects undertaken to increase production and employment, reduce costs and accelerate economic growth. It is also grossly unfair to thousands of shareholders who are denied their legitimate dues, such as bonus shares or new capital issues requiring Government approval....

I would, therefore, earnestly recommend that the blacklist scheme, or at least its penalising feature, be withdrawn or suitably modified.

With warm regards,

Yours sincerely,
J.R.D. Tata

The Political Scene

FROM C. RAJAGOPALACHARI[*]

15 May 1961

Dear Mr. Tata,

I write to you in your capacity of the chief of the Tata Industrial concerns and to seek your attention and assistance to the Swatantra Party....

You are aware how the Swatantra Party is suffering from many handicaps in the material aspects associated with party organisation and how on the other hand the ruling party enjoys enormous advantages in the same respect besides commanding the opportunities and scope available to a party in power....

I therefore request that even if you help the ruling party with funds for its political and electioneering activities, it would also be just and proper for you to help a party that seeks to build an efficient check on its errors. While you may exercise your judgment and help the party in power, I respectfully urge that in the interest of good government and parliamentary democracy, the national interests in general as well as the particular interests of those engaged in the industrial and commercial progress of the country justify adequate assistance being also given to efforts calculated to build up and bring an opposition party into effective operation. Indeed I claim your

---

*   C. Rajagopalachari (1878-1972); Governor-General of India, 1948-1950; Chief Minister, Madras; Home Minister in Nehru's cabinet; Governor of West Bengal; one of the founders of the Swatantra Party; Bharat Ratna recipient, 1954.

generous help in proportion to the greater difficulties and handicaps such a movement suffers from, by reason of the Congress party being in office and in the enjoyment of power incidental in a "Welfare State".

Your decision will serve to give a lead to all others who are like you engaged in the patriotic work of promoting the prosperity of the country. No democracy can govern well in the absence of a strong opposition and I trust you will deeply consider the situation and come to our assistance....

Yours sincerely,
C. Rajagopalachari

TO PANDIT JAWAHARLAL NEHRU

Bombay
16 August 1961

My dear Jawaharlal,

Because of my life-long friendship, I feel I must write to you about a decision we have recently taken in Tatas which I do not want to reach you from outside sources.

As you know, ever since Independence Tatas have supported the Congress in all successive elections. Actually, our support to the Congress goes much further back than that, in fact to the days of Motilalji. Even though we may not feel happy about some of the policies of Congress and Government, particularly in the economic field, we intend to continue that support. We have been conscious of the fact that under your leadership the Congress has been and continues to be dedicated to the creation and maintenance of a democratic welfare state and to the welfare and betterment of its people; also that they have provided the stable and vigorous administration and the sense of unity without which the country might have sunk, and could still drift into chaos or some form of dictatorship as has happened to so many other under-developed countries in the world since the war.

At the same time, we have been perturbed by the total absence of any responsible and organised democratic opposition which we feel is an equally indispensable element of any permanent democratic organisation of society. As a result, we have been increasingly worried about the future, however distant, when the strong and outstanding leadership which you have provided may no longer be there. I am one of those who believes that the single party regime under which we have lived since Independence has been up to now a good thing for the country as it has provided the stability and the means of concentrating the national energies and resources on orderly development, which would have been impossible without a strong and continuing administration.

But even you will agree, I think, that if continued indefinitely this situation contains the seeds of trouble and risk in the future. However good any political party and its administration may be, it is inevitable that people will ultimately want a change and that some elements in the political life of the country will come to disagree with some of the Congress Party's policies and seek the means of trying out their own ideas.

In the absence of any other democratic non-extremist party, the only alternatives today available to such people are either to go into the political wilderness where their services will be lost to the country or to turn to the Communist Party or some other equally undesirable extremist party....

In these circumstances and after many many hours of thought and discussion amongst ourselves, we have come to the conclusion that it is indispensable in the national interest that an effort should be made to displace the Communist Party as the second largest party in Parliament. The only party which, it seems to us, offers any possibility of developing ultimately into a responsible and democratic opposition, is the Swatantra Party which, after all, consists mainly of people who have been fostered by the Congress, have spent many years within the Congress and, while conservative in outlook, are not reactionary or communal or extreme rightists.

I personally doubt that the Swatantra Party can achieve anything substantial in the coming elections, but we believe there is a good chance that they could make sufficient headway to ensure that they replace the Communist Party as leaders of the opposition, however small in relation to the Congress their Members in Parliament may be. If they were totally to fail, they would have no alternative but to disappear altogether from the scene leaving the field, however limited, to extremist parties. I will not pretend that we are not to some extent influenced by the fact that the economic views or policies of the Swatantra Party are nearer to those of the business and industrial community than those of any other party in the country, not excluding the Congress, but I hope you will believe me when I say in all sincerity that this is only a secondary consideration. We have therefore come to the conclusion that in addition to continued support to the election funds of the Congress we should also contribute, although on a lower scale, to the funds of the Swatantra Party....

Hoping you are well and with affectionate regards,

Yours very sincerely,
Jeh

FROM PANDIT JAWAHARLAL NEHRU

New Delhi
18 August 1961

My dear Jeh,

I have your letter of the 16th August. Thank you for your long letter explaining to me what you have decided and the reasons for it....

During the fairly long life that I have devoted to political and like matters, I have tried to follow, with more or less success, certain paths aiming at certain objectives. I suppose that, as was natural, I have learnt from experience and occasionally varied the policies I pursued somewhat. But basically I think I have been fairly consistent. This is so because I firmly believed in them. Naturally if I do so and think that those policies are beneficial for the people of India, I must continue to follow them.

You are, of course, completely free to help in any way you like the Swatantra Party. But I do not think that your hope that the Swatantra Party will emerge as a strong Opposition is justified. I think that it will be disappointed at the turn of the next General Elections. It seems to me that it has no roots in the thinking of either the masses of India or the greater part of the intelligentsia...

All good wishes to you.

Ever yours,
Jawaharlal Nehru

TO CHESTER BOWLES[*]

Bombay
15 December 1971

Dear Mr. Bowles,

I am sure you have been following developments in the Indian sub-continent with concern. We all know that war is always an unmitigated tragedy, for, apart from the loss of life, the human suffering, and the waste of resources, war embitters relations between countries and their people for a generation or more. This is perhaps unavoidable, but what surely can, and should, be avoided is the poisoning of relations with other countries not directly involved in the conflict, and particularly those with whom close bonds of friendship and cooperation have been long established.

I am writing to you today[**] because this is happening in a most grievous way at this moment between India and the U.S.A., to whom India has been tied not only by bonds of friendship and a common political philosophy, but also for us by bonds of gratitude for all the help America gave in abundance since we achieved Independence. We remember also her support to our cause during our struggle for freedom.

Although there have, at times, been differences between our two countries on world political issues and events, and, on occasion, one side may have been irked by the stand taken by the other, the relationship has throughout been one of mutual friendship and respect. Indians have recognised the incredible material achievements of the U.S. and the sacrifices it made in World War II and in helping the world to recover from it. Americans have, I think, recognised the immensity of India's problems,

---

*   Chester Bowles (1901-1986); Ambassador to India, 1951-1953 and 1963-1969.
**   This letter was sent to around thirty prominent Americans.

the privations of its people, and the great efforts made to alleviate them. Americans have also appreciated the fact that India is the world's largest democracy, with a Constitution inspired by your own and devoted to the same basic ideals.

Innumerable Indians like myself, who are uncompromisingly dedicated to the cause of freedom and democracy, and unalterably opposed to tyranny and totalitarianism, are conscious that without the U.S.A. freedom might have vanished from much of the earth.

You will therefore appreciate the dismay with which we have viewed the tremendous harm done to the relations between our two countries by the attitude officially adopted by the U.S. Government in the last few days in regard to the Indo-Pakistan war.

That, amidst the confusion of events, claims and counter-claims on both sides as to the nature and timing of military activities, the U.S. Government should prefer to believe that the war started because of military intervention by Indian troops on the borders of East Pakistan, rather than by the sudden massive air raids on Indian aerodromes made by the Pakistan Air Force in a pre-emptive attempt to destroy the Indian Air Force, is something that we would disagree with, but could understand.

That the U.S. Government should find itself more in sympathy with Pakistan in its bloody repression of over half its people, which drove ten million of them to flee from their homes and seek refuge in India, than with India which gave them that refuge and now fights in support of their liberation from one of the most brutal tyrannies ever inflicted on a people, is much harder to understand and accept.

But the U.S. Government goes much further. Ignoring the horrors perpetrated in East Bengal over a period of eight months which preceded and caused the war, it publicly accuses India of aggression, and shares with Communist China alone, the honour of openly attacking us in the U.N. and bringing pressure to bear on us by a naval presence in our waters. This, predictably, has had an appalling impact on an embattled people in the middle of a war which, to them, is a wholly just one and in which their very survival is at stake.

The universal reaction in Government, in Parliament, in the Press, and in every organised group in the country, has been swift, unanimous and disastrous for Indo-American relations. From being a friend and supporter, America has, in the eyes of all, become an enemy, second only to Pakistan and on a par with Communist China. As a result, the cause of Indo-American friendship and cooperation is today in jeopardy, to the grievous detriment of both countries. In fact, in the present context, the loss to America seems to me the greater of the two, for in return it can only obtain, or retain, the friendship and support of a discredited and soon to be defeated military dictatorship, while it will have driven India even further towards an understanding with another country.

It is not for me to criticise the American Government's judgement of events and the conclusions they may reach on such judgement, however erroneous they may seem to me, but, because there is so much about America and its people which I love and admire, I feel entitled to utter to you and other American friends a cry of anguish and sorrow. There is already, I believe, a considerable body of public opinion in the United States which does not approve of the stand taken by the American Government. Perhaps nowhere in the world is public opinion more potent in influencing governmental policies than in the United States.

If you believe, as I do, that Indo-American understanding and friendship is a great force for good in this strife-torn world which should not be wantonly cast away; if you feel, as I do, that the alienation of the goodwill and affection of over five hundred million people is an appalling price to pay for whatever debating points the U.S. Government may want to score against India by openly taking sides in this war, I plead with you to use your influence to help prevent the further deterioration of a situation which is already fraught with the gravest consequences and may soon pass the point of no return. This, I suggest, would require at least that the U.S. Government remain neutral as other countries have done in supporting a call for a ceasefire.

The war may probably end quite soon, and there is little time, if any is left at all, to influence its aftermath so far as relations between our two countries are concerned. If therefore you decide, as I hope you will, to take some action in the matter, I would urge that it be without delay.

With kind regards, and warm wishes for Christmas and the New Year.

Yours sincerely,
J.R.D. Tata

FROM CHESTER BOWLES

29 December 1971

Dear Mr. Tata,

I was very glad to get your thoughtful and concerned letter. Believe me, I share your concern as do millions of other Americans.

The recent actions of the Nixon Administration have, in my opinion, been impossible to defend.

The one positive development was the extraordinary TV and newspaper coverage which the American press gave to the war in both East and West Pakistan. Even the best newspapermen seem to prefer to write about crises than positive developments or long-range plans, and ours is no exception. However, the American press and TV commentators who descended on India en masse to report a war began in the process of reporting that war to discover India and to get some inkling of the remarkable economic and political developments that have been taking place there. As a result the U.S. press has generally changed sharply in its orientation and I am hopeful that now more newspapermen will go there to write in greater depth.

Another thing I think you would be pleased about here is the number of Indians, many of whom had become American citizens, who came forward to work their hearts out to help India in its present difficulties. A large percentage of the Indian student population here in the U.S. (about 8,000) have been forming committees, rallies, local TV and radio discussions, etc. It was good for them, good for India too and also good for the United States.

I have strongly opposed President Nixon in previous campaigns and I shall certainly oppose him in the one coming next fall. I believe a change in our government is essential not only for our own benefit but for that of the world....

I appreciate your writing me and hope you will do so again. If there is anything we can do on this end to help we shall try to do it.

My warmest regards,

Sincerely,
Chester Bowles

FROM MRS. INDIRA GANDHI

New Delhi
10 February 1972

Dear Jeh,

Thank you for sending me your letter to some Americans and their replies. They make interesting reading. I have also received many such letters.

We certainly want lasting friendship with the United States. Unfortunately the policy postures and doctrines which America adopts in pursuit of what it supposes to be its global interests create conflicts where none need exist. During my recent visit, I urged President Nixon to undertake a new appraisal of the realities of our subcontinent, especially when it is evident that America's assessment of Pakistan had been proved wrong....It is astonishing that with all their resources and concern abroad, the American administration should be so lacking in accurate information.

Those in America who have a deeper understanding of historical forces and the currents of foreign policy have been unhappy with their government's stance. So are most of the better educated Americans. But the average person persists in a stereotyped view of India's ingratitude despite U.S. aid.

....You have done well in drawing pointed attention to Pakistan's aggression. Business leaders and academic men are often more effective in creating an awareness of the facts than diplomatic or publicity machinery.

With regards,

Yours sincerely,
Indira Gandhi

TO MRS. INDIRA GANDHI

Bombay
25 February 1972

Dear Indira,

    Many thanks for your letter No. 41-PMH/72 of February 10, in reply to mine of February 2 enclosing a copy of a letter I had written to a number of influential friends in the U.S.A., and copies of some of the replies I had received. I have since received further replies, with which I need not trouble you.

    By and large, most of the replies to my letter have been favourable to India, and some of them downright critical of the U.S. Government. A few of them, however, while friendly and genuinely regretful of the breach in Indo-American relations, have shown concern firstly at the fact that we were the first to cross the Pakistan frontier in force, and secondly that we did so in support of a secessional rebellion. Some were evidently victims of the view spread by Washington that India intended, after completing their Eastern campaign, to attack in force in the West with a view to destroying Pakistan.

    With affectionate regards,

Yours very sincerely,
Jeh

TO SIR FREDERICK TYMMS

Bombay
25 July 1975

Dear Frederick,

Thelly and I were both delighted and touched at receiving your letter of the 11th July. Let us henceforth accept without argument the admiration that we have for each other!

I was surprised to learn that you claim the age of 86. Are you sure you have not absent-mindedly added a decade? If not, I am happy and congratulate you on being so fit and strong at such an age that you are able to stand the hard work of hours of digging in your garden....

We are indeed living in a difficult period of our so called modern civilisation. It is extraordinary that similar economic problems and troubles seem to hit, at the same time, advanced countries like Britain, U.S.A. and Australia, and under-developed ones like India, and even more so that the political forms of democracy, invented and developed over the centuries in Britain, should be found wanting in England itself as well as, more understandably, in India. So far as the present political situation* in India is concerned, all I can say is that I hope it is only a temporary phenomenon....

I am beginning to wonder, looking around the world, whether the pure British liberal concept of democracy remains relevant to the modern world, even in very politically mature nations like Britain, for such democracy requires a high degree of self-discipline and civic sense....Perhaps, western civilisation, as we have understood it, has begun the process of decadence resulting from its own affluence, which in

---

* The State of Emergency declared by Prime Minister Indira Gandhi.

the past has overwhelmed previous advanced and affluent civilisations. Today, one sees a frightening absence of character, morality and compassion except in times of war or catastrophes. Possibly, there is a need now for some measure of authoritarian enforcement of discipline for democracy to survive if we are to avoid it being replaced by pure totalitarianism.

Sorry for all this boring philosophising....

Yours ever,
Jeh

TO GENERAL K.M. CARIAPPA[*]

Bombay
16 August 1977

My dear General,

Many thanks for your letter of July 30. You must be living in an inaccessible Shangri-la, as your letter took nine days to reach me!

I am afraid I have no clear impression as yet in respect of "the order of things in our country today". I am not sure that even our Government has either! It is time things began to move hopefully in the right direction.

Unfortunately, we don't seem able to differentiate between what is important and urgent and what is not; so today one hears as much about prohibition, urine therapy and Coca-Cola, as about rural development and finding employment for our thirty million unemployed! I have always felt, and in fact made a speech on the subject some time ago, that considering that India's problems are mainly economic and not political, it was a grave mistake for us to have adopted the British Parliamentary system under which our Ministers have necessarily to be Members of Parliament and therefore politicians. One form or another of presidential rule, such as the French have, would have been far more suited to our character. It is an interesting fact that under the French Constitution any M.P. who becomes a Minister has to resign from Parliament! ...

With all good wishes,

Yours sincerely,
J.R.D. Tata

---

[*] General K.M. Cariappa (1900-1993); First Indian Commander-in-Chief of the Indian army, 1943-1953; was later made Field Marshal.

TO JAYAPRAKASH NARAYAN

Bombay
17 November 1978

Dear Jayaprakashji,

Many thanks for your letter of November 11th in answer to mine of October 23rd. ....I shall certainly do my best to be present at the function,* but as you will see from my letter to him I do not want to be one of the speakers at the public meeting to be held that day under the presidentship of Rashtrapati Reddy....

As you probably know, I have, unlike other industrialists and businessmen, always believed that the industrial and business community should keep aloof from politics and never seek to influence politicians except publicly and openly in regard to economic matters. Although Tatas have, perhaps, suffered from such a policy, I have never regretted it and feel that if it had been universally followed the business life of this country would have been cleaner than it has been, and the business community would not be faced with so much hostility and mistrust as it is today....

With kindest regards,

Yours sincerely,
J.R.D. Tata

---

* Rajaji Centenary Committee Celebrations in Delhi.

TO CHAUDHARY CHARAN SINGH[*]

Bombay
26 November 1979

My dear Chaudhary Saheb,

I am very grateful to you for the time you spared to meet me when I paid a courtesy call on you in Delhi on the 23rd instant....

I was most interested in the view you expressed that the parliamentary system we had adopted could not meet India's political requirements and that we should change over to a presidential system. You were surprised when I told you that I had advocated such a change as far back as 1968, in a speech I delivered in Bombay, and again last month when I addressed the Maharashtra Chamber of Commerce....

I was sorry to find you somewhat despondent at the dismal situation prevailing in many parts of the country today. This I hope is just a temporary consequence of the break-up of the previous Government and pre-election fever. As I mentioned to you, I am more worried about the breakdown of law and order, particularly in Bihar, which is gradually bringing the coal and power situation on which the economy of the country so largely depends to a catastrophic crisis.

I was dismayed at learning from you that the Central Government could not intervene as law and order was constitutionally a State matter. In that case, it would seem that if the Constitution were ever to be amended in order to introduce the presidential type of Government advocated by you, it should certainly include a provision enabling the Central Government to intervene when a breakdown in law

---

[*] Chaudhary Charan Singh (1902-1987); Prime Minister of India 1979-1980.

and order occurs which, as in this case, is serious enough to jeopardise the political or economic life of the country as a whole.

With renewed thanks and kindest regards,

Yours sincerely,
J.R.D. Tata

Family Planning

TO PANDIT JAWAHARLAL NEHRU

Bombay
13 January 1953

My dear Jawaharlal,

I would like to thank you very much for giving Mody, Shroff and me an hour of your valuable time during our recent visit to Delhi.

We greatly appreciated the opportunity of unburdening ourselves to you of some of our worries and doubts on various trends and developments in the country. In such a short time we could touch only sketchily upon a few issues....

One subject, which there was no time for me to mention and about which I am increasingly perturbed, is the population problem of our country. I am convinced that with the possible exception of a drastic increase in the minimum legal age of marriage which presents insuperable political and sociological difficulties, none of the remedies discussed upto now, including mechanical and chemical contraceptives, continence, the rhythm method, etc., can produce results on a big enough scale and quickly enough to make any appreciable difference.

There is, however, one avenue which offers tremendous possibilities, namely, the development of a simple, safe, effective and cheap anti-fertility hormone or drug to be taken orally. Research in this direction has been carried on abroad for some time....

I do not, of course, suggest that the successful control of the growth of our population will automatically solve all our economic and social problems. But it would go a long way indeed and would at least ensure that any increase in our agricultural and industrial output and in our social services would result in a corresponding rise in our standard of living instead of being largely absorbed by the increase in the population. It is only necessary to imagine how much easier Government's and your personal task would be today if our population had remained at the 300 million or so at which it stood some thirty years ago, or if you could count on its remaining substantially at the present level for the next fifty years, instead of doubling itself during this period, as it will, if the present rate of growth is maintained.

I earnestly advocate this line of research, my dear Jawaharlal, in all humility but at the same time in the sincere belief that it will, if successful, remove the most serious threat not only to the success of our present and future five-year plans but to our very survival as a modern, democratic nation.

With affectionate regards,

Yours very sincerely,
Jeh

FROM PANDIT JAWAHARLAL NEHRU

New Delhi
21 January 1953

My dear Jehangir,

Thank you for your letter of the 13th January. I was glad to have a talk with you, Mody, Shroff and Pan.* I gave the gist of our talks to Deshmukh and T.T. Krishnamachari. It may be possible for us to have a joint talk in future. I agree with you that it is necessary that we should be clear about these matters and understand each other, even though we might not agree on all matters. Such talks help in promoting some measure of understanding. We have to deal with enormous problems and we can only succeed in solving them by a large measure of cooperation. Perhaps the old orthodox method of approach is not wholly suited to a completely changed environment and different conditions. My own mind is constantly trying to explore and I want all the help I can.

You have raised the question of population. Broadly speaking, I agree with you that we should tackle this problem. But we have to proceed with care so as not to raise a hornet's nest around us which might make progress more difficult. Also progress in this direction cannot be fast enough in the near future to react on our economic problems. However, we have to think of the distant future also.

I agree with you that it is not possible for obvious reasons to raise the minimum legal age of marriage much more. In fact, in some Western countries the marriage age is becoming less and less. I do not mean the legal marriage age, but in practice.

---

* P.A. Narielwala joined TOMCO as a junior assistant in 1928. He became Director of Tata Industries in 1949; Director-in-Charge of Tata Chemicals and TOMCO in 1957; later became Chairman of some Tata companies.

I also agree that the various mechanical and chemical contraceptives as well as the rhythm method can hardly be expected to produce any large-scale results within an appreciable time. The new method to which you have referred does offer possibilities of quicker and more widespread results. We should keep in touch with it....

Ever yours,
Jawaharlal Nehru

TO PANDIT JAWAHARLAL NEHRU

Bombay
3 January 1959

My dear Jawaharlal,

For years I have been very much interested in the population problem as I have felt that it presented the most serious obstacle in our country to rapid economic and social progress. None of the means of birth control proposed or seriously propagated up to now seem likely to make a real impact on the problem because of the ignorance, poverty and dispersal of the greater part of our population. It would seem, therefore, that the most effective solution lies in the development and widespread distribution of a harmless fertility-inhibiting drug or hormone in the form of a pill or tablet which could be made available at little or no cost to the women of India.

There is evidence that such a pill is today well beyond the stage of wishful thinking or distant scientific feasibility. Research already done on the subject in various parts of the world, including India, would seem to show that concentrated effort backed by adequate and by no means prohibitive funds, could achieve complete success within a very few years.

Unfortunately, the stimulus for pushing ahead with this type of research is lacking in the very countries best equipped to achieve success, because they have themselves no population problem of their own and also because of the strong inhibiting influence of the Catholic Church. India, because of its resources, scientific status and background of religious and philosophical tolerance, can take effective action herself or support action elsewhere.

While by all means continuing with all other studies and activities undertaken upto now in the field of family planning, India should, I earnestly suggest, sponsor and subsidise large-scale research in the development of "anti-fertilisers" both in India and abroad. It should, in particular, investigate the work done in the field of oral contraception by Dr. George Pincus, Research Director of the Worcester Foundation for Experimental Biology, Shrewsbury, Massachusetts, U.S.A....

Wherever Government find that useful and promising work has been done in the "anti-fertiliser" field, they might offer facilities and funds on an adequate scale for further research and development, preferably in India itself but, if necessary, in the countries concerned. Once it became known that the Government of India were prepared to support research in the development of "anti-fertilisers", I believe that some of the world's great research institutions and drug manufacturers would be encouraged to undertake crash programmes of research and manufacture....

I sincerely believe that the solution of this appalling problem is within our grasp provided we go after it with all the means at our disposal and do not hesitate to spend a few crores in the process. As important as any other factor, however, is your personal lead in the matter. Whether you like it or not, my dear Jawaharlal, the fact remains that the only sure way of ensuring action in any direction in our country today is for the P.M. to show personal interest in the subject and to say that he wants results!

With warm wishes for the New Year,

Yours very sincerely,
Jeh

P.S. Please do not take the trouble to answer this letter. I would like to feel that I could occasionally write to you on matters of public interest without burdening you with the need to write back...

Jeh

TO DR. SUSHILA NAYAR[*]

Bombay
8 July 1964

Dear Dr. Nayar,

Re: Population Control Oral Contraceptives

I am most grateful to you for the trouble you have taken in writing your letter of the 6th June...

I am glad to learn that you agree that oral contraceptives would provide the most effective means of population control. I note, however, that you are doubtful about the present anti-fertility pills on the market, such as Searle's ENOVID, because they have to be taken for twenty consecutive days every month and also because it is not certain that they may not cause thrombo-phlebitis. It is true that the need to take them regularly for twenty days a month is a drawback but as their efficacy in preventing conception is virtually hundred percent, I do not think that this would materially affect the ultimate results. While a small proportion of women, who want to control the size of their families, may occasionally forget to take their daily pill and a small proportion of those may as a result conceive, the treatment would be effective in the vast majority of cases....

I note that your Ministry is conducting experiments with these pills and that careful schemes of observation and research have been worked out for this purpose. Such research will presumably take years to complete and considering that it has already been done abroad and that today some four million women are allowed to

---

[*] Minister for Health, Govt. of India (1962-1967); Chairman, Indian Red Cross Society (1964-1967); freedom fighter and a Gandhian social worker.

take these pills regularly in the U.S.A. and Europe, it is clear that the Health Ministries and the Medical Professions of Europe and America do not consider that they involve a hazard to health and that further research is required. Need we be more Royalist than the King? The stakes for us are so high and the need for action so desperately urgent that, with the greatest respect, I feel it would be wrong to hesitate to take advantage of a powerful available instrument in the solution of the gravest and most urgent problem facing the country....

I am, of course, all in favour of continued research to improve and refine the pills, cheapen their cost, and simplify their use, but this work could go on even while oral contraceptives now available were being widely distributed in the country.

I do hope, dear Dr. Nayar, that faced with the threat of a real catastrophe, unless a solution to the problem of the population explosion is found within the next ten years, the Health Ministry will, in consultation with the Planning Commission and the Finance Ministry, undertake a crash programme of birth control on an immeasurably larger scale than at present, and on all fronts, i.e. sterilisation, the pill, education, rhythm method, etc....

With kindest regards,

Yours sincerely,
J.R.D. Tata

TO DR. KARAN SINGH[*]

Bombay
30 October 1974

My dear Karan,

I recently read with interest your inaugural address at the National Symposium on Labour and Population Policies held in Delhi on the 15th April. I also followed as much as appeared in the Press here of your speech at Bucharest...

I must confess I was unhappy at reading the view you have expressed that family limitation is not regarded by Government as a national requirement, and also that over-population is not a main cause of India's poverty, but poverty is the main cause of the massive increase in our population.

While it may be true that in many countries population growth has declined as living standards have risen, this has not been so everywhere, and in any case such decline has invariably occurred with considerable delay. The tremendous rise in living standards of most European countries, including Britain, France and Scandinavia in the past century, was not accompanied by a significant decline in their population. The same applies to Brazil and other South American countries where the birth rate remains high notwithstanding a high rate of economic growth.

On the other hand, Japan achieved her spectacular reduction in birth rate at a time between 1947 and 1957, when her income per capita was only $250 per annum and she was still described in World Bank literature as an under-developed country. Her success was due to an intensive programme of birth control and to nothing else. In fact, it is noteworthy that Japan's birth rate has begun to rise again *since* she achieved her present very high standard of living.

For us, therefore, to rely on rising standards of living for stemming the rising flood of our population would be, I submit, a piece of wishful thinking of the most dangerous kind which could only lead us to disaster before the end of the century. For, while there is no certainty that rising economic standards will automatically reduce our population growth, our rate of economic growth per capita has been, and is still so low that even if the theory proves right in our case, it might well take us fifty years or more for rising standards of living to produce a significant impact on our population problem.... While it may be true that excessive population is not the only cause of our continuing poverty, the fact surely cannot be questioned that it is a principal cause of it.

Furthermore, there are two important factors which do not seem to have been taken into account in coming to the view you have expressed. One is that there is still, by world standards, considerable scope for a further decline in our mortality rate. As population growth represents the difference between births and deaths, a reduction in both would leave us with much the same growth rate. The second is that, according to Government's own assessment, some 40% of our population live today below the poverty line. Any gains in our GNP will, for many years, rightly be directed largely at bringing up this grossly under-privileged section of our population, comprising about 225 million people. Even were this to be achieved, after a couple of decades, by which time we shall have added a further 300 million or so to our population, the average standard of living of the nation as a whole will still be amongst the lowest in the world and, therefore, hardly adequate by itself to make an impact on our birth rate....

In the light of all these considerations, facts and figures, I respectfully submit that, if the views you have expressed represent the present thinking of Government in dealing with the population problem, and provide an indication of their current and future programme and policies, there is indeed cause for concern and alarm. At the very least such views, expressed by so important a spokesman of Government as its Minister of Health and Family Planning, cannot but seriously dampen the enthusiasm of people ready to work and to devote themselves wholeheartedly to the cause of family planning, who will now have reason to feel that if in Government's own view the population problem is nothing to worry about, why should they?

I was also somewhat surprised at the concern you expressed at the percentage of women workers in our country showing a steady decline, which you considered "unfortunate, retrograde and against Government's declared policy as it would necessarily have a negative impact on the family planning movement". Throughout the world, the large-scale employment of women has come after a high degree of male employment...has been achieved. It therefore seems inevitable that there should be a decline in the employment of women in our country....

Furthermore, I cannot see how decreasing job employment amongst women can, as you suggest, have a negative impact on the family planning movement. If they are employed, which would mostly be in the same place or town as their husbands, their opportunities to create babies would remain unimpaired, whereas if they are unemployed, a large proportion of them are likely to live in their villages where the opportunities for becoming legitimately pregnant would obviously be lessened!

Having voiced disagreement with your views on some points, may I say how glad I was at your statement at the above-mentioned symposium, that family planning must be transformed from a programme of the Government of India into a genuine mass movement, because it recognised that we shall have to rely in future increasingly on private individual and collective initiative and effort....

I greatly welcome also the favourable views you expressed of the potential impact of family planning efforts in the industrial sector and your assurance of support for such efforts by both employers and unions....

With warm regards,

Yours sincerely,
Jeh

TO RAJIV GANDHI

Bombay
18 April 1988

Dear Rajivji,

I was delighted to learn from newspaper reports that, while addressing the full meeting of the Planning Commission on 8th April, you had asked for policy papers on seven strategic areas, including family planning. I congratulate you for your timely attention to these important questions....

I have maintained that, contrary to the belief of many people that our population problem is an age-old one, influenced by age-old beliefs, and therefore not amenable, except over centuries, to modern scientific solutions, it actually is a very recent one, mainly caused by dramatic improvements in health standards and resulting decline in the death rate, particularly in infant mortality. Fortunately, since the launching of a comprehensive programme to eliminate disease and promote family welfare, we have acquired the knowledge, the skills and the tools to overcome the obstacles. What we need is a strong and sustained commitment by Central and State Governments backed by people's convinced participation.

Factors like age at marriage and female literacy have been rightly identified as being perhaps the most relevant obstacles to bringing down the birth rate which, unfortunately, has been near-static for a decade....

With warm regards,

Yours very sincerely,
J.R.D. Tata

TO PROF. ASHISH BOSE[*]

Bombay
12 October 1992

Dear Ashish,

On my return from New York after receiving the U.N. Population Award I send you herewith the verbatim text of my acceptance speech, as you are one of the very few, if any, whose views on our population problem I greatly respect and agree with.

It was a brief 18-minute speech in which I had to limit my views or recommendations to the minimum, and yet felt it important to try to explain how the countries of Europe, all of which, just like India at the beginning of this century, accepted the burden of large families, had been literally transformed in one or two generations into universally accepting the small family norm, in contrast to the continued situation in India.

...I sought to explain it by the almost universal existence amongst their people of child-bearing age of two basic beliefs of which the bulk of our people are ignorant or have remained impervious. Hence the need, if my assumption is reasonably correct, to make it, in our continued pursuit of population stabilisation, a priority in our country to try to convince parents, or newly married young people, on the one hand, of the imperative necessity of a good education for their children or, at least, training in employment-oriented skills, and, on the other, of the latter's crippling high cost which they just could not afford to bear except by adopting the small family norm. This was, admittedly, an oversimplistic approach to our problem, but I believe a correct one in comparison.

---

[*] Prof. Ashish Bose was Head, Population Research Centre, Institute of Economic Growth, New Delhi.

I would appreciate your reaction to the above and also to the view expressed to me by Home Minister S.B. Chavan, whom I met in London, namely, "India is doomed unless we succeed in controlling our population growth which we can achieve only by making family planning compulsory!"

With all good wishes,

Yours sincerely,
J.R.D. Tata

Business Ethics

TO GIANNI BERTOLI

Bombay
23 May 1949

My dear Gianni,

    Many thanks for your letter of the 19th and for the cherries which you either forgot to send or which have disappeared into someone else's stomach between Geneva and Bombay, for they have not arrived here yet. I doubt if they ever will!

    I am not sure how the cherries and, before them, the chocolates and cheese parcels were sent by you, but if they were sent by the crew, I would prefer if in future none were sent at all except as fully documented freight, in which case, of course, you must charge my account with the cost. Apart from the possibility of illegality of carrying undocumented parcels on board, I don't want to take advantage of Air-India International which, as you know, is a semi-Government concern. In any case, the *kursiwalla* must give the right example! Many thanks nevertheless for the cherries which Thelly and I have tasted in our imagination at least!

    With love to you both,

Yours
Jeh

TO C.C. DESAI[*]

Bombay
6 December 1951

My dear Desai,

Thanks for your D.O.No.Works.FY.4(165) of the 26th November regarding Shri J.J. Ghandy's proposed appointment to the Board of Directors of the Sindri Fertiliser Factory.

Although the general policy of our firm in such matters is that our Directors do not accept directorships in other companies not connected directly or indirectly with Tatas, this naturally does not apply to Government concerns, work for which we would treat as a matter of national service and not of business. So far as I am concerned, therefore, I have no objection whatever to Ghandy joining the Board of Sindri and the matter is entirely one for his own decision. I hope, however, that it will not involve him in much extra work as he is already overloaded....

Yours sincerely,
J.R.D. Tata

---

[*] Secretary, Ministry of Works, Production & Supply, Government of India.

TO COUNT NICOLO CARANDINI[*]

Bombay
15 July 1960

My dear Nicolo,

Re: Offer of Free Living and Travel Facilities to Alitalia Passengers

I am writing to you with some hesitation as I am not sure how far you are personally committed to the above scheme. At the same time, I feel we are sufficiently good friends for me to tell you frankly what I feel in the matter and to seek your assistance and cooperation.

As you are aware, ENIT[**] has, since the beginning of May this year, offered to all Indian travellers to Italy eight days' free holiday in Italy including living and travelling expenses within that country provided they travel to and from Italy by Alitalia. Air-India and all the other airline members of IATA operating to and from India have naturally taken a serious view of this scheme which gives a decisive and most unfair competitive advantage to Alitalia. All the operators feel that the scheme is clearly in violation of the spirit, if not the letter, of its resolutions, as it is tantamount to a rebate in the price of a return air ticket between India and Italy....

It is clear that such an offer provides a powerful incentive to travel by Alitalia rather than by any other carrier and in fact our experience since May and that of other airlines operating between Europe and India has shown that the offer has diverted a tremendous amount of traffic to Alitalia. There can thus be no question

---

*   President, Alitalia, Rome.
** Ente Nazionale Italiano per il Turismo – Italian State Tourist Board.

whatever as to the competitive advantage which the scheme has given to Alitalia to the detriment of all other carriers.

What throws a particularly unabashed light on the matter is that in Bombay, which is the main centre in the context of this scheme, the ENIT Office is located in the Alitalia Office, and the Alitalia Manager and the ENIT Manager are one and the same person!....

We protested to the local Alitalia management on the 20th June,...but have not been favoured with a reply so far. We understand, however, that Alitalia takes the stand that they have nothing to do with this offer which is made by the Government of Italy and that they are therefore helpless in the matter. I suppose that from a purely legal point of view, it is possible in this case to differentiate between the Government of Italy and Alitalia and thus to claim that the competitive advantage derived by Alitalia is purely fortuitous, that Alitalia are not responsible for it and that the scheme does not infringe IATA traffic regulations. But I cannot believe that you would personally approve of such a legalistic stand.

Apart from the grave injury done to Air-India and other airlines whose traffic is being stolen by this grossly unfair and unethical means, I wonder if Alitalia have fully appreciated the possible repercussions within IATA and of the ultimate consequences to themselves. We in Air-India are proud of IATA and proud to be a member of it....

Is there any reason why the scheme adopted by the Italian Government, and to which Alitalia is presumably a willing party, should not be adopted by most other Governments owning airlines? This would obviously be the end of IATA and leave all international airlines floundering in chaos.

I, therefore, appeal to you as a man of honour who, I am sure, would not knowingly approve of unethical practices, to throw your weight on the side of fair and clean business and to do whatever is required to obtain the immediate withdrawal of this scheme which, may I add, has aroused condemnation from all quarters including, of course, our Government and has already done much damage to the good name and reputation of Alitalia.

I shall be most grateful for an early reply to this letter, indicating your own views in the matter and the action you propose to take.

With kind regards,

Yours sincerely,
J.R.D. Tata

TO KHAN BAHADUR C.B. TARAPORVALA*

Bombay
13 July 1962

My dear Taraporvala,

I am sorry to learn that you will not be attending our next Board meeting, as I was anxious to discuss a personal matter concerning your own membership of the Board with you. I am therefore reluctantly compelled to do so by letter.

You are one of the Directors retiring from the Telco Board by rotation at the next Annual General Meeting which is to be held on the 28th of August. I need hardly tell you how much we have appreciated your presence on the Board and your cooperation which you have unstintingly extended to us throughout the last twelve years...

The point at issue concerns your membership of the Board of Hindustan Motors Limited which you joined last year. To be quite frank with you, as I am sure you would want me to be, we are unhappy about your being a Director of Hindustan Motors as well as of Telco. Although Tatas' relations with the Birlas are excellent, there is no doubt that there is a very considerable competitive element between the two firms in regard to their and our operations in the auto industry.

I of course have confidence in your judgment and impartiality and know that you would not consciously divulge any information about our activities which we would not want them to know. Still, there is always a chance of an inadvertent disclosure and from your own point of view, I feel that you are bound to be placed at some time or another in an uncomfortably ambiguous position. Furthermore, I think you

---

* TELCO Director, representing the Nizam of Hyderabad.

will agree, now that you know the conflict of interest that arises, that it would not be right in principle for you to hold both Directorships. We would naturally be anxious that you should remain on the Board of Telco and that we should continue to have the benefit of your support, advice and counsel, but we hope that, if it is your wish to remain one of us, you would find it possible to divest yourself of your directorship in Hindustan Motors. If, on the other hand, there were some special reasons which made you feel you could not give up your Directorship of the latter, and in consequence preferred to resign from our Board, we would be extremely sorry, but we would reluctantly have to accept your decision....

I sincerely hope you will treat this letter in the genuine spirit of friendship and understanding with which I have written it.

I would be obliged if you would kindly let me know before the Board Meeting on the 24th, at which resolutions about the retiring Directors will have to be passed, what your decision is.

With kind regards,

Yours sincerely,
J.R.D. Tata

TO RAMKRISHNA BAJAJ[*]

Bombay
1 April 1966

Dear Shri Bajaj,

Thank you for your letter of the 26th March.

I am sorry I must once again ask you to kindly excuse me from attending the meeting which you propose to hold towards the end of April to discuss the "Draft Principles of Fair Business Practices", a copy of which you forwarded to me earlier....

As I have said in another letter of today's date to you and the President of the Indian Merchants' Chamber, what to me is of primary importance is not so much the pronouncement of principles, of which one hears all too much these days, but how these can be translated into action. My own belief is that this will largely depend upon the extent to which the business community is willing to apply moral and social pressure upon all those who claim to subscribe to these principles, to ensure they adhere to them and apply punitive sanctions against offenders. Unless the individual organisations, which form the business community, are willing to be forthright in this way and openly ostracise those who are known to offend its principles, and do so regardless of the personal consequences that might follow, I see no practical way in which your ultimate objective can be achieved....

Yours sincerely,
J.R.D. Tata

---

[*]   Chairman, Bajaj Group of Industries.

TO M.A.S. DALAL[*]

Bombay
24 June 1971

My dear Maneck,

On the 21st instant, I received a parcel of bandages sent, through you, by Lord Harewood for some friend of his in Madras. I was upset at this breach of the Airline's regulations in which I was made to be involved. In future, please do not hesitate to turn down such requests from anybody. If anything is sent to me, it should be sent properly documented and through the Customs....

Yours sincerely,
J.R.D. Tata

---

[*]   Regional Director, U.K., Air-India, London.

TO RAI BAHADUR M.S. OBEROI[*]

Bombay
19 August 1974

Dear Rai Bahadur Oberoi,

I am sorry for the long delay in answering your letter of the 26th June, in which you complained that Air-India was showing undue preference to the Taj Mahal Hotel in the business that it passed on to it and giving too little to the Oberoi-Sheraton.

From the time the Oberoi-Sheraton opened, I gave instructions that a fair and reasonable share of the business should go not only to the Oberoi, but to other hotels in Bombay. On questioning the senior management of Air-India on the subject, the following views have been expressed to me.

The Taj has been in existence for seventy years, out of which it has served Air-India and its predecessors, Air-India Limited and Air-India International Limited, for thirty years.

The Oberoi-Sheraton has been in existence less than two years.

The Taj has always gone out of its way to look after Air-India's business and passengers, often at some sacrifice of its own interests and of the convenience of its other patrons.

Most of Air-India's passengers or their tour sponsors specify preference for the Taj.

The Taj has invariably responded to Air-India's approaches for special concessions and facilities for tourists brought to India by Air-India. Recently, the Taj readily responded to our request that tourists brought in under an air/sea cruise scheme should not be charged for the few hours by which they arrive ahead of the normal

---

* Chairman, Oberoi Group of Hotels.

noon check-in time, while the Oberoi-Sheraton reluctantly agreed to give only a 50% discount....

I find that during the first six months of this year, of the 50% of passengers for whom bookings were made in Bombay by Air-India, under 50% were allotted to the Taj and the balance divided between the Oberoi-Sheraton and other hotels mostly at Juhu.

Apart from the booking of passengers, Air-India places a considerable amount of its non-room business with the Oberoi-Sheraton, including a number of special conferences which were held at the Oberoi and not the Taj. A large farewell party to Bobby Kooka, on his retirement, at which I presided, and many other banquet functions have been held at the Oberoi in preference to the Taj, while, because of the proximity of the Oberoi-Sheraton to the Air-India building, a good deal of the entertainment business of Air-India is done at the Oberoi-Sheraton.

In the circumstances, I cannot share your view that undue preference has been given to the Taj. As Chairman of Indian Hotels, I have deliberately kept right out of any allocation of business as between hotels, and have left it entirely to the Management...

With all good wishes,

Yours sincerely,
J.R.D. Tata

TO A.N. HAKSAR[*]

Bombay
22 December 1977

My dear Ajit,

I am sorry for the long delay in replying to your letter to me of the 16th November...

I note that you have had negotiations with the owners of the Searock Hotel, and I hope that they have fructified to your satisfaction....

Your letter gives me the opportunity to assure you once again that, while each of us may, naturally, seek the best opportunities for promoting the growth of our respective companies, we consider Tatas' and ITC's role complementary rather than competitive, and we are glad that a firm of ITC's prestige and resources is playing a growing part in the development of the Indian hotel industry. There is such a dearth of hotel accommodation in our country that there is ample room for both of us, and indeed for many others. No single firm, however enterprising or resourceful, is capable of meeting the current or likely demand for hotel accommodation during the next decade or two, particularly in centres like Bombay and Delhi where the shortage is critical....

With best wishes for the New Year,

Yours sincerely,
J.R.D. Tata

---

[*] A.N. Haksar (b.1925) joined ITC Ltd. in 1948, was its Chairman from 1969 to 1983 and became Chairman Emeritus after retirement.

TO JUSTICE S.P. KOTWAL*

Bombay
1 August 1979

Dear Justice Kotwal,

We, in Tatas, have long recognised that the responsibilities and obligations of an industrial enterprise transcend the normal ones to its owners, to its employees, and to the consumers of its products or services, and that they should encompass the welfare of, and service to, the local community and society as a whole, particularly where its operations are large and established in the countryside. Jamsetji Tata clearly recognised such social obligation well ahead of his time and, in planning the town of Jamshedpur which would house the Company's employees and their families, he laid clear guidelines on the subject. Those who followed him in guiding the destinies of the Company and the local management adhered to his concept of a company's responsibilities and Jamshedpur, today a fairly large town with some 600,000 souls, bears the imprint of Jamsetji's philosophy.

In 1970, the Company decided, along with other Tata companies, to incorporate its social obligations into its Memorandum and Articles of Association, which were amended to include the following clause:

"3A. The Company shall have among its objectives the promotion and growth of the national economy through increased productivity, effective utilisation of material and manpower resources and continued application of modern scientific and managerial techniques in keeping with the national aspirations; and the Company shall be mindful of its social and moral responsibilities to the consumers, employees, shareholders, society, and the local community."

---

* Retired Chief Justice of the Bombay High Court.

For many years the above concept was applied mainly for the benefit of the residents of Jamshedpur and particularly of the employees of the Company and their families. In recent years, however, in recognition of the fact that while industrialisation has benefited the people of urban areas, it has, with some exceptions, left untouched the bulk of the population which lives in the country's rural areas, we have felt that the Steel Company should extend its welfare activities to surrounding areas of the countryside, and are in the process of finalising a plan of assistance to over a hundred and fifty neighbouring villages within an area of about 300 sq. kms.

We believe that the Steel Company has substantially lived up to its obligations and responsibilities, not only to its shareholders, its employees and its consumers, but also to the community and the nation. However, with private sector industry, particularly large companies such as ours, increasingly in the public eye, accused of a harmful concentration of economic power and threatened with nationalisation, my colleagues and I feel that the time has come when we should put our performance and our role in the economy and the country to the test of an independent social audit by a small group of persons whose judgment and views would command universal public respect and confidence.

At a recent meeting the Board approved of this proposal and of my recommendation that you should be invited to head a small Committee which should include Prof. Rajni Kothari, a leading economist, and Mr. P.G. Mavlankar, an independent Member of Parliament. I hope you will be willing to respond to this invitation and agree with the other two names proposed....

Looking forward to your favourable reply, and with kind regards,

Yours sincerely,
J.R.D. Tata

PROMINENT PERSONALITIES, FRIENDS AND OTHERS

Prominent Personalities

Friends

Others

Even though JRD tried to maintain a low profile in the media, and had an "intense dislike" for making speeches, he loved to write letters to his friends, business associates, ministers and government officials on topics close to his heart.

Among his friends JRD could count some national and international celebrities and others who were respected figures in their own fields. As his biographer says, "While JRD may not have actively sought out celebrities, inevitably many have crossed his path." There were, among, others Mahatma Gandhi, Rabindranath Tagore, Motilal Nehru, Louis Fischer, Henry Kissinger, Yehudi Menuhin and Le Corbusier, some of whom he knew well. JRD had enormous respect for Mahatma Gandhi and politicians like Vallabhbhai Patel and C. Rajagopalachari. But at a personal level he was close to Pandit Jawaharlal Nehru and Indira Gandhi.

Among politicians, next to Nehru, he had a deep sympathy for Jayaprakash Narayan (J.P.). JRD responded to J.P.'s occasional appeals for help to his social causes but their relationship went deeper than that.

Amongst international celebrities, there were George Woods—advisor to the World Bank—and his wife Louie Woods, who were quite close to JRD. Others included David Rockefeller who invited him to become a member of the International Advisory Committee of the Chase Manhattan Bank, economist J.K. Galbraith and Robert McNamara, president of the World Bank.

Amongst national celebrities one person whom JRD knew very closely was Dr. Homi Bhabha, the pioneer of India's nuclear energy programme. JRD played an important part in helping Dr. Bhabha to launch a programme which made India in a matter of two decades virtually self-sufficient in nuclear science.

On 19 August 1943 Dr. Bhabha wrote a letter to JRD saying, "... the lack of proper conditions hampers the development of science in India at the pace which the talent in the country would warrant." In his reply, JRD said, "If you and/or some of your colleagues in the scientific world will put up concrete proposals backed by a sound case, I think, there is a very good chance that the Sir Dorab Tata Trust…will respond."

Dr. Bhabha set up the Tata Institute of Fundamental Research which became the cradle of atomic science in India. The rest, as they say, is history.

Amongst JRD's friends in India there were some journalists and other professionals.

Several people whom he did not know personally wrote to him out of love and admiration and he made it a point to answer most of these letters.

Prominent Personalities

FROM PANDIT JAWAHARLAL NEHRU[*]

Allahabad
4 March 1942

My dear Jehangir,

   Within the next few days you will get an invitation which probably you will not be able to read as it will be in Hindi and Urdu. So I hasten to tell you that this is about Indira's marriage which is fixed for March 26th in Allahabad. It is perhaps too much to expect a very busy captain of industry in these strenuous times to attend to such functions. But of course if you and Thelly could come we would be happy.

Yours sincerely,
Jawaharlal Nehru

---

*   Copy of handwritten letter.

TO PANDIT JAWAHARLAL NEHRU

Bombay
11 March 1942

My dear Jawaharlal,

Thanks very much for inviting Thelly and me to your daughter's wedding and for your kind letter. It was nice of you to take the trouble of writing personally.

Thelly and I would naturally love to take advantage of this opportunity of meeting you again and of congratulating, and giving in person, our best wishes to Indira.

The difficulty however, lies in the fact that it would take up three days in all. I am afraid I am not much of a "captain of industry", but I am certainly being kept as busy as if I were one! I am particularly heavily booked during that week.

I hope, therefore, that you will forgive me if we don't manage to come and will not think that we don't want to.

Apart from that I fear that you will have your hands so full with all the people who will be coming from all parts of India that we would be a nuisance to you. Unless, of course, you allowed us to stay at a hotel. In fact, if later on I found it was possible for me to get away from Bombay and, at the last moment, we flew over, it would be only if you promised to let us stay at a hotel!

If we are unable to see you this time, I sincerely hope we shall see you in Bombay soon after. Isn't it time this city got another visit from the great man? I hope you are very fit and with renewed thanks and best wishes from us both.

Yours ever,
Jeh

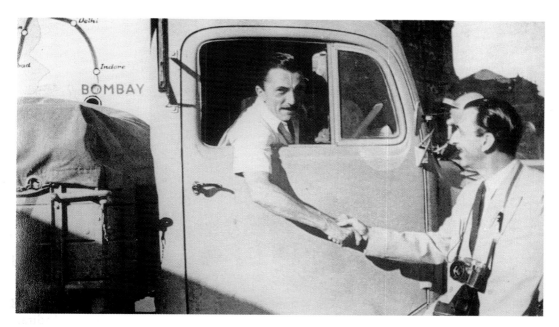

(top): JRD shaking hands with his brother D.R.D. Tata. Mercedes-Benz trucks participate in the Geneva-Bombay International Motor Rally with DRD taking part in it, January 1955.

JRD with Fateh Singh Rao Gaekwad and Y.B. Chavan (extreme left).

JRD with Pandit Jawaharlal Nehru.

With Indira Gandhi.

JRD with Pandit Jawaharlal Nehru after the Delhi-Bombay demonstration flight.

JRD and Thelma Tata with Indira Gandhi at London Airport.

Indira Gandhi visiting a school run by Thelma Tata for underprivileged children.

JRD with David Rockefeller, head of the Chase Manhattan Bank and also a close friend.

With Prince Philip at the Duke of Edinburgh Study Conference at Oxford.

With Prof. J.K. Galbraith, one of the world's leading authorities on economic matters.

JRD with Acharya
Vinoba Bhave.

With Jayaprakash Narayan.

JRD with Morarji Desai and Naval at
the inauguration of the J.N. Tata
Memorial Centre in Navsari in 1978.

Citation

Honoring...

Mr. Jehangir R. D. Tata of Bombay, India

in formal recognition of his magnificent contributions to the profession of Management through unselfish, intelligent and humane work in behalf of the industrial and business people of the great nation of India. Presented this Twenty-fifth day of September, Nineteen hundred and Fifty-three, in recognition of his being honored as the NAF INTERNATIONAL MAN OF MANAGEMENT, in the City of Milwaukee on the occasion of the Thirtieth Annual Convention of The National Association of Foremen.

Edward O. Seito
PRESIDENT

J. E. Bathurst
EXECUTIVE VICE PRESIDENT

F. W. Sterub
CONVENTION COUNCIL CHAIRMAN

Kershner
SECRETARY-TREASURER

In 1953, at its Thirtieth Annual Convention in Milwaukee, the National Association of Foremen honoured JRD with the International Man of Management award.

Then President of India, R. Venkataraman confers the Bharat Ratna on J.R.D. Tata at Rashtrapati Bhawan in March 1992.

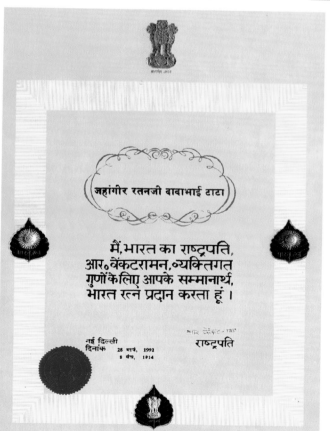

जहांगीर रतनजी दादाभाई टाटा

मैं, भारत का राष्ट्रपति, आर॰ वेंकटरामन, व्यक्तिगत गुणों के लिए आपके सम्मानार्थ, भारत रत्न प्रदान करता हूं ।

नई दिल्ली
दिनांक 28 मार्च, 1992
8 चैत्र, 1914

राष्ट्रपति

The medal; and (left) the citation.

JRD was promoted to the rank of Commander of the Legion of Honour by the French Government in 1983: Award and Plaque.

FROM SARDAR VALLABHBHAI PATEL[*]

Poona
9 October 1945

My dear Jehangir,

It is more than three years since we met last before my arrest in August 1942 in Bombay. Since my release I have been mostly confined to this clinic except for short intervals when urgent public duty called me away. I wanted to meet you when I was in Bombay for three days on the occasion of the A.I.C.C. meeting, but I could not find time owing to pressure of work.

I am writing this to you in the hope that you may be able to assist me in an urgent matter of public importance. In the coming Central Assembly elections the Congress has to set up two candidates from the Bombay City general constituency. There is no difficulty in getting both the seats, but I want your help in securing the services of an expert. If you can permit and persuade Dr. John Matthai[**] to agree to stand as a Congress nominee and contest one of these seats on its behalf, you would be doing a great service to the country's cause. His services in the Central Assembly at this critical juncture would be of immense value. If he would accept a Congress ticket I would see that there is no difficulty in winning the seat in the elections.

---

[*] Sardar Vallabhbhai Patel (1875-1950), the "Iron Man of India", was Deputy Prime Minister in the Nehru Cabinet.
[**] Dr. John Matthai joined Nehru's Cabinet and was elevated to the position of Finance Minister. He resigned from the Cabinet on account of differences of opinion with the Prime Minister and rejoined Tatas.

As the date of nomination is drawing near I would request you to send me a reply as soon as possible.

I have written this on my own behalf, but if you agree I will place it before my Committee.

Yours sincerely,
Vallabhbhai

TO SARDAR VALLABHBHAI PATEL

Bombay
12 October 1945

Dear Sardar Saheb,

    Thanks for your letter of the 9th instant, which I received the day before yesterday. I showed it to Dr. Matthai, and discussed the matter with him. He fully appreciated the importance of your invitation and the opportunity for national service that it offered to him. He seemed favourably inclined at first, but wished to give further thought to it before making up his mind. This morning he sent me a letter which I am passing on to you in the original, in which he explains the personal difficulties which come in the way of his accepting your invitation.

    I am very sorry that he is unable to stand for election, because I am convinced that his great ability, personal qualities and his expert knowledge of economic matters would enable him to render great service to the country as a member of the Central Legislature, and also because I felt it was a compliment to our Firm that this offer should be made to one of its Directors.

Yours sincerely,
J.R.D. Tata

FROM SARDAR VALLABHBHAI PATEL

Poona
13 October 1945

My dear Jehangir,

Thanks for your letter of the 12th instant with its accompaniment. I am grateful to you for the efforts you made at my suggestion. I fully appreciate the reluctance of Dr. Matthai in entering into the troubled waters of political life and his consequent hesitation. However, I am glad that both of you have appreciated the spirit which prompted me to make that offer. I believe there will be occasions in future when we may need his services in a line which may not be so unsuitable to his temperament. I hope that in that case both you and he will agree to help us....

Thank you very much for your good wishes,

Yours sincerely,
Vallabhbhai

FROM GHULAM MOHAMMED

Karachi
28 August 1947

My dear Jeh,

   You will excuse me for not having written to you earlier to thank you for all your kindness and understanding shown to me during the 21 months I was with Tatas. I have developed during this period the highest regard for you and consider you as one of the leading Indians of the day and I wish there were a few more like you! Though our association has ceased, I shall continue to cherish genuine feelings of regard and friendship towards you and wish you all success I hope you will not mind helping us by giving me particulars of four- or five-seater aeroplanes suitable for top executives for tours....

   With kindest regards,

Yours sincerely,
Ghulam Mohammed

TO GHULAM MOHAMMED

Bombay
5 September 1947

My dear Ghulam Mohammed,

Many thanks for your letter of the 28th August, and for your kind remarks which I very warmly reciprocate. It was, I assure you, a matter of great regret for me to part with you, but I felt somewhat compensated by the knowledge that by releasing you, I was making a useful, though indirect, contribution to the very important work you are doing for your country, and for which you are so eminently fitted. I shall always retain the most pleasant memories of my all too brief association with you, and a warm regard and friendship for you personally....

I shall send you, within a couple of days, the information about "executive" aeroplanes for which you ask.

Yours,
Jeh

FROM PANDIT JAWAHARLAL NEHRU

New Delhi
4 July 1948

My dear Jehangir,

Thank you for the lovely cherries you sent me today. Where did they come from? Were they brought from Europe in one of your Constellations?...

Thank you also for your attempt to send me the stamp, etc., of the Air Mail carried by your Constellation to Europe. As a matter of fact you did not wholly succeed in the attempt largely due to the lack of intelligence of the people who deal with my mail. I get a very large number of letters daily, over 1,500 or so, and a number of people open them and sort them out. Only such letters as they think worthy of my perusal or which may have special marking, reach me. In the case of this particular letter of yours the card inside reached me and the envelope had been torn away. I tried to find it but without success. In future if you wish any of your letters specially to reach me, please mark it on the envelope "FOR HIMSELF".

I have had plenty of information from various sources, both official and non-official, about the running of your air service to Europe. All accounts agree in speaking well of it and praising it for its general efficiency. Congratulations. Perhaps I might use it sometime or other....

Yours,
Jawaharlal Nehru

TO PANDIT JAWAHARLAL NEHRU

Bombay
12 July 1948

My dear Jawaharlal,

On my return from Delhi I found your kind letter of the 4th, for which I thank you very much.

I am sorry that the Souvenir Airmail cover of our inaugural flight was lost in your office. I am, however, sending you another one in case it may be of interest to you, or to any member of your family.

Thanks for telling me how to mark letters addressed to you in order to ensure that they reach you direct. I shall use the method sparingly.

I am happy to know that you had good reports about our international service and am delighted to hear that you may use it some time this year....

Yours ever,
Jeh

FROM PANDIT JAWAHARLAL NEHRU

New Delhi
16 March 1949

My dear Jehangir,

As you know, we have been negotiating an agreement with Blumenfeld on behalf of a French company for the processing of monazite sands in India and the extraction of rare earths and minerals from this sand....

The company for the processing of monazite sands from Travancore has now to be formed and Messrs. Wadia, Gandhi and Co., Solicitors, Bombay, have been asked to draw up the constitution of the proposed company. The fixed capital of the company will be rupees fifty lakhs and the working capital rupees ten lakhs....

The Board of Directors of the company will consist of seven members. These will be:

3 nominees of the Government of India,
2 nominees of the Government of Travancore,
1 member representing Industry, and
1 member representing Science.

The Atomic Energy Commissioners have suggested three names of industrialists for the seat on the Board of Directors which is to be reserved for a representative of Industry. They have strongly suggested your name for it and placed it first in their list. Further, they are anxious to have you as Chairman of the Board...I hope that you will agree to this, at least for some time. This is a very special venture of ours having great potentiality and we would like to give it as good a start as possible. Hence, our desire to have you as Chairman...

Will you please consider this matter and let me know, at your earliest convenience, whether you will accept the chairmanship of the Board of the Company which is being formed for the processing of monazite sands from Travancore?

Yours,
Jawaharlal Nehru

FROM PANDIT JAWAHARLAL NEHRU

New Delhi
4 April 1949

My dear Jehangir,

So you are back again. I hope your skiing has done you good and that you are quite fit now.

I suppose you know that I am leaving for England on a brief visit soon. I shall go by Air-India from Bombay on the 19th night. I expect to reach Bombay the same afternoon by the Viking Service from Delhi.

I want to give you a little trouble. I should like to take a parcel of mangoes with me for the Mountbattens. I suppose you will be able to get fairly good Alfonso mangoes by the time I go. I do not want to add too much to my luggage. So do not give me too many.

Love,
Jawaharlal

TO PANDIT JAWAHARLAL NEHRU

Bombay
7 April 1949

My dear Jawaharlal,

Your letter of the 16th March, inviting me to become a Director and Chairman of the new chemical company which is being formed for the processing of monazite sands under an agreement with a French company, was received by me in Switzerland the day before I left for India. It was, therefore, not possible for me to reply to it earlier.

I greatly appreciate the confidence in me evidenced by your requests. As you know, my services are always at your disposal, and if after reading this letter you still think that my appointment as proposed is necessary, or even desirable in the interests of the project, I shall bow to your wishes.

While I do not claim that I am more over-burdened with work than others, it is a fact that, during the last few years, I have been compelled by sheer lack of time, health and energy to withdraw from a number of activities within and outside Tatas, and to give up directorships and chairmanships in a number of companies, including some of our own. As recently as a couple of months ago I decided, to my regret, to give up administrative charge of Air-India and Air-India International, as I found it impossible to spare the necessary time. You will, therefore, appreciate that apart from the additional strain it would put on me, it would be somewhat inconsistent, and in fact embarrassing, for me to increase my "outside" commitments while at the same time reducing my work and responsibilities in the Firm, whose paid servant I incidentally am. I know that Bhatnagar and others think that the work of the Chairman of this new company will not amount to much, and that consequently, the time and energy to be devoted to it would be small. From experience, however, I know that this is never so in practice, as I am unfortunately one of those who cannot undertake a job without taking a deep and detailed interest in it. In this instance, the absence of Managing Agents or of a Managing Director would be an additional factor resulting in the Chairman having to give quite a lot of time to the activities of the company, particularly in the early stages.

There are other considerations which, I respectfully suggest, militate against my appointment as Chairman. I feel, for instance, that it is neither fair, nor desirable, to appoint as chairman of state corporations, businessmen or industrialists who are actively engaged in their own business. Then again, the very special nature of the present project, with its association with thorium and therefore with atomic energy, would make it desirable to keep the control of the Board and Management in the hands of a Government official.

If you think that the managerial and business experience of our Firm would be specially useful, I feel that Pan* would have more time to devote to the project and would be capable of contributing more than I to it. If, however, you still feel that I should be connected with the scheme, I hope you will only make me a Director of the company, and not its Chairman. I need hardly add that even if I am entirely unconnected with the company, I shall always and gladly be available for any consultations, negotiations, etc.

With kind regards,

Yours very sincerely,
Jeh

---

*   P. A. Narielwala.

TO PANDIT JAWAHARLAL NEHRU

Bombay
13 April 1949

My dear Jawaharlal,

Thanks for your letter regarding the mangoes for the Mountbattens. I shall do my best to have them ready on the 19th; one basket will be for yourself.

The only thing that worries me is that, owing—I believe—to the cyclone which damaged the mango trees on the west coast, the crop is expected to be very poor this year, and in fact no mangoes have come on the market yet. In case they are so delayed that there will have been no arrivals by the 19th, I shall arrange for three or four dozen to be sent to Lord and Lady Mountbatten on your behalf as soon as they are available.

Please do not worry about the weight on your flight, as mangoes carried by the Prime Minister are of a very special kind, to which the laws of gravity do not apply, and which therefore weigh nothing!

Thelly and I are looking forward to seeing you this week.

Yours sincerely,
Jeh

FROM PANDIT JAWAHARLAL NEHRU

New Delhi,
7 May 1949

My dear Jehangir,

This is just a brief letter to express my great appreciation of the quality of the Air-India International Service. I have now travelled on four occasions between India and England in it and the more experience I have had of it, the better I like it. I think that Air-India International have played not an unimportant part in raising the prestige of India abroad. Indians in other countries have told me of the thrill they feel when they see one of these aircraft with the Indian National Flag painted on it sail down gracefully in foreign airfields. Foreigners have also been much impressed. So, congratulations....

I suppose you have received a letter from Lady Mountbatten to thank you for the mangoes which were appreciated very much. I sent some of these mangoes to Princess Elizabeth, as it was her birthday. Apparently they reached the King, who enjoyed them thoroughly. Among other recipients of your mangoes were Attlee and Stafford Cripps. So you see they went pretty far....

Yours ever,
Jawaharlal

TO PANDIT JAWAHARLAL NEHRU

Bombay
11 May 1949

My dear Jawaharlal,

I was touched by your personal letter of the 7th May, for which I thank you very much. It was kind of you to have taken the trouble and found the time to write.

Your approval of Air-India International's service means a great deal to all of us and we were delighted to read in the papers that, on arrival at the London Airport, you said some kind things about our service. We deeply appreciate the remarks you made then and those now contained in your letter. All of us, including myself, who are connected with Air-India International think of it not merely as another airline and commercial venture, but as an institution which is privileged, in its own small way, to represent our country abroad. We, therefore, feel that in striving to achieve and maintain the highest possible standards, we are doing something to keep up India's prestige abroad. It is nice to know that this has been appreciated by our Prime Minister!...

I am happy to know that the mangoes you took pleased so many people. I received a very nice letter from Lady Mountbatten....

With affectionate regards,

Yours ever,
Jeh

TO C. RAJAGOPALACHARI

Bombay
5 May 1950

My dear Rajaji,

I have been shown the passenger card with the kind remarks you wrote during your recent flight on one of our planes from Madras. These heartening words from you have been deeply appreciated by our staff, and on their behalf and my own, I thank you very much for your kind thought and for the kind words which you have taken the trouble to express.

We were honoured in having you as a passenger, and I hope that we will have the privilege again in the future. I particularly hope that you will be able one day to fly by Air-India International on a trip abroad, as the standards are even higher on our overseas service than on our domestic services owing to the much larger and more modern aeroplanes we use for the former, and to the fact that they are pressurised.

I was particularly struck by your approval of "Better Acquainted"....Your favourable comments are particularly heartening because both "Better Acquainted" and "Foolishly Yours", though approved by most people and universally so by foreigners, have raised adverse criticisms from some of our Indian passengers and friends, including one of our Directors. It is considered by them that the flippant humour of these books and the fact that they make fun of everybody, including ourselves, is not in keeping with the dignity of our country and our people and of a semi-nationalised company. My own view is that a sense of humour is, to a large extent, synonomous with a sense of perspective and I have often felt that in many ways India would be in a better way today if we had the ability to laugh at ourselves and see the humorous side of things and situations. I therefore find it refreshing and encouraging that a person of your eminence, and one who can hardly be charged with having become unduly westernised, should have appreciated our little effort at amusing our passengers....

With kind regards,

Yours sincerely,
J.R.D. Tata

TO PANDIT JAWAHARLAL NEHRU

Bombay
5 May 1953

My dear Jawaharlal,

As you will be spending an hour and a half in Bombay on the 28th of this month on your way to England, Thelly and I would be happy if you would have tea at our Juhu shack during the interval between your arrival from Delhi and your departure for London. I understand from Pan that he has suggested this to you and that you thought it would be convenient. The plane is scheduled to arrive at 3.30 in the afternoon and to leave at 5 p.m. As there will no doubt be some sort of reception for you at the airport when you arrive and a send-off when you go, you will, I expect, have to spend at least five to ten minutes at the airport on both occasions. We must also allow for at least fifteen minutes for your drive to Juhu and back. This will leave just about an hour for you to spend at Juhu....

The mango season is now in full swing and although some eminent Northerners occasionally challenge the claim of the Alfonso to superiority over all other kinds, I have no doubt about it and am having a basket delivered to your house with this letter to prove it. If you will allow me I would also like to place two baskets on board your plane when you leave for England as I am sure you will want to give some to friends there. If you would like more than eight dozen, please do not hesitate to let me know and I will arrange accordingly....

With affectionate regards,

Yours,
Jeh

FROM PANDIT JAWAHARLAL NEHRU

New Delhi
7 May 1953

My dear Jehangir,

Thank you for your letter of the 5th May and for the mangoes. I shall not argue with you about the relative merits of various kinds of mangoes. I know some people are not open to reason. Let it be enough that Alfonsoes are very good mangoes.

Thank you for your intention to send some mangoes with me. The number you mention is quite big enough. Please do not exceed it....

Jawaharlal Nehru

TO JAYAPRAKASH NARAYAN

Bombay
4 January 1955

My dear Mr. Jayaprakash,

I thank you very much for your kind letter of the 24th December....

I am a genuine believer in the concept that those in whom fate has placed control of means of production, with or without personal wealth of their own, should treat the control and powers which they exercise as a trust for the people. I must however confess that I do not share your understanding of the role of the capitalist system or its place in history. With great respect, I wonder whether you are not making the mistake of viewing the capitalist system as it was many years ago and not as it is today or in the form into which it is clearly developing all over the world. It is true that such evolution is somewhat uneven and that progress has been less in economically backward countries such as ours than in the more advanced democracies of the West, but the trend is clear and unmistakable and I am convinced that those who are today so confidently sealing the fate of the capitalist system on behalf of history are likely to change their mind in due course or to regret the change which they will have brought about. I believe that in most parts of the world the system of free enterprise, far from dying, will be given a renewed lease of life in recognition of its ability and willingness to serve the community well and also from a revulsion against the unpleasant reality—as distinct from the myth—of State socialism.

I also feel that in thinking that the benefits and future prospects of the system are confined to America, you are unfairly ignoring its achievements, even in the social sense, in countries like Switzerland, Scandinavia, Holland, Western Germany, etc., and also in England. I sincerely believe that with adequate safeguards the cooperative system and evolved capitalism are, in their respective fields, the most effective, if not the only, forms of economic organisation combining decentralisation of economic power with efficiency. State ownership and control of all economic activities cannot exist for long without centralised control of political and social activities. Between the two, enormous powers are placed in the hands of a few, leading ultimately to dictatorship in one form or another.

To be quite frank, I find it difficult to understand these days how, in the face of the experience of the only countries which have adopted State socialism exclusively or on a predominating scale, socialists, particularly in our country, reconcile their vociferous advocacy of nationalisation and State enterprise with their belief in democracy. In my view the two simply cannot go together.

The Gandhian concept does avoid the pitfalls of centralised socialism. It is, I am prepared to accept, an ideal type of organisation in rural areas and even perhaps in small-scale industry, although I believe that modern, large-scale cooperative enterprise operating largely according to capitalistic methods is more effective. I have grave doubts, however, that the Gandhian concept can operate effectively in a modern, highly industrialised society, and particularly in those sectors of industry which cannot function except by means of large industrial plants and mass production.

Furthermore, I wonder whether it is a practical proposition for a country which seeks a rapid rise in the material standards of its people, which in turn cannot be achieved without massive industrialisation, to organise itself on Gandhian lines without isolating itself completely from the rest of the world.

Finally, may I say that while I admire and envy the faith that men like you and Vinobaji have in human society's capacity to transform itself in a few years into a body of selfless and dedicated men and women, I cannot share it. I note that the human beings of today are little better, in terms of human qualities, than their ancestors of thousands of years ago, while there are lots more of them! In endeavouring to help them to improve their condition of life, I would not hesitate to harness some of the selfish but otherwise harmless urges which seem to form such a large part of the human character, including the urge for self-betterment, the urge for private ownership—whether of a piece of land, a cow, a house, a motorcar or a bank account—as incentives towards greater production for the good of all....

...I wish you happiness in the New Year and success in your work.

Yours very sincerely,
J.R.D. Tata

TO JAYAPRAKASH NARAYAN

Bombay
10 May 1955

Dear Mr. Jayaprakash,

In my letter to you of January 4th I had mentioned that on my return to India in March I would arrange a meeting of my co-Trustees at which we would discuss the details in regard to my contribution to the Bhoodan (and Sampattidan) Movement. I am glad to inform you that such a meeting was held a few days ago and that a favourable decision was reached.

I understand that Minoo Masani informed you a few days ago that the amount of the contribution to Sampattidan would be Rs. 10,000/-, that being one-sixth of my estimated net income for the current year. The figure that he mentioned was based on my personal income and I feel that the more correct and proper way of computing my income for this purpose would be to include in it the income of the Trust as if it were my own income. On this basis, one-sixth of my net income would come to Rs. 11,000/-, and this is the amount that the Trustees have sanctioned as an annual contribution to Sampattidan for the next five years....

I assume that this letter will take the place of any form that might normally have to be filled in by a donor to Sampattidan and contains all the information that you need....

Yours sincerely,
J.R.D. Tata

FROM ACHARYA VINOBA BHAVE[*]

Cuttack, Orissa
15 June 1955

Shri Tata,

I am informed by Shri Jayaprakash Narayan that you have made your contribution to Sampattidan...

The main thought that underlies Sampattidan is that every propertied man, whether big or small, should consider himself trustee of his wealth. This noble thought was given to us by Gandhiji. I am only his follower and for the last two or three years, while touring on Bhoodan work, I have been expounding this point of view to the people. The donation of one-sixth of one's income by way of Sampattidan is the first step towards this ideal. I hope that one who takes the first step will gradually accept and implement the entire concept of trusteeship....

Pranams from
Vinoba

---

[*] Original in Hindi. Acharya Vinoba Bhave (1895-1982) was a veteran Gandhian who led the Bhoodan movement. He received the Bharat Ratna in 1983, and the first Magsaysay Award.

TO LE CORBUSIER*

Bombay
12 November 1957

My dear Le Corbusier,

I was delighted to receive a copy of the beautiful book published by Boesiger of the Editions Girsberger, Zurich, containing your complete works for 1952-57. It was most kind of you to have thought of sending me a copy which now has pride of place in my library. Although a layman's appreciation of the work of Le Corbusier is probably of little value, may I warmly and sincerely congratulate you on your tremendous and continuing contribution to architecture and decoration.

You seem to have discovered the secret of keeping eternally young in spirit, for one cannot help being struck by the continuing boldness of your creations. The master is still the master. I hope you will be spared for many years more so that you may continue to lead the way to better living....

With affectionate regards in which Thelly joins me,

Yours very sincerely,
Jeh

---

* Le Corbusier (1887-1965) was an internationally renowned architect and town planner. Planned the city of Chandigarh.

FROM DR. HOMI BHABHA[*]

Bombay
30 March 1960

My dear Jeh,

The construction of the Canada-India Reactor is now nearing completion and trial runs of different parts of it will be started shortly, after which one area after another of this very complicated project will be closed permanently to all except those who have to do some work in this area. The reactor is expected to reach criticality early in June.

The Canada-India Reactor is one of the most powerful research reactors in the world and one of the largest isotope producers. It has cost Canada and India jointly a total sum equivalent to approximately $17 million. While parts of the project will always be open for visits by important members of the Government and the public, certain areas which can be visited now will become inaccessible. Perhaps the best time for visiting the reactor would be during the first two weeks of April....

Yours,
Homi

---

[*] Dr. Homi Bhabha (1909-1966); Chairman, Atomic Energy Commission; the pioneer of India's nuclear energy programme.

TO DR. HOMI BHABHA

Bombay
11 April 1960

My dear Homi,

Many thanks for the visit to the C.I.R. this morning and for the arrangements made to show us this immensely interesting project. I was most impressed. I hope the reactor's commissioning next month will be free from any undue teething troubles. I look forward to seeing it in operation at some convenient time later in the year.

Thanks again.

Yours ever,
Jeh

TO MRS. VIJAYALAKSHMI PANDIT*

Bombay
30 May 1964

Dear Nan,

Need I say how desperately sorry Thelly and I are at the passing of Jawaharlal and how deeply we feel for you?

I shall ever be grateful to you for arranging for us to meet Jawaharlal and talk to him for a while a few days before he died. We won't ever forget that we owed it to your thoughtfulness and kindness.

Jawaharlal's passing is so immeasurably great a loss for the country as a whole and for the hundreds of millions of its people that it seems wrong and selfish to think of one's own sense of loss. But Jawaharlal was that kind of a man who made you feel he was part of your own life and I grieve at his passing, more than I can say.

An era has passed with him, which he adorned and enriched. For me it began one day in 1922 when I first met him with you at "Soonita". Even though we met thereafter at rare intervals, the fact that I knew you both and had your friendship has meant much more to me.

He is no more but to me it is a real consolation to know that you are there. I realise, dear Nan, how much, much greater your loss and your grief is than ours and I can only hope that the love and sympathy of your friends like ourselves will be of some help to you, however minute, in this tragic hour....

With our deep and affectionate sympathy,

Yours ever,
Jeh

---

* Copy of handwritten letter.

TO LOUIS FISCHER[*]

Bombay
25 January 1965

My dear Louis,

How kind and thoughtful of you to send me a complimentary and charmingly autographed copy of your *Life of Lenin* which I have just received. Even though I am somewhat frightened by the number of its pages, I am looking forward very much to reading it, or most of it!

I was particularly interested in reading the glowing reviews of the book from which it is clear that it is not only an outstanding biography but also one of the most important contributions made up to now to a better understanding of contemporary world history. I am awed by the magnitude of this piece of work and by the depth and range of your "scholarliness". I doubt that any single scholar-author has done as much as you have in explaining and illuminating through your biographies and other books the history of this turbulent and awesome era in world history....

Yours sincerely,
Jeh

---

[*] Louis Fischer (1896-1970), noted journalist and writer, was the author of *The Life of Mahatma Gandhi* (1950).

FROM MRS. LOUIE WOODS[*]

Washington
8 February 1965

Dear Jeh:

   …Your tea has arrived per schedule, thank God. I do hope that you have left in your Will that I am to continue to get that tea in case you die before I do. I do not think I can live without it now….

Louie

---

*   Wife of JRD's friend George Woods. JRD used to send her packets of Lopchu tea which she liked.

TO MRS. LOUIE WOODS

Bombay
12 March 1965

My dear Louie,

Thank you for your amusing letter of the 8th February. I am glad that the tea arrived in time to save your life now that you find you cannot live without it. I have considered your suggestion of making a provision in my Will to ensure that you continue to receive the tea after my death, but as I do not expect anything to be left of my estate after paying taxes, I am making other arrangements to ensure continuity of supplies even while I am waiting for you on the other side. I only hope we will both go to the same place!...

I hope you are both keeping well and that George is not under too much pressure. Our love to you both,

Yours ever,
Jeh

FROM GEORGE D. WOODS

Washington
29 January 1968

Dear Jeh:

That was an exceedingly interesting piece in the London *Economist* a few weeks ago about your businesses. I started to say I wish there was more publicity of this sort coming out of India but, of course, this is not possible because there is only one "Tata". You may be justifiably proud of your organisation, the job it does with a minimum of constructive collaboration from the Government bureaucracies, and also of the very high regard in which it is held throughout Western Europe and North America....

Warm regards,

Cordially,
George

TO GEORGE D. WOODS

· Bombay
19 February 1968

Dear George,

I only received your very nice letter of January 29 after meeting you in Delhi and I could not, therefore, thank you for it at the time.

I suppose that, considering the political-cum-ideological background against which we have had to operate since the War, Tatas have not done too badly, but not half as well as I had hoped we would, and I am sure we could have, in a more propitious environment. I am afraid that in spite of all the lessons of the past twenty years, there is no real change in Delhi's attitude towards "big business", nor have our politicians and bureaucrats realised that what seems big business to them would be little more than peanuts elsewhere....

Getting to know you and your friendship have been amongst the most rewarding experiences of my career. I do hope our paths will continue to cross from time to time. My one regret is that I will never be able to see you and Louie in your Portuguese retreat!

With renewed thanks for your letter, and with affectionate wishes to you both in which Thelly joins me,

Yours very sincerely,
Jeh

TO CHESTER BOWLES

Bombay
28 *March* 1969

Dear Mr. Bowles,

...I am happy that I shall meet you in Bombay on the 31st at the Braddocks' dinner.

I would like you to know that I am one of the countless people in this country who will be sorry indeed to see you go. In your two tenures of office as Ambassador, you have succeeded in identifying yourself with the people of our country and earning their friendship and confidence to an extent that is rare indeed.

I know that it is fashionable these days to be, or at least to sound, anti-American. Here, as elsewhere, the Vietnam war has done some damage, although I am one of those who believe that however tragic that war is, it is in part India's war. Had the U.S. allowed the take-over by North Vietnam, armed by Russia and China, it would not have taken long for neighbouring countries to fall even more quickly and the Communist power to engulf the whole of South-east Asia up to our very doors.

Unfortunately, we as a people are inclined to prefer readymade ideas and slogans rather than to think things out for ourselves. We are thus gluttons for propaganda and our Leftist friends have squeezed all they could out of the Vietnam war and racial troubles in the States.

The point I am leading to, however, is that such propaganda would have been far more successful but for the role that you played as American Ambassador. If your successor does half as well as you have done, he will have served his country well indeed!

Wishing you and Mrs. Bowles a safe and comfortable journey home, and hoping we shall meet again some day,

Yours very sincerely,
J.R.D. Tata

TO YEHUDI MENUHIN*

Bombay
1 April 1969

Dear Yehudi,

    Thank you so very much for the two wonderful records you have kindly sent me of Beethoven's *Violin Sonatas* and Tchaikovsky's *Swan Lake Suite*. I am delighted to have them, particularly coming from the Maestro himself....

With affectionate wishes to you and Diana,

Yours ever,
Jeh

---

*   Internationally famous violinist Yehudi Menuhin had a deep interest in yoga and Indian philosophy and contributed greatly to the awareness of Indian classical music in the West.

FROM DAVID ROCKEFELLER*

New York
6 August 1969

Dear Mr. Tata:

I am writing to invite you to serve as a member of the International Advisory Committee of the Chase Manhattan Bank. This Committee was established four years ago to advise the officers and directors of our bank on matters relating to our rapidly expanding international business. We were fortunate in being able to persuade Mr. John Loudon, formerly Chief Executive Officer of the Royal Dutch Oil Company, to be Chairman of the Committee....

The International Advisory Committee meets twice a year, usually for a day and a half....

Our agenda normally includes some discussion of various aspects of the bank's foreign operation plus a discussion on some particular topic or area of the world which is of special interest at the time. In addition to our own officers, we normally try to get one or two outside speakers for luncheon and evening meetings....We try to leave ample opportunity for discussion of each topic so that we can get the benefit of the thinking of the members of the Committee....

From the bank's point of view, the Advisory Committee has served a very useful function in bringing us the collective thinking of a very outstanding group of men on some of our sensitive policy and management questions in the international area. I believe most of the Committee members too seem to have enjoyed the meetings

---

*   Chairman, Chase Manhattan Bank (1946-1981); Supporting Chairman of the Bank's International Advisory Committee (IAC). JRD joined the Committee to represent India at his request and continued for 21 years.

and have attended with exceptional regularity considering the distances some of them must travel.

At the time the program first started, we made it clear that we thought it desirable that there be some rotation of members and of countries represented on the Committee. Accordingly, this year three or four members will be dropping off and we will be adding new members representing countries heretofore not represented on the Committee. We feel that it would be most important for us to have a representative from India. It was our unanimous conclusion that you would be the ideal candidate from your country were you willing to accept our invitation. I very much hope that you will see your way clear to do so....

I look forward to hearing from you.

Sincerely,
David Rockefeller

TO DAVID ROCKEFELLER

Bombay
14 August 1969

Dear Mr. Rockefeller,

I thank you very much for your letter of August 6 and for your flattering invitation to me to serve as a Member of the International Advisory Committee of the Chase Manhattan Bank. I am happy to respond to it in the belief that, apart from such small service as I may be able to render as a member of the Committee, I shall be serving the cause of international trade, understanding and goodwill. I know that I shall greatly enjoy meeting and talking with such a distinguished group of men, and that I shall myself gain much from attending these meetings....

With renewed thanks and kindest regards, and looking forward to the pleasure of meeting you in September,

Very sincerely yours,
J.R.D. Tata

TO THOMAS BATA[*]

Bombay
25 October 1971

Dear Mr. Bata,

Thank you very much indeed for your letter of October 9, which I was glad to receive.

I happen to be Chairman of more than one Company. Although you have not mentioned the name of the one to whose annual report you refer, I assume that it was that of the Tata Iron and Steel Company....

I am encouraged to know that you seem to share the views I hold and give vent to year after year, and only wish that they created a more responsive impression amongst the powers-that-be in our own country! With your own very large operation in India, you are, I am sure, very familiar with the problems with which Indian industry has to contend. One can only continue to do one's utmost to bring home to Government some of the economic realities which they have preferred to ignore up to now, and to hope that one may ultimately prove convincing!

With kind regards and all good wishes,

Yours sincerely,
J.R.D. Tata

---

* Chairman, Bata Shoe Organisation, Czechoslovakia.

TO JOHN ROCKEFELLER

Bombay
17 December 1974

Dear Mr. Rockefeller,

Many thanks for your letter of the 3rd instant, sending me a copy of the speech you delivered at the Bucharest Conference. I have read it with deep interest and, if I may say so, with admiration.

Unfortunately, from the newspaper reports I have read, and others I got directly from members of the Indian delegation, the Conference did not apply itself to the basic population problem in the rational manner in which you did in your speech, but allowed itself to be heavily politicised. This was perhaps inevitable, in view of the fact that it was a political conference of Member-nations within the U.N. system, at which all or most countries were represented by Ministers or Government officials. Still, it is a tragedy that, at a time when there is such a need and scope for a dispassionate study of the great human problems and crises of the age, and, where possible, for worldwide cooperation in solving them, opportunities for discussion in United Nations bodies or in conferences like the Bucharest one are so often used for purposes of political propaganda which divide people instead of uniting them in a common cause.

Nevertheless, I am sure that some good will ultimately come out of this Conference, if for no other reason than that for the first time all the countries of the world have, by attending it, openly admitted the existence and importance of the population problem.

I would agree with you that on a global basis population policy should be placed "solidly within the context of general economic and social development", which is, incidentally, the line taken by our own Government, rather than concentrated on family planning alone. However, in a country like India, where more than two-thirds of the people are illiterate, mass media of communications are sorely lacking, and the population problem has already reached critical proportions, there is some justification for concentrating mainly on family planning, albeit as part of a medicare package, rather than treating family planning only as one of the many elements of economic and social development. There is just not enough time, before disaster overtakes us, to wait for higher standards of living, brought about by economic development, to motivate people to limit their families....

With warm regards and all good wishes for Christmas and the New Year,

Yours very sincerely,
J.R.D. Tata

FROM JOHN ROCKEFELLER

New York
27 December 1974

Dear Mr. Tata,

Thank you for your letter of December 17th in regard to my Bucharest talk. Your reaction to the talk was as gratifying as it was appreciated.

I do agree with you that India and two or three other countries in your part of the world have a very special problem which makes it difficult to go as far as one would wish in combining family planning and development. However, there must be at least a minimum on the development side if in my judgment the results are to be more effective than have proven to be the case so far.

What I have in mind of course is the urgency factor on the one hand, and on the other the fact that only something like fifteen per cent of the people of your great country have responded to family planning programs. There are of course many factors involved, but a key one must be incentive.

I appreciate so much your letter and the copy of the one that you wrote to Karan Singh, the Minister of Health and Family Planning. Your own continuing interest in the population problem is gratifying indeed and gives heart to those in other countries who have the same concerns and objectives.

I hope that our paths may be crossing again before too long. Please let me know when you next come to New York.

Sincerely,
John Rockefeller

TO PROF. JOHN KENNETH GALBRAITH[*]

Bombay
26 February 1975

Dear Kenneth,

It was a great pleasure to meet you again after such a long interval. I enjoyed tremendously listening to your speech at the seminar at the Taj, and also meeting you at our informal lunch the next day.

I have since read with interest your Bhagat Memorial lecture delivered in Ahmedabad on February 9th on "Socialism in Rich Countries and Poor." I have been closely concerned with the Indian steel industry for over forty years. I was, therefore, somewhat surprised to note the contents of the third paragraph of your address which reads as follows:

> There was the fact that, here, if some things were not done by public agency, they were not done at all. The new Indian steel industry, mostly a public enterprise, one knew in those days was not a model of efficiency. But a steel industry existed. That was more than could be said for the development prior to the public initiative that followed Independence. That in the first hundred years of the iron age, India achieved a steel capacity of less than a million tons capacity was hardly an exhibit for private enterprise. In the West private enterprise could in a general way be counted upon to fill such gaps. In India this was by no means so certain.

---

[*]   John Kenneth Galbraith (b. 1908) was Ambassador to India (1961-1963) and author of *The Affluent Society* (1958).

You would normally be about the last man I would risk joining issue with, but you have given me such a good opportunity to do so in complete safety, that I cannot resist it! The example of the inadequate development of the steel industry by private enterprise which you have cited, is hardly a good one for supporting the unexceptionable point you make that public agencies must do the essential things that private agencies cannot or will not do.

Jamsetji Tata conceived, and began actively to pursue his project for establishing steel manufacture in India in the 1890s, and the first steel plant in India was established at Jamshedpur by his heirs towards 1910, in the face of the severest odds and in the most unfavourable industrial and financial environment imaginable. India then enjoyed neither political nor economic freedom, and on the economic front the British were only concerned with extracting from it cheap primary products and cheap labour, reserving India to themselves as a market for their finished goods. Far from being late, Jamsetji Tata's and his successors' efforts were so far ahead of their time under the conditions then prevailing, that their request for encouragement and a modicum of support from the then government, met with derision, as evidenced by the remark of a high government official who, when approached, said that he would "eat every pound of steel that Tatas would make".

I, therefore, feel it was a little unfair of you, apart from not being really relevant, to accuse Indian private enterprise of showing little initiative in achieving less than one million tons of capacity in the first hundred years of the iron age. Had it not been for the Tata Iron and Steel Company and, from 1939, for the Steel Corporation of Bengal, later merged into the Indian Iron and Steel Company, both private enterprises, there would probably have been no steel industry established in India until the 1950s. This, therefore, was an example of a thing having to be done by private enterprise or not done at all, rather than the opposite! Indian private enterprise cannot, therefore, fairly be charged with having failed to establish a steel industry in India or of having been unduly tardy in doing so.

The next point is whether your implied assumption, that the admittedly inadequate rate of growth of the Indian steel industry once established was because of a lack of enterprise on the part of the private sector, is correct. Actually, the responsibility rests exclusively with the Government of India who, for the last thirty years, balked our efforts to expand the Jamshedpur plant, except on one occasion only when, in the 1950s, they permitted us to add a million tons to it. Under the strict Government control of the prices to be allowed to the steel producers, which have been in force since World War II, prices have been restricted, year after year, to levels so far below those prevailing in other countries as to leave the industry with no possibility of expanding, and barely enough to maintain existing capacity by replacing worn-out equipment. Even after Government became themselves the largest producers in the country, the same policy continued to prevail with the result that the public sector plants made heavy losses year after year. Over the years, the prices allowed to the Indian producers in both the sectors, depending on the product-mix, were not much more than half of the prices earned by producers in other countries. If I may quote from my Chairman's statement to the Steel Company's shareholders last year:

> The argument sometimes advanced in the past that the Indian consumer was entitled to some return for the sacrifices he had made in paying higher prices during the period of protection from 1923 to 1939, was wholly specious, for it conveniently ignored the fact that the sum total of these sacrifices was less than Rs. 11 crores spread over sixteen years, whereas the amount by which the industry in both sectors was made to subsidise the consumer in subsequent years, has come to the formidable total of over Rs. 4,400 crores, of which no less than Rs. 1,565 crores were contributed by our Company alone!
>
> (Note: Rs. 11 crores in 1923/39 rupees would be equivalent to about Rs. 100 crores in 1939/74 rupees, while, at the average dollar/rupee rate of exchange prevailing in the past 35 years, Rs. 4,400 crores would be equal to $8.8 billion and Rs. 1,565 crores to $3.1 billion.)

Throughout this long period, I pleaded, in vain, year after year, for a reasonable increase in prices, which would enable us to finance a continuous expansion of our capacity through a combination of plough-back of retained earnings, fresh issues of capital and borrowings. If Government had responded, there is no doubt that the private sector of the steel industry would have been much larger than it is today.

With warm wishes,

Yours sincerely,
J.R.D. Tata

FROM PROF. JOHN KENNETH GALBRAITH

Cambridge, Massachusetts
18 March 1975

Dear JRD,

I've read your letter with close attention and I'm persuaded that you have a point. I have used this example in the past; and I must confess it was without proper investigation of the circumstances of the industry in the British period. I will be more careful about my examples in the future.

On the second point I also agree with you—although you are not arguing, I believe, with any point that I made in my lecture. My reference there was to the earlier time. I have always felt that the effort of the Indian government to protect its own industries against private competition was a mistake. There is everything to be gained from allowing public and private enterprises to serve as yardsticks, each against the other. And there is equally everything to be gained from the added output.

I am very glad you wrote me, for it allows me, as I've said, to correct a mistake that better research would have avoided. It also gives me a chance to thank you for the pleasant lunch in Bombay and the joy in seeing you again after all these years.

Yours faithfully,
John Kenneth Galbraith

TO DR. HENRY KISSINGER[*]

Bombay
21 November 1979

Dear Henry,

I am sorry for the delay in writing to thank you for your charming inscription in the copy of that little book of yours, *White House Years*, which you so kindly presented to me. I waited until I had a chance to read a good part of the book, and particularly the 77 pages of "The Tilt", which, naturally, received extensive press coverage in India. To my pleased surprise, it was not over-critical, as might have been expected from the reaction at the time of your thoughtful gesture in sending the *Enterprise* into the Bay of Bengal to entertain us.

So far as I am concerned, the chapter made clear to me the larger geo-political issues which motivated your tilt, although I still deplore the adverse effect it had on Indo-American relations, always under adverse pressures from friends of the Soviets of whom there never is a shortage in our country.

On one point that you have made, however, I cannot help remaining doubtful, and that is the belief that, had it not been for American intervention, with the help of the Soviets India intended to launch an all-out attack on West Pakistan to recover the part of Kashmir which it had acquired by subterfuge and force in 1947, as well as to destroy its military power, leading to its final dismemberment. I was personally in fairly close touch with Delhi at the time, and also had occasion to talk to high-ranking military chiefs after the war. I do not, of course, know what contrary evidence was

---

[*]   Dr. Henry Kissinger (b. 1923) was Secretary of State of the United States of America, 1973-1977. He and JRD were members of the International Advisory Committee of the Chase Manhattan Bank.

furnished to you at the time, but I still believe that no such adventure was seriously contemplated although it was naturally discussed as a possibility and supported by some hawks in our country....

I am continuing my reading of the book with immense interest and look forward, hopefully not too soon, to the next volume which you have announced. Apart from the fascination of the events and views you express, your felicitous use of the English language and the humour which you obviously find difficulty in suppressing at times make it the lightest heavy book I have ever read!

With warm regards and renewed thanks,

Yours sincerely,
Jeh

FROM ROBERT McNAMARA*

Washington
17 *June* 1981

My dear JRD,

As you may know, I will be retiring from the World Bank at the end of this month. These past thirteen years have been the most fulfilling and rewarding of my life, and I am deeply grateful for all the support that you have given both to the work of the Bank itself, and to me personally.

If there is ever anything, in the years ahead, that you feel I can do to assist in meeting the problems of the international community, I want you to call on me. Although not wealthy, I am fortunate in that I need not choose my activities on financial grounds, and I propose to devote myself to things that interest me, that broaden my understanding, and that promote peace and security in an increasingly interdependent world.

The 1980s will clearly confront us with a whole spectrum of tangled problems. The difficulties are formidable, but not insuperable if the developed and developing countries alike can act in ways that are consistent with their growing interdependence, and serve the long-range interests of all. In any event, if there is any practical way in which I can be helpful, I very much want to be.

With warm personal regards, and with my very best wishes, I am

Sincerely,
Bob

---

* Robert McNamara was the Secretary of Defence (1961-1968) during the Kennedy and Johnson administrations in the U.S.A. He was also President of the World Bank.

TO ROBERT McNAMARA

Bombay
10 July 1981

Dear Mr. McNamara,

I was touched by your letter of June 17 written on the eve of your retirement from the World Bank.

The Bank's outstanding performance and remarkable growth during your tenure as President is universally recognised as having been due in very large part to your inspired leadership over the past thirteen years. We in India have a special reason to be grateful to you, for it was your sensitive understanding of the plight and needs of LDCs which enabled the Bank greatly to increase its support and encouragement to them, while the growing priority you have attached to agriculture, health and population problems has, to my knowledge, had a valuable influence in creating in our Government and bureaucracy a greater awareness of the importance and urgency of these long neglected subjects. Under your leadership the Bank has indeed become more than a bank and the prestige and influence it commands today in the economic world is tremendous, for which the credit is deservedly attributed mainly to you.

I hope that your continuing interest in the promotion of peace and security in our increasingly interdependent world will include the population problem which, serious in the rest of the world, threatens to be catastrophic in India and makes every other problem more intractable. As President of the World Bank you have already done much to arouse international alarm on the subject....

In closing, may I extend to you my warmest personal wishes for many years of good health and rewarding work, and success in any task that you undertake in the years to come in the interests of international understanding and development.

With kindest regards,

Yours sincerely,
J.R.D. Tata

FROM DAVID ROCKEFELLER

New York
6 *December 1989*

Dear Jeh,

I am sure that many people have sent you copies of the article which appeared about you in the *New York Times* about a week ago. I thought that it was a particularly accurate and sensitive piece. You have been running one of the world's great industrial empires for some fifty years in a country where capitalism, no matter how enlightened, has not been popular. You have run that empire efficiently and profitably, but in a manner that was done with a degree of grace and humanity that caused your leadership to be accepted despite an unwelcoming climate. You have also lived your life with a degree of simplicity and lack of ostentation which has made it virtually impossible, even for those who would have found you an attractive target, to be critical of you. In short, in an era when, alas, far too many ambitious and greedy entrepreneurs are tarnishing the image of the market economy, at the very time when socialism has proven to be a failure, you have been a shining example of the way captains of industry ought to behave in our modern society.

Apart from the foregoing, I wanted to take this opportunity to say how much your participation on the Chase International Advisory Committee has meant to all of us over the years. You have always been modestly restrained in speaking out at the meetings, but, whenever you do speak out, everyone listens to your words with great attention.

For Peggy and me, your friendship has been and continues to be something that is very meaningful to us. We send you our warmest best wishes for Christmas and the New Year. Congratulations again on your many achievements and, above all, the example you have given your friends and admirers around the world.

Sincerely,
David

TO DAVID ROCKEFELLER

Bombay
16 January 1990

Dear David,

I am sorry I could not write earlier to thank you most warmly for your letter of December 6....

I was deeply touched by your over-kind remarks which greatly exceeded the merit of what I may have done, or tried to do, in the difficult period of years in which our politicians chose to adopt for the country a form of socialism which, apart from being impractical, seriously impeded our economic growth and the private sector's contribution to it. The situation was not made easier by the simultaneous introduction and maintenance of personal taxation at levels which led, inevitably, to a serious diminution of ethical values and the development, at great cost to the country, of a parallel economy, much of which still prevails today. Perhaps, an additional cause of the moral debasement that has taken place in the business community in our country is that the industrial development in the private sector has, as elsewhere, been in the form of a massive and over-hurried transition from trade and finance, the main occupation of Indian business in the past, to industry, with the opportunities it offered to make money with little regard for moral values or for the public good. Unfortunately, the situation was aggravated by the fact that, in India, as in other regimented countries, the Government, the politicians and the bureaucrats made sure, by their laws and their policies, to lace such opportunities with the maximum of delay, impediments and disincentives.

It is particularly good of you to tell me, once again, that my participation in the IAC* has been of some value and interest....It might have been more purposeful if

---

* International Advisory Committee.

the course of events in India had been of greater interest to the international business world as they surely will one day. We must blame ourselves for the greater interest which some of our Asian neighbours have aroused or the success they achieved for themselves. We are learning, but slowly!...

Yours sincerely,
Jeh

TO DAVID ROCKEFELLER

Bombay
3 April 1991

Dear David,

I feel it my duty to tell you of an important event in my career which has taken place on the 25th March, namely my decision to relinquish the chairmanship of Tata Sons Ltd., Tatas' parent and oldest company, to the Board of which I was appointed in 1926 and to the chairmanship of which I was elected in 1938. In the years that followed, as I think you know, I became the chairman of most of the companies in the Tata group, including those that were established during my chairmanship. During the last ten years or so I voluntarily relinquished my responsibility as head of these companies in favour of colleagues who had played an important managerial role in their growth and progress. These minor events were recorded in most business newspapers....

The reason I write this letter is that ever since you honoured me by inviting me to join the Chase International Advisory Committee (IAC) I have been aware of our sound decision that such membership was reserved for persons who were themselves leaders in their own field of business or industry. From the start I considered the IAC membership as a prestigious one and also a very pleasant one which provided me with the opportunity to be associated with you and the fine group of men whom you appointed as members.

All good things must, however, come to an end, and having stepped down from my last chairmanship in the Tata group, I think the time has come for the Chase to put me to pasture, as I have suggested to you more than once in the past. If you felt the continued need for an Indian member, I believe you could do no better than to choose Ratan N. Tata, now Chairman of Tata Sons Ltd.

Pending this recent happening, I had arranged to attend as usual the meeting of the IAC on the 28th to 30th April....I would in any case have wished to call on you to say goodbye and to thank you again for the wonderful memories I acquired in those 21 years as a member, and for the warmth of the friendship you and your colleagues have throughout extended to me.

With affectionate wishes to you and Peggy,

Yours ever,
Jeh

TO THOMAS BATA

Bombay
23 *October 1992*

Dear Mr. Bata,

It was with great pleasure and interest that, on my return from an extended trip abroad, I found a copy of your autobiography* which you had kindly sent me. I have for decades been greatly interested in the achievements and tribulations of your great organisation in the changing world of the post-Russian Revolution and the rise of world communism. It was therefore not unexpected to me that a large business enterprise such as yours located in Eastern Europe would be attacked by communism, and I was happy of the opportunity to read the Bata story at length and to appreciate the measure of your dramatic struggle, and success, against the political regime established in Czechoslovakia.

We in Tatas have been fortunate in that even when our political leaders were inclined to admire and favour Soviet policies, their opposition to private enterprise in our country and their socialist policies did not go anywhere as far as in your own country. They did nationalise some industries such as the airline industry, of which I was personally the creator in India, banks and insurance companies, but they fortunately did not impede the continued growth of major industries.

Mr. Nehru did, from the beginning of his political life and leadership in India, become greatly sympathetic to, and influenced by, Soviet policies. Interestingly enough, in some of the Tata activities, such as the tea business and, similarly, the hotel industry of which we are the leaders in India, we have, in recent years, and at the

---

* *Bata: Shoemaker To The World* (with Sonja Sinclair), Stoddart Publishing Co. Ltd., Toronto, 1990.

Soviets' own instance, established a close collaboration with them. We are, naturally, relieved that during the past few years the socialist and pro-Soviet trend has largely faded out in India and the present government has understood the realities of modern industrial and business life and are acting upon this....

An additional and even more important reason for my interest in the Bata story is the similarity that has existed between our two organisations, particularly in our treatment of, and relations with, labour. Although Tatas did, some decades ago, have some initial trouble with unions, we found it possible to convince them not only of our good intentions but of our honest and active support of good trade unionism.... There seems to have been throughout a unique similarity in the philosophy of Batas and Tatas!

Many thanks again for sending me your autobiography, and with warm regards,

Yours sincerely,
J.R.D. Tata

Friends

TO ROMESH THAPAR[*]

Bombay
9 August 1947

My dear Romesh,

Many thanks for your letter of the 30th of July. I note that you are now a gentleman of leisure, which is quite appropriate for a member of the Party.

With reference to your application for a post in the Foreign Service, Press Attaché Section, I suppose its fate will now depend on your friend, Krishna Menon. As a fellow Bolshevik he should support it. I have no objection at all to your having given my name as a reference, although I do think it is a sad commentary on the present condition and frame of mind of the proletariat, that its leaders are reduced to seeking the support of bloodsucking capitalists such as myself! However, I shall cooperate out of enlightened self-interest, as I may one day have to come to you for similar support under somewhat altered circumstances. I would be content with a minor post,

---

[*] JRD had a fascination for men on the other side of the political fence. Romesh Thapar was one such Left-leaning ideologue who in later life, with his wife Raj, founded the influential journal, *Seminar*. He was educated in England and applied for a job in the Foreign Service and gave JRD's name as reference. JRD's reply is both good-humoured and ironic.

say, as Commissar for industries with a couple of 'dashas', three American cars and a few servants (including a member of the Secret Police) thrown in....

Yours,
Jeh

P.S. I have looked up the dictionary, and find that a Jay is "a noisy, chattering, European bird of brilliant plumage", and, figuratively, "an impertinent chatterer or simpleton".

For future reference please note therefore that my name is spelt "Jeh", in abbreviation of "Jehangir" and that any resemblance between me and the bird is purely coincidental.

Jeh

FROM PROF. K.T. SHAH

Bombay
14 December 1948

My dear Mr. Tata,

You must have, by this time, got 22 volumes containing 25 Reports of the Sub-Committees of the National Planning Committee.* Four more are at various stages of completion, such as printing or binding, and will be ready, I hope, very soon. I had planned 25 Volumes to contain 29 Reports of Sub-Committees; but have had to expand the Series slightly to include Reports of 2 Ad Hoc Sub-Committees on the basic Principles of Planning and Administrative machinery needed for carrying out the Plan. The (Draft) Report of the Main Committee is yet another Volume, making in all 27 Volumes in the Series....

The Series has been, generally speaking, well received in the press, even though it has not been advertised much....

You are, I know, not a Member of the National Planning Committee; but as you have helped us very materially in enabling me to bring out the volumes, I am writing this to request you, if you can find time, to see me some time before the 26th inst. when I am going back to Delhi....I should like to see you and have a cup of tea with you.

Yours sincerely,
K.T. Shah

---

* The Indian National Congress appointed the National Planning Committee to study various aspects of the economic development of India. Pandit Jawaharlal Nehru was its Chairman and Prof. K.T. Shah, Secretary. Reports of this Committee were published with financial help from JRD.

TO PROF. K.T. SHAH

My dear Prof. Shah,

Many thanks for your letter of the 14th December. We have received the 22 volumes containing the 25 reports of the various Sub-Committees of the National Planning Committee. May I congratulate you on the remarkable progress of this work in the face of so many difficulties. It is, however, nothing more than I expected from a man of your ferocious energy!

As regards my meeting you in the near future, as you know I always enjoy the rare occasions on which we do meet and on which the Marxist lion (or is it wolf or bear?) accepts a cup of tea from this capitalist lamb (or is it sheep or goat?), but I must request you to excuse me from fixing a meeting before the end of December...

With best wishes,

Yours sincerely,
J.R.D. Tata

TO SIR SHRI RAM[*]

Bombay
22 April 1950

Dear Sir Shri Ram,

Thanks for your letter of the 4th April regarding the Indraprastha College for Women.

The matter will have to be put up to the Trustees of the Sir Dorabji Tata Trust and I would therefore suggest that the Principal or the Registrar of the College should write to the Secretary of the Sir Dorabji Tata Trust, Bombay House, Bruce Street, Bombay, enclosing a copy of the appeal and also sending the last report of the College showing its accounts. This information is invariably required by the Trust Management.

I am a little surprised that a published appeal on behalf of a College imparting higher education up to the M.A. degree, should be written in such poor English. It is one of our Indian failings, I am afraid, to think that the outward form of things is unimportant, as a result of which we see only too often badly finished goods, badly worded and typed reports and correspondence and generally poor presentation....

With kind regards,

Yours sincerely,
J.R.D. Tata

---

*   Chairman, D.C.M. Group, Delhi.

TO D.F. KARAKA[*]

Bombay
18 May 1951

My dear Dosoo,

    I was distressed to read the leading article in your issue of *Current* of the 9th instant entitled *"Now Let Them Die"*, not because of the criticism you have expressed on the food policies of the Government of India, but because of the offensive language you have chosen to use in addressing Pandit Jawaharlal Nehru. While, in a democracy, it is the privilege of the Press freely to express views against the policies of Government, there is no reason why this should not be done in decent and reasonably polite language and without descending to the level of personal abuse....

Yours sincerely,
Jeh

---

[*]   Editor, *Current*, a weekly, published from Bombay.

TO NOBORU NARUSE*

Bombay
19 April 1952

Dear Mr. Naruse,

I was happy to receive your letter of the 18th February which I found on my return from a fairly prolonged absence abroad.

I certainly remember our trip on the *Hirano Maru* 34 years ago. I suppose you know that the ship was torpedoed off the coast of England on that same trip. We seem to have been exactly the same age, as I shall be 48 years old this summer.

I am glad to know that you have safely survived the upheavals of recent years and that you are doing well in the Kinsho Trading Company. I wish you the best of luck and success in whatever you do.

I have been kept increasingly busy all these years and I suppose will go on being so until the end of my days. I often wish that I was back in the days of the *Hirano Maru*, playing with friends on board like yourself and free from the anxieties and troubles of today. However, life has been on the whole kind to me and I cannot complain....

With best wishes,

Yours sincerely,
J.R.D. Tata

---

* JRD's childhood friend from Japan.

TO DINSHAW DAJI[*]

Bombay
12 May 1953

My dear Daji,

...In the almost universal cry for nationalisation in this country, no one seems to think of the potential danger of concentrating enormous economic power into the hands of a small political-cum-bureaucratic minority.

In our country political immaturity and economic illiteracy aggravate the tendency of our people, except in the spiritual field, to avoid thinking *through* any problem that faces them. Slogans and over-simplification provide easy and glib solutions requiring no mental strain. Thus socialism, to most of them, boils down merely to the ownership by the State of all means of production and no differentiation is made between socialism, communism and state capitalism, nor is it realised that full-scale socialism or state capitalism is inherently incompatible with democracy as understood in the West. The concentration of all economic power and patronage into the hands of a few at the top of a national pyramid must ultimately lead to a similar concentration of political power and therefore to a totalitarian regime. Few realise that in fact capitalism with suitable safeguards is one of the most democratic forms of economic organisation as it is based on wide diffusion of economic power.

For the prejudice against capitalism in India the depredations and selfishness of the majority of Indian businessmen have been largely responsible. But it is an interesting fact that the more advanced countries of the West originally went through the same process. For instance, the first generations of British and American industrialists and

---

[*]   Noted lawyer.

businessmen were just as unscrupulous and callous as some of our industrial black sheep. It took two or three generations and a lot of legislation to control malpractices to create the present high standards of business morality in those countries. Unfortunately in India our industrialists and businessmen, most of them first-generation-wallas, do not realise that they are not going to be given the time to reform that their counterparts in Western countries enjoyed. They are even unmindful of the grave they are busily digging for themselves!...

Yours sincerely,
J.R.D. Tata

TO G.D. BIRLA

Bombay
24 January 1958

My dear Ghanshyamdas,

Thank you for sending me the enclosed article which I return after having read it with interest.

I have given up nicotine, and hardly ever drink coffee or alcohol. According to others, I should give up meat. What I would like best to give up is work!...

Yours sincerely,
Jeh

TO R.K. KARANJIA[*]

Bombay
10 August 1961

My dear Russy,

Thanks for your letter of the 28th July. It is nice of you to say that you would like to renew our old contacts, but quite frankly I wonder what purpose it could serve for us to meet.

There is such an abyss between what you and I stand for in the things that count in life that there is no possibility of a "meeting of the minds". Your support of communist philosophy, methods and action while purporting to defend democratic ideals, is a matter entirely between yourself and your conscience and so is your interpretation of the responsibilities and ethics of a publisher and editor. I have my own views on the subject which you can hardly expect to change by meeting me. I have no expectation of changing yours, nor the inclination to attempt to do so. We would only, therefore, waste each other's time. Life is short and difficult as it is and there is enough tension between individuals and peoples without creating occasions to add to it....

Yours sincerely,
Jeh

---

[*] Editor, *Blitz*, published from Bombay.

TO MRS. LOUIE WOODS

Bombay
11 November 1963

My dear Louie,

...I saw the "amusing" pictures taken during the meeting and all the men, including, I fear, the President of the World Bank, looked either like members of a rogues' gallery, or candidates for the nearest lunatic asylum! So, if you happen to forget your promise to get some of these pictures which include me and to send them to me, I for one shall not weep!...

I shall be most happy to come back to Washington and stay longer as you suggest. There is a very simple way to arrange it: if George is prepared to advance to Tata Steel the two hundred odd million dollars we are seeking from the World Bank, I shall be happy to come and stay in Washington for negotiations for as long as he and you like!

Thelly joins me in sending you both our love and our respectful regards to the man who sits on that lovely pile of money.

Yours ever,
Jeh

TO MRS. VERRIER ELWIN

Bombay
6 March 1964

Dear Mrs. Elwin,

On my return to India from a prolonged business tour abroad, I was shocked and saddened by the news of Verrier's[*] death.

I had the good fortune to come in contact with him from the very beginning of his dedicated career in India and ever since considered it a privilege to have him as a friend. There is no one I have known for whom I have had greater admiration and affection. I am sure he will live, for the rest of their lives, in the hearts and minds of all his friends and also the innumerable people to whose welfare he dedicated his life. If only there were more Verrier Elwins in this world, it would be a better and happier place to live in.

On behalf of my wife and myself, I extend to you and your children our deepest sympathy and condolences in your grievous loss.

Yours sincerely,
J.R.D. Tata

---

[*] Verrier Elwin (1902-1964), anthropologist and writer, was a pioneering scholar of Indian tribes. JRD helped him to bring out some of his books.

TO N.J. NANPORIA[*]

Bombay
24 January 1968

My dear Nanporia,

I was happy to receive your letter of January 9 which brought us news of you and Shiraz, and to learn that you are now well-settled in Singapore and like it there.

Indian politics may be more interesting and exciting than those of Singapore, but you must have had a surfeit of the former, as we all do here, and I envy you the more restful atmosphere of your part of the world. The people there may be less mature and sophisticated than we are, but considering the use we seem to be making of our maturity we could do with less of it and more of the simpler and more practical approach of the other people of South and South East Asia....Thelly joins me in sending you and Shiraz our best wishes.

Yours sincerely,
J.R.D. Tata

P.S. I hope you are both well.

J.

---

[*] Editor, *The Straits Times*, Singapore. Earlier editor of *The Times of India*, Bombay.

Others

TO S.J. PANDYA[*]

Bombay
30 April 1951

Dear Mr. Pandya,

Many thanks for your letter of the 20th instant written from the T.S.S. *Jal Jawahar*, enclosing a postcard of the Cairo Museum.

I was interested to learn of the God "TATA", of whom I am of course a direct descendant!

I hope you have a very pleasant holiday.

With best wishes,

Yours sincerely,
J.R.D. Tata

---

[*] Pandya visited the Cairo Museum where he saw a statue of a god named Tata.

TO MISS MAHALAKSHMI KESHAVA RAO

Bombay
21 *June* 1971

Dear Miss Rao,

I thank you for your letter of the 8th June, asking me to clarify the gender of our Jumbos and the reason why we have changed it from the female to the male.

The only way I can answer your interesting question, is that ships and aeroplanes seem to be androgynous, at least in the manner in which they have been named and referred to over the years. Thus, all ships are referred to in the feminine although most of them are named after male persons! Some of them, however, like the famous Empress ships of the Canadian Pacific Line, were named in the feminine. The same odd and irrational tradition seems to have been adopted for aeroplanes. In the case of Air-India's new planes, affectionately referred to as Jumbos because of their size, there are of course both male and female elephants! I hope this answer clarifies this important international problem!

You will be glad to know that our Jumbos, whatever their sex, have up to now behaved like gentlemen, while looking like beautiful ladies.

Yours sincerely,
J.R.D. Tata

TO PRAVIN KUMAR DIN DAYAL[*]

Bombay
10 May 1976

Dear Pravin Dayal,

Thank you for your letter of the 28th April....

From this reply you will note that your assumptions that I would throw your letter in the dustbin, that your feelings would be hurt, and that an industrialist like me would never reply to you, were wrong!

I note that you are sure to become an industrialist, and ask for my advice. At this early stage of your life the best advice I can give you is to do your best in college in order to prepare yourself for an industrial career. If you have a bent for mathematics and technical subjects, I would advise you to become an engineer. If you do not have such a bent, I would advise you to seek a B.Com. degree or a legal degree, as any one of these would be of great value to you in the future. As your father is a company executive, presumably in Mahindra Ugine, I do not see why you feel there is no one to advise you and I suggest you consult him too.

Finally, I would strongly recommend that you improve your knowledge of the English language which will be important to you in the future, and also try to be precise and methodical in whatever you do. Your letter shows that you are still somewhat deficient in this respect. For instance, although I received your letter on the 22nd April, it is dated 28th April!

With best wishes for a successful career,

Yours sincerely,
J.R.D. Tata

---

[*] JRD advises a college student who aspires to become an industrialist.

TO PROF. A.K. SAHNI[*]

Bombay
16 August 1978

Dear Professor Sahni,

I am sorry for the delay in replying to your letter of July 17th, received on the 24th July.

I do not think I have much to contribute to the acquisition of knowledge by your students. They know, as well as I do, that success in one's career depends on two main factors—the innate abilities of the individual which are a gift of nature, and the use made of them in life. Life is undoubtedly a hard one for most people in our country, and opportunities to live a full and rewarding life come to the few who have taken the fullest advantage of them, first in their school and college education, and later in their working years, to maximise their talents and capabilities.

It is a sad and disheartening fact that in our country so much of the limited time available to young people fortunate enough to acquire a college education essential to their later progress, is wasted in fruitless political and other agitational pursuits, such as we read about so often in the papers today. The task of building the India of our dreams will need the dedication and hard work of every educated man and woman in the country, and material success will come mainly to those who face up to the challenges and obstacles placed before them with courage and determination.

I was fortunate in my younger days to be given exceptional opportunities to play a part in promoting and serving worthwhile causes and enterprises. If I were to

---

[*]   Professor, Indian Institute of Management, Bangalore.

attribute any single reason to such success as I have achieved, I would say that success would not have been possible without a sustained belief that what I did or attempted to do would serve the needs and interests of our country and our people.

Yours sincerely,
J.R.D. Tata

FROM MRS. R. LALWANI[*]

Bombay
9 April 1985

Dear Mr. Tata,

I owe you an explanation and an apology! On Monday, 18 March, approximately at 8 p.m., I drove out of Sterling Apartments and approached Pedder Road. There was no way I could get into the extreme left hand lane of the road as I normally do, to make a 'U' turn....The 'U' turn signal turned green and your chauffeur started agitating as your car could not move. It must have taken me five seconds to take in the situation, and in the meantime you leaned out of your car and shouted something rude, being obviously impatient to get home....

It was a genuine unforeseen error on my part and I admit I stopped in the wrong lane and obstructed your car for a period of five seconds....This behaviour coming as it does from you, Mr. Tata, really surprised and shocked me rather than angered me. If you could be so agitated in a chauffeur-driven limousine, you can imagine the plight of a working housewife and that she can understandably make such an error in Bombay traffic which is one of the worst in the world especially when the signs are no help to the drivers on the road.

Whereas I do apologise for obstructing your car, I have offered you my explanation and must regrettably point out that I was appalled at your ungentlemanly behaviour at that moment. My impressions of you have been that of a gentleman par excellence.

Mrs. R Lalwani

---

[*] A former air-hostess of Air-India.

TO MRS. R. LALWANI

Bombay
24 April 1985

Dear Mrs. Lalwani,

I was both surprised and sorry at receiving your letter of the 9th instant, but also very appreciative of the trouble you took in writing to me. I regret I could not reply to you at once as I have only just come back from abroad and your letter lay unopened at my house until my return at the end of last week.

I was surprised because I frankly have no recollection of the incident you mention and sorry because it was indeed a serious lapse on my part to have, as you say, shouted something rude, the exact words of which you, mercifully, do not mention.

I have always had a somewhat Rajput-like chivalrous sense of respect for women and I can't imagine the circumstances in which I could have behaved rudely towards one of them, which I would myself consider inexcusable whatever the provocation.

In the circumstances, all I can do is to tell you how sorry I am and to convey my sincere apologies to you, which I hope you will accept along with these few flowers as a token of my contriteness, and my hope that you will regain the impression you previously had of me, mentioned in your letter.

With kind regards,

Yours sincerely,
J.R.D. Tata

TO PROF. J.C. HARAN[*]

Bombay
4 December 1986

Dear Professor Haran,

I thank you for your letter of November 22 which I read with interest and from which I was glad to learn that you were not bored by *Keynote*.

Thank you also for sending me a copy of your booklet *You and Your Studies*....

You must be a somewhat rare specimen of a university professor with an original mind combined with a sense of humour. If I had been one of your students, I would have enjoyed and appreciated your booklet. I have, in the last year or two, had occasion to meet university students in a number of question-and-answer sessions which I found to be an excellent means of learning how the brighter students of our country think and what interests them, and I must confess to being disappointed with their apparent lack of interest in important issues and happenings outside their immediate field of study....

I have been particularly dismayed at the fact that, at all my meetings with students in question-and-answer sessions, not a single one has so far raised the issue of excessive population growth which has added 350 million souls to our population in the past 30 years or so and is, today, the most grievous and intractable problem facing the country....

With good wishes,

Yours sincerely,
J.R.D. Tata

---

[*]   Professor, Gogte Institute of Technology, Belgaum.

TO SANJAY KUMAR GUPTA*

Bombay
20 May 1987

Dear Mr. Gupta,

Thank you for your letter of the 29th April, asking for my suggestions and guidance regarding your intended career as a pilot. Of all the technical careers, that of a pilot is perhaps the one that requires the greatest self-discipline, not only in his or her own interest, but also that of passengers whose lives are in his hands, as also the safety of costly equipment. We Indians are not by nature as self-disciplined as the people of some other countries like the Japanese, the Swiss and the Scandinavians. My only advice to you is that, apart from working hard to acquire the best possible skill, you should never make an exception in the pursuit of discipline and safety.

I wish you the best of luck and success,

Yours sincerely,
J.R.D. Tata

---

* Student of Indira Gandhi Rashtriya Uran Akademy, Rae Bareli.

FROM ASHISH BHARADWAJ*

Baroda

Respected Uncle J.R.D.,

I am 14 years old Ashish Bharadwaj, extending new year greetings to you in my own special way.

Sir, recently in an elocution competition I was asked to speak on the topic:

"TATA IN TIMBUKTU".

I was dumb-founded, but in a few moments a few scenes flashed in my mind (which I am sketching for you), and I delivered a humorous story. The audience liked it very much, and so I thought it would be fun sending you the same....

I am curious to know what you feel about it....

With my very best regards,

Yours,
Ashish Bharadwaj

---

*   This school student from Baroda sent JRD a story, accompanied by a sketch of JRD flying an aeroplane.

TO ASHISH BHARADWAJ

Bombay
24 January 1989

Dear Ashish,

Thank you for your undated letter which I have just received, and for your greetings for the New Year which I warmly reciprocate.

I found the story "Tata in Timbuktu" quite interesting. It shows you have a talent for writing and imagination. Whatever you choose to take up as a career, you should continue to develop your writing talent which should make life for you, now and later on, more satisfying and fulfilling.

With best wishes,

Yours sincerely,
J.R.D. Tata

TO MISS FARAH PESI TAVARIA[*]

Bombay
7 April 1989

My dear Farah,

Thank you for your long letter of February 6, which I have just seen on my return from a trip abroad. I realise that I have been a very poor correspondent and you must wish you had selected a better "uncle" who could be more helpful to you!

From what you write I was sorry to learn that even at this early age you already have the sort of problems and worries which you should be spared....

In any case, don't lose heart, for in the course of your life you will, I hope, find as I have, that some events that seemed very serious at the time turned out to be less so when looking back on them in later life. I have had my share of such disappointments and set-backs, and am still alive and optimistic!...

Yours affectionately,
"Uncle" Jeh

---

[*] Reply to a letter from a girl from Poona seeking JRD's advice on facing life.

THE LAST LETTERS

JRD left on his last visit to Geneva on 7 October 1993. Before leaving he dictated some letters to his secretary. One of them was to Dr. Gritli Mitterwallner, a German Indologist and family friend, informing her about the death of Gool Contractor, his personal physician.

The other letter, addressed to A.V. Krishna Murty of the Indian Institute of Science, Bangalore pertained to the operations of the Department of Aerospace Engineering, a subject dear to his heart.

JRD was always concerned about human relations in Industry and took the initiative in setting up the Personnel Department of Tata Steel in 1943. His last communication from Geneva was a condolence letter to Mrs. Laxmi V. Gopal, the wife of V.G. Gopal, the President of the Tata Workers' Union, Jamshedpur who was murdered on 14 October 1993.

JRD was admitted to the Geneva State Hospital on November 4 and he passed away on 29 November 1993.

TO DR. GRITLI MITTERWALLNER[*]

Bombay
6 October 1993

Dearest Gritli,

    Many thanks for your letter of 27 September which I received today. Yes, Gool's tragic passing away has been a tremendous loss and I miss her very badly....
With our love and warm wishes,

Yours ever affectionately,
Jeh

---

[*]   A German Indologist who was a family friend.

TO PROF. A.V. KRISHNA MURTY[*]

Bombay
6 October 1993

Dear Prof. Krishna Murty,

I thank you for your letter of September 13 and its enclosures, reviewing the work and functions of the Department of Aerospace Engineering. I am happy that my remarks at the last Court meeting induced you and your colleagues to undertake the review.

I must confess to you that I am poorly impressed by the fact that after all these years India's aeronautical science and industry should have such a dismal record of designing anything worthwhile in the form of any kind of aircraft, including the simplest type of training aircraft, in total contrast to the achievements of many countries in the world, including Brazil and China. With due respect to our aeronautical scientists or manufacturers like Hindustan Aeronautics, I cannot see any valid reason for our still being so far behind others.

With all good wishes,

Yours sincerely,
J.R.D. Tata

---

[*] Chairman, Department of Aerospace Engineering, Indian Institute of Science, Bangalore.

FROM RATAN TATA[*]

Bombay
14 October 1993

Dear Jeh,

As you may have already heard, V.G. Gopal was shot dead this morning as he was getting into his car at the Union office. His bodyguard was also killed.

I am going to Jamshedpur tomorrow morning and will attend the funeral. The union met this afternoon and elected a new President (Mr. Benjamin). The vacuum has therefore been filled—at least for the time being.

With affectionate regards,

Yours,
Ratan

---

[*] Copy of handwritten letter.

TO DR. J.J. IRANI[*]

Camp Geneva
15 October 1993

Dr. J.J. Irani[**]

I was shocked and distressed to learn of the ghastly and fatal assault on Mr. V.G. Gopal. I would much appreciate it if you would kindly arrange to convey my sympathy and condolences to his colleagues in the Tata Workers Union and to the bereaved family of the security guard, and the following message to Mrs. Gopal:
Mrs. Lakshmi V. Gopal, Jamshedpur
I was shocked and grieved to learn of the brutal and fatal assault on your husband whom I had known for many years and whom I held in the highest esteem and regard. I extend to you and the members of your family my deepest sympathy and condolences in your tragic and irreparable loss.

J.R.D. Tata, Camp Geneva

---

[*] JRD's last telegram sent from Geneva.
[**] Managing Director, Tata Steel.

J.R.D. Tata: Chronology at a Glance

1904   Born on July 29 in Paris.

1909   R.D. Tata purchases a house at Hardelot. Young JRD grows up here.

1909-17 The family moves between Bombay and Paris. JRD attends Cathedral School
        in Bombay.

1917-18 The family lives at Yokohama, Japan. Moves to France after the War.

1923   Mother Sooni passes away.
        Spends a year in a "Crammer" School in England.

1924   Drafted into the French army for a year.

1925   Joins Tatas as an apprentice.

1926   Father R.D. Tata passes away. JRD inherits his directorship in Tatas.

1929   Renounces French citizenship.
        Secures pilot's licence, the first in India.

1930   Marries Thelma Vicaji.
        Stands second in the Aga Khan aviation race for flying between India and U.K.

1932   Aviation Department of Tata Sons set up.
        Aviation service inaugurated with him flying between Karachi and Bombay.

1938   Appointed Chairman of Tata Sons.
        Aviation Department renamed Tata Air Lines.

1944   Draws up the Bombay Plan.
        Sets up the J.R.D. Tata Trust.

1945   Initiates the setting up of the Tata Institute of Fundamental Research.
        Leads the first delegation of industrialists to the U.K. and U.S.A.

1946   Tata Air Lines renamed Air-India Ltd.

1948	Air-India International incorporated as a joint sector venture.
	Appointed a member, Indian Delegation (third session), UN General Assembly, Paris.
1952	Appointed a member, Executive Committee, the International Air Transport Association (IATA).
1953	Aviation industry nationalised. Two Corporations formed. JRD appointed Chairman of Air-India International.
	Selected "International Management Man" by the National Association of Foremen, Milwaukee.
1954	Nominated Officer of the Legion of Honour by the French Government.
1955	Awarded Padma Vibhushan by the Government of India.
1958	Elected President of IATA.
1962	Re-enacted Karachi-Bombay flight to commemorate 30th Anniversary of Indian Civil Aviation.
1964	Knight Commander of the Order of St. Gregory the Great (Papal Honour).
1966	Made Honorary Air Commodore, Indian Air Force (IAF).
1969	Appointed Member, International Advisory Committee of the Chase Manhattan Bank, U.S.A.
1970	Appointed Chairman, Governing Board, Family Planning Foundation, New Delhi.
1974	Made Honorary Air Vice-Marshal, IAF.
1978	Honoured with Knight Commander's Cross of the Order of Germany.
	Chairmanship of Air-India terminated by Prime Minister Morarji Desai.
1979	Presented the Tony Jannus Award.
1980	Re-appointed Director Air-India by Prime Minister Indira Gandhi.
1981	Conferred Doctor of Law (Honoris Causa) by the University of Bombay.
	Appointed Member, Auroville International Advisory Council.
1982	Re-enacted Karachi-Bombay flight to mark the golden jubilee of Indian Civil Aviation.
1983	Bestowed with the rank of Commander of the French Legion of Honour.
1985	Presented the Gold Air Medal by the Federation Aeronautique Internationale.
1986	Awarded the Bessemer Medal of the Institute of Metals, London.
	Received Edward Warner Award from the International Civil Aviation Organisation.

1988	Awarded the Daniel Guggenheim Medal and the Dadabhai Naoroji Memorial award.
1991	Stepped down from the Chairmanship of Tata Sons in favour of Ratan Tata. Established the JRD and Thelma J. Tata Trust.
1992	Awarded the U.N. Population Award and the Bharat Ratna.
1993	Awarded the Doctor of Literature (Honoris Causa) by Tata Institute of Social Sciences, Bombay. Passed away on November 29 in Geneva.

Index (From)

Index (To)

La Francisée d

"The Spirit of St. Louis"